The PLANE that changed the WORLD

Dedicated to my wonderful and understanding wife, Mary Sue Lusk Ingells, whose love, faith and never-ending support made it possible for me to take the time to write this book . . . With all my love . . .

The PLANE that changed the WORLD

A biography of the DC-3 by Douglas J. Ingells

Aero Publishers, Inc.
Fallbrook, California

Library of Congress Catalog Card Number

66-28792

Printed and Published in the United States by Aero Publishers, Inc.

Preface

August 19, 1966
National Aviation Day

The first flight of a heavier-than-air, power-driven, man-carrying flying machine was made at Kitty Hawk, North Carolina, on December 17, 1903. Orville Wright, co-inventor of the aeroplane with his brother Wilbur, both unknown bicycle builders from Dayton, Ohio, made the flight in a cloth and wood frame machine, covering a distance of 120 feet and remaining aloft with full control for a total of 12 seconds. In that fraction of a minute, it can be said the wing joined the wheel and the sail as a prime mover of people and things. The ocean of air around us made a port city of virtually every spot on this earth; the airplane was the *Santa Maria* and the airport was the *Sky Harbor* of the Air Age. The new vehicle of the air which the Wrights gave us has changed the way people think and act, work and play, and the way we live on this planet.

It is fitting, perhaps, that this is being written on National Aviation Day, 1966. Orville Wright, had he lived, would be 95 years old on this date. He would delight in the peacetime wings of commerce that fill the world's skies. But he would deplore the use of the airplane as a weapon of war. In the many interviews this writer had with Mister Wright, the inventor stressed this point more than any other: *that it was his (and Wilbur's) greatest wish to see the aeroplane become a machine dedicated to bringing the peoples of the world closer together, opening up new vistas of trade and commerce in the great air ocean!*

More than anything else, these repeated expressions of this great man, listened to by a very young reporter who aspired to one day write a book, influenced this writer to chose as his subject the DC-3 airplane. Certainly no machine has done more to bring the world of nations closer together, and in war and peace, its wings have been a shining symbol of the great leap forward in transportation.

By resolution of the Congress of the United States in 1939, President Roosevelt was asked to designate August 19 as National Aviation Day, because "the rapid development of aviation has made it a profound influence in world affairs." Paradoxically, at that time, the Douglas DC-3, flying under the flags of nations of the world, was carrying more than 90 per cent of all the world's air commerce. It would soon play another vital role as the "winged workhorse" of World War II, and to hundreds of millions of persons, this plane more than any other, was, and is, one of the most beloved aircraft ever built.

"The Plane That Changed The World" is more than a story of a machine with wings. It is a story of men with vision, of engineers and scientists; men who worked with their hands on the production line, tens of thousands of them; men of Wall Street who had the faith to back a struggling, infant air transport industry; men born to the sky who loved to fly; of small towns and big cities linked together in the greatest air transport system the world has ever known; the story of a revolution in transportation that unshackled the bonds of earthlings and put them on the stairway to the stars.

Preface (continued)

Work on the book really began almost a quarter of a century ago, high in the skies over the mountainous terrain near Albuquerque, New Mexico. The author was flying with Jack Frye, then president of Transcontinental & Western Airlines, Inc. (it is now Trans World Airlines and we were "up front" in the small, twin-engined Lockheed "Electra" which Frye used as an executive ship. It was there in the cockpit that Frye related the story of the concept which was born with the tragic death of Knute Rockne in a cloth-covered, and veneer Fokker airliner that crashed in a Kansas wheat field.

"We knew we had to come up with a different kind of airliner, a bigger faster, all-metal ship," Frye said. "The result was the Douglas DC-1. Few people have ever heard of this airplane. There was only one ever built, but it was the prototype that gave us a modern airliner . . . You should write a book about the DC-1 . . . "

Since then the author has been gathering material for this book – the book that he promised Jack Frye would one day be written.

In researching and writing this book, the author has interviewed the men who saw the vision, conceived the concept, and make their dream of a practical, useful flying machine come true. He has talked with hundreds of pilots who have flown the DC-ships across ten thousand skies. He has flown in the first Douglas DST, Sleeper Transports, in the early 14-passenger DC-2's, in the first C-33 military cargo versions, with air evac crews in the "flying hospitals," with the first parachute troopers in training at Fort Benning, Ga. when they made the DC-3 a *Skytrooper,* in the tow-planes that pulled aloft the first glider troop transports, the C-47 "locomotives," in the DC-3 that was made into a glider, in the deluxe chair-car version of the DC-3, in the standard 21-passenger "Model T" of airliners, and in the posh DC-3 executive planes. He has combed the files of the Douglas Aircraft Company historical records, selected hundreds of photographs from among tens of thousands, and dug through files of virtually every major airline using this type of aircraft. The author has tried to put together this material in entertaining, narrative form to tell the story of this fabulous thing with wings. It seems, however, the story is never-ending. She has found herself another war now in far off Viet Nam and no one knows how much longer she will write history in the skies.

The truth is, this is her story. It is really more autobiographical than biography. It is the plane talking, not the author. Were it only possible for one to write such history as she has done in engraving the name of DOUGLAS across the heavens.

Douglas J. Ingells

Acknowledgements

It would be virtually impossible to express my appreciation and gratitude to the many persons who helped me in gathering the material for this book. So many have contributed their time, and made possible my perusing through their scrapbooks and files, that to list them by name would fill more pages than the entire book. The names of many of these to whom I am indebted appear in the text itself, and I hope that the material appears in a manner of which they can be proud.

There is one person whom I should like to particularly thank for all his efforts and helpful suggestions: Mr. Crosby Maynard, Assistant to the Vice President of Public Relations, Douglas Aircraft Co., Santa Monica. Crosby, through the years has helped me to set up interviews with various Douglas people from whom was gleaned many of the personal background stories of the early development stages of the DC-1, DC-2 and DC-3 aircraft. He has given me the most encouragement to continue this project when at times I thought of giving it up. He also has given his time to read proofs and make suggestions here and there which most certainly have helped to make this a better story. Others of the Douglas public relations staff whom I shall never forget for their helpfulness include A. M. Rochlen, Don Black, Hugh Gagos, Al Chop (now with NASA) and Ray Towne. Their efforts in helping me to dig out material and pictures, I hope, will be rewarded when they see the finished book.

The task has also been made easier by so many other public relations staffers with the various airlines of the United States and some foreign carriers. Although this work certainly was not put together from PR releases, without them it would have been almost impossible to ascertain dates, names and places. Many of those who supplied this data are lifelong friends. I should like to mention a few: Jim Devine, Bill Van Dusen, Red Sutherland, Gordon Williams, Harold Mansfield, Gordon Gilmore, Bob Helmer, Willis Player, Elmer Thompson, Chapin Leinbach, Dick Fernald. They and the great industry they represent – *American, TWA, Pan American World Airways, Eastern, United, Douglas, Boeing,* and all the others – helped provide many pictures and background to enrich this story.

I also want to pay special tribute to Richard A. Woodbury, of North Central Airlines who provided so much inspiration, sweat, blood and tears to make possible the filming of the motion picture short subject – "The Plane That Refused To Die" – parts of which are adapted from this book. And to Mr. William C. Dempsey, vice president and general manager of WZZM-TV, Channel 13, Grand Rapids, Michigan, Burdick Myre, assistant program manager and Arnold Street, cinematographer, who produced, directed and made the TV motion picture version.

I am also grateful to Jim Straubel, John Loosbrock, and Dick Skinner of AIR FORCE Magazine for their cooperation in supplying material and photographs. Thanks also to Major Jim Sparks and the gang in the Pentagon for their efforts in helping with the picture version.

There are others, some personal friends, whose encouragement and support helped greatly to make this project more pleasant: Gregory (Joe) Melonas, Ernie Andresen, Bruce Draper, Ray Hollick, Bill Karlsen, George Dearborn,

Acknowledgement (continued)

Paul and Marlene Toeppen, Elaine and Lorree Lewis, Morgan W. Anderson, Walt Listing, R. J. "Joe" Cunningham, A. Ivan Pelter, Mrs. William Siebert, Benny Mercer, and Mrs. S. W. Conkling, my mother, for their encouragement and patience listening to my telling so many times of "The PLANE that changed The WORLD."

There is one other, Colonel Carroll V. Glines, co-author of "THE GRAND OLD LADY" – story of the DC-3, who helped so much in getting photographs and data from the USAF historical files.

I also want to thank Miss Marcia Johnson, my faithful typist, who knows this story now better than anyone else having typed the manuscript so many times.

Especially, too, I want to thank my publisher, Mr. Ernest J. Gentle and the staff at Aero for their understanding and efforts in presenting this book. Also my deep appreciation to Eleanor (Mrs. Gentle) for the hospitality extended me on the many visits to the Gentle home.

Douglas J. Ingells

AUTHOR'S NOTE: Some of the material in this book has appeared previously under the author's name in AIR TRAILS, AIR PROGRESS, FLYING, AMERICAN MODELER, AIR FORCE MAGAZINE. The author wishes to thank these publications for permission to use this material again in a different form. Also: Certain excerpts throughout the text from other books is used with permission of the publishers, credit being given where the material appears.

AGELESS WINGS

This aircraft, a sleek and shiny plush interior DC-3, was born in 1939. She is still flying after 84,000 hours and twelve million miles of air travel. She has worn out 550 main gear tires, 25,000 spark plugs, 68 pairs of engines, burned more than eight million gallons of gasoline, and taxied well over 100,000 miles. The airframe is 90 per cent original, and, inside and out, "728" is still a queen of the skies. Her "ageless wings" probably more than any other member of the DC-family, represent the design integrity and ruggedness of "The PLANE That Changed The WORLD."

(North Central Airlines Photo)

CHAIRMAN OF THE BOARD

October 21, 1966

Dear Mr. Gentle:

I appreciate your courtesy in making available advance proofs of The Plane That Changed the World by Douglas J. Ingells.

It can be no secret that we at Douglas have a sentimental affection for the DC-3 which appears to be shared by many people throughout the world. We would, of course, be sensitive to the accuracy and detail embodied in the history of any Douglas product but because the DC-3 does have a special place in our hearts, any volume memorializing this airplane would inevitably receive most attentive scrutiny.

With this in mind, may I say that I thoroughly enjoyed Mr. Ingells' book. I have undertaken to set right a few minor errors of fact, but on the whole, he is to be congratulated on painstaking research and interesting prose.

I am glad that your firm saw fit to publish this work and I hope that it provides many readers the enjoyment it gave me.

Sincerely,

Donald W. Douglas

Donald W. Douglas

Mr. Ernest J. Gentle
President
Aero Publishers, Inc.
329 Aviation Road
Fallbrook, California

DWD:mh

DOUGLAS AIRCRAFT COMPANY, INC. / SANTA MONICA, CALIFORNIA

Table Of Contents

Chapter

THEY DESIGNED THE PLANE THAT CHANGED THE WORLD

Almost thirty-five years ago, in 1932-33, these men all worked on the design and production of the Douglas DC-1 transport, prototype of the fabulous Douglas DC-3 airliner. L. to R.: J. O. Moxness, Franklin R. Collbohm, E. H. Burton, Donald W. Douglas, Sr., James H. Kindelberger, W. Bailey Oswald, George Stompl, J. L. Atwood, [illegible] of the DC Skyships to sell the public on the utilization of this new mode of travel. Photo was made in 1959 on the flightline adjacent to Douglas Aircraft Company's Santa Monica plant where the DC-1 was born. DC-3 in background and the "probe" which Mr. Douglas is holding were being used to gather test data for the DC-8 program. (Photo by Stan Raymond.)

Chapter One

Out Of A Kansas Wheat Field

The youngest airline executive in the U.S., at 29, Jack Frye, Vice-President in Charge of Operations for Transcontinental & Western Air, Inc., could look out the window of his office at the Kansas City airport, TWA's main base, and see the planes takeoff and land. Himself a qualified transport pilot, Frye loved to fly. Roaring motors, the song of the sky, quickened his heart and inspired his imagination. Often times when he heard the sound, he would get up from his desk and glance out the window watching the big airliners as they thundered into the sky.

Invariably, he checked his watch by the arrivals and departures. Frye was a stickler for maintaining schedules. He had learned it the hard way, flying the mail. Timetable reliability was one yardstick by which he measured a successful airline.

On this particular morning he was overly concerned. The westbound plane was still on the ground. Already it had been delayed for more than an hour, and there was a VIP on the passenger list. Knute Rockne of Notre Dame was flying to Hollywood to be technical advisor for a feature film.

Frye went to the window and looked out. The scene was blurred. A drizzling rain was falling. There were ominous thunderheads in the sky. But the murky weather was moving out fast. The rain was stopping. He had checked the weather ahead. The sun was shining in Wichita, the next scheduled stop.

He could see the plane sitting there, parked in front of the passenger loading ramp. It looked ready to go, but there was no activity about. Then, suddenly, things began to come to life. Captain Bob Fry (no relation) and Jesse Mathias, co-pilot, in their snappy uniforms, walked briskly out to their charge. Mechanics swarmed around the airliner.

Soon the passengers began filing out of the terminal waiting room. Frye counted them as they climbed up the little ladder steps into the cabin. There were six, including Rockne. Frye recognized the latter, who was last to board the plane.

The door slammed shut. The engines whined, coughed and started with a throaty

Fokker F-10 Trimotor. (TWA Photo)

roar, their staccato blasts splitting the morning air. Ground crews pulled away the wheel blocks. The plane began taxiing out to the end of the runway. Frye watched the take-off and went back to his desk.

The big Fokker airliner was airborne at 9:15 A.M.

It was March 31, 1931.

"The death of Rockne started a revolution in air transport equipment," Frye said, recalling the Fokker crash. "It proved our planes were growing obsolete to a point of sacrificing safety. The honeymoon in the Lindbergh cottage was over."

He was referring to the fact that TWA in the thirties was known as "The Lindbergh Line," and had gained a lot of business and prestige because of the famous flyer's known association as a technical advisor and stock holder in the company. The name Lindbergh was magic in building public confidence in flying. Unfortunately, the fate of Rockne, sports idol of millions, tore down this same confidence. His death was a staggering blow to the struggling, infant airline industry.

The ill-fated airliner was completely demolished. The plane did not burn as sometimes reported in newspapers. (Kansas City Star Photo)

Less than an hour later, the airliner lay a twisted mass of cloth and wood, aluminum and steel, in a wheat field on the farm of Stewart Baker near Bazar, Kansas. Rockne, Fry, Jesse Mathias and the five others were all dead.

According to Baker's son, Edward, who saw the crash, the plane had come tumbling down out of the clouds with part of its wing fluttering after it. Then, with a terrifying sound, the craft plunged, nose first, into the ground.

II

Ten years later, talking with Jack Frye about the Rockne incident, we were sitting in the same office from where Jack had seen the ill-fated plane start off on its flight to eternity. In 1941, Frye was President of the airline. And outside, we could see a big four-engined TWA Boeing "Stratoliner" taking on her passengers. Progress had changed the scene.

Newspapers across the nation blamed the airline and the aircraft manufacturer relentlessly. Some of the editorials condemned air travel and aviation in general. Some of the accounts were biased and unfair. Most of them were full of technical inaccuracies and meaningless theories as to what had caused the accident. The Rockne thing put the spotlight on air transportation's mistakes and misfortunes, not on its accomplishments.

The adverse publicity was something that Rockne, himself, would have abhorred.

The Fokker Trimotors were among the best commercial airliners ever built. They had spanned the oceans and flown over the North Pole, a popular transport with the early family of airlines during the so-called "Lindbergh Era" 1927-32. Note the cowlings on this F-10 which helped increase the ship's speed, an early effort at streamlining. (TWA Photo)

TWA was also flying the larger Fokker airliner, the F-32, a thirty-two passenger, four-engine aircraft. Hanging from the huge wings were two nacelles, each housing a tractor-type and pusher-type radial-air-cooled engine. (TWA Photo)

Indeed, he would have been the first to come to the defense of the airlines. The famed coach and builder of men, was one of the strongest proponents of air travel. He took a plane whenever schedules permitted, and complained when air service was not available.

On one hot Saturday afternoon, a close friend revealed, Rockne invited humorist Will Rogers, to sit on the bench with him to watch Notre Dame's Fighting Irish battle it out with Southern California's Men of Troy on the gridiron. Rockne is reported to have remarked: "Just think, Will, someday we'll be able to see the game here in South Bend together in the afternoon. Then, after it's over, we'll hop a plane and I can see you do that rope trick on the stage in New York the same night. Neither one of us will have to be away from the job very long at either end of the line."

But Rockne was dead. The machine in which he was killed was a high-wing monoplane capable of carrying 10 passengers. Its fuselage was constructed of steel tubular frame covered with fabric. The wings were built entirely of wood with internally-braced spars and ribs of spruce, and covered with thin layers of veneer. The ship had three powerful motors, one in the nose, and one on each side of the fuselage hanging in cone-shaped housings, or nacelles, beneath the wing supported by a strut arrangement.

Designed by Anthony Hermann Gerhard Fokker, the Dutch aeronautical genius, the Fokker trimotored transports were considered among the finest planes ever built. These ships were world famous. The *Josephine Ford* in which Commander Richard E. Byrd was first to fly over the North Pole in 1926, was a Fokker trimotor. So was the *America* that Byrd flew across the Atlantic a year later. Fokkers had also flown the Pacific - Maitland and Hegenberger in *The Bird of Paradise;* Sir Kingsford Smith's, *Southern Cross.* The *Question Mark,* an Army Fokker trimotor, held the world's endurance record.

In this country, the Fokkers were manufactured by the General Aviation Corporation in St. Louis, Mo., a subsidiary of General Motors Corporation, under a special licensing arrangement. At the time GM was also interested in TWA which partly accounted for the airline using

Fokker equipment.

With such a record of reliability and patronage, what happened? What killed Rockne and the others?

Jack Frye (left) and Tony Fokker.
(Kansas City Star Photo)

Tony Fokker, himself, flew to the scene of the crash. The designer was furious and threatened to sue the airline. He maintained that the ship never should have been allowed to take off under existing weather conditions.

Naturally, TWA conducted its own investigation. Frye had an explanation. He said their belief was that the ship had flown into severe icing conditions. Ice had formed on the wings, weighing them down to the breaking point. This deduction coincided with the eye-witness account of the death dive. The ship had come apart in mid-air. But why? This was the point on which nobody could be sure. They could only surmise what might have happened.

The Bureau of Air Commerce crash investigators were more positive in pinpointing the cause. Under the Air Commerce Act of 1926, this government agency had jurisdiction over all private and commercial aviation. It was, in effect, the forerunner of the Civil Aeronautics Administration, the Civil Aeronautics Board and today's Federal Aviation Agency.

For days and weeks following the Rockne accident, Government crash detectives probed the wreckage searching for clues that might lead to the cause. They found what they believed to be a structural failure in the Fokker's wing. Their official report said that there were signs of rot in the wooden spars and ribs. As a result, the Government "red-tagged" all aircraft of this type, requiring a periodic inspection of the internal wing construction.

That action spelled the end of the Fokker airliners, according to Frye. "In order to conduct the inspection," he explained, "it was necessary to rip off the thin plywood covering on the wings, which meant a major repair operation. The time required, and the expense, would have put us out of business. We had to turn to a different type of airliner."

It was Jack Frye's job to find such a plane.

Jack Frye, who became President of TWA, poses beside the rudder fin of a TWA "Skysleeper," one of the first DC-3's that TWA ordered.
(Kansas City Star Photo)

III

Born in Sweetwater, Texas in 1902, Frye first got interested in flying, when a barnstormer pilot made a forced landing with an old Curtiss pusher biplane on the Frye ranch. Right then, Jack got the youthful notion that being a flyer was more glamorous than being a cowboy and he decided, someday, he would learn to fly. Before he was eighteen, he had hitch-hiked to California, met up with a wartime flyer, and in exchange for working on the aviator's plane, Frye got free flying lessons.

Not long after that he started giving flying lessons himself. Later, with two partners. W. W. (Walt) Hamilton, an automobile builder, and Paul Richter, a movie stunt pilot, he started the Aero Corporation of California. To begin with, it was just a small flying school operation and an aerial taxi service. But soon, they landed the sales agency for the popular Eaglerock biplane, one of the first post-war aircraft designed for private and commercial use. Business was good. They sold sixty planes the first year. The profit was about $500 on each sale.

Aero Corporation of California was started with this Fokker, single-engined transport. Pilot rode in cockpit directly behind propeller blast. (TWA Photo)

On a trip east delivering one of the Eaglerocks, Frye met Tony Fokker at the factory in St. Louis. The pair hit it off right from the start, and before leaving, Jack had made a deal to sell Fokker planes on the West Coast. Aero Corporation bought one of the Fokker F-7 transports, a single-engine, seven-passenger monoplane as a demonstrator. Frye flew it back to Los Angeles.

They sold five of the Fokkers, and then decided to keep one, and start an airline operation they had been thinking about. Standard Airlines was born, a subsidiary of the Aero Corporation. Carrying passengers only, the airline operated between Los Angeles and El Paso, Texas. Movie stars and their guests filled up the seats on almost every trip, flying to secluded desert hide-a-ways.

Standard Airlines also used the Fokker F-10 trimotors as this early Airline time-table illustrates. The airline was one of the first privately-owned passenger-carrying, scheduled operations in the U.S. (TWA Photo)

Harris M. "Pop" Hanshue (Western Airlines Photo)

Standard Airlines was one of the first scheduled airline operations in the country, started in 1926. Moreover, it was the only airline which didn't have a mail contract that was showing any profits. This factor, probably more than anything else, caught the calculating eye of Harris M. "Pop" Hanshue, President of Western Air Express, a major airline on the West Coast and one of the five original private air transport companies to be awarded a Government contract to fly the mail.

Hanshue, a shrewd operator, reasoned that if he could get control of Standard, it would bolster Western's passenger operation because of the Movie Colony "gravy train." At the same time, it would extend WAE's system into the rich southwest, with the possibility of getting more mail pay for the additional cities served.

Looking over the potential property, Hanshue made a flight in the Standard Airlines' Fokker to Phoenix and back. On the return trip he offered Frye and his partners $1,000,000 in Western stock for the Aero Corporation, lock, stock and airline. The Three accepted, and part of the deal also kept Frye, Richter and Hamilton on the WAE payroll as executive pilots. Later in 1928 when Western Air Express merged with Transcontinental Air Transport (TAT) to become Transcontinental & Western Air, Inc., the trio went along. Frye was made a vice-president of the new company in charge of all its flight operations.

In 1931, faced with the problem of get-

A later model of the Fokker, the F-7, was used by Standard Airlines on its Los Angeles to El Paso operation. (TWA Photo)

ting rid of the Fokkers, Frye was a little bitter about the whole thing. He still had a lot of faith in these airplanes, and he never did swallow the story about the wood rot. Although he admitted it might have been a rare case, caused by some unusual circumstances and maintenance carelessness. Anyway, there wasn't much he could do about it because of the Bureau of Air Commerce mandate involving the wings. The Fokkers had to go.

"The kind of plane we were really looking for hadn't been built yet," Frye declared. "There was need for an entirely new and revolutionary air transport, a bigger, faster plane, designed especially with passenger comfort and eye appeal in mind."

IV

Up in Seattle, Washington, home of the Boeing Airplane Company, the kind of progress Frye envisioned was being manufactured. Frye read about it in the papers in June, 1931. Boeing test pilots, Slim Lewis and Erik Nelson, flying in a revolutionary twin-engined bomber design, the XB-9, set a cross-country record from Seattle to Dayton, Ohio. The story also leaked out that Boeing had a twin-engined transport plane, built along the lines of the new bomber, on the design boards. They called it the Model 247. The design was reported to be a low-wing, all-metal monoplane, capable of carrying 10-passengers in a roomy, soundproofed cabin, at speeds approaching 200 miles per hour!

If and when, the Boeing design materialized, it would be a challenge to TWA, because of the Boeing association with United Air Lines. There were only two real giants in the air transport industry, such as it was in the early thirties, – TWA and United. Boeing was affiliated with United because of Boeing Air Transport, a subsidiary of the Boeing Airplane Company, which had been merged with Nation-

On the Western leg of its transcontinental "Mainline Airway." United Air Lines was flying these Boeing biplane trimotors. Note the triple-tail design. (United Air Lines Photo)

al Air Transport and Varney Airlines to become United Air Lines.

United's route was the "mainline airway" pioneered by the Post Office mail flyers. It stretched from New York via Cleveland, Chicago, Omaha, Denver, Elko, Nevada, across the northern middle U.S. with the western terminus at San Francisco. TWA's was the more southerly route New York, Pittsburgh, Columbus, Kansas City, Albuquerque, Phoenix and Los Angeles. Both carriers had juicy mail contracts, but they would do almost anything to get the passenger business away from each other. Getting the lead with faster, better equipment was one way to run the other fellow out of the sky.

United had jumped the gun. The Boeing Model 247 was no myth. Frye heard about it again, when United announced it was buying sixty of the planes and completely re-equipping its entire fleet with the most modern airliners ever built.

Moreover, when he contacted Boeing to see if TWA could buy some of the 247's, he got the cold shoulder. The answer was a blunt "No" – not until the United order was completed. Then, of course, it would be too late for TWA to get in the race.

"The chips were down," Frye described

Illustrative of the competitive environment among the two major transcontinental air carriers in the early 30's was United's introduction of the first stewardesses. Here, grouped around the square-door entrance to a Boeing 80A Tri-motor, wearing a dashing uniform of green wool twill, complete with "shower cap" tam are (front from left) Margaret Arnott, Inez Keller, Cornelia Peterman, Harriet Fry, Jessie Carter, Ellis Crawford and (in doorway from left) Ellen Church (UAL's first stewardess), and Alva Johnson. All nurses, the young ladies of the air, flew the San Francisco-Chicago route of Boeing Air Transport, a pioneer division of United.
(United Air Lines Photo)

The Boeing Model 247, a ten-passenger, high-speed, low-wing transport, one of the first airliners to start the modern trend toward comfort aloft. The 247 was almost twice as fast as the Ford Trimotors and the Fokkers. (United Air Lines Photo)

the predicament. "We got together, our whole engineering staff, operations and sales people, and put down on paper all the requisites that we thought should go into the ideal passenger air transport. There were some strong ideas on the subject. The project got a top priority rating. There wasn't much time to lose."

By the end of July, 1932, they had the specification finalized. Frye sent letters to different aircraft manufacturing companies – Glenn L. Martin in Baltimore, Consolidated in San Diego, the Curtiss-Wright Corporation in St. Louis, General Aviation, and the Douglas Aircraft Company in Santa Monica, California.

That letter was to have far-reaching implications. It precociously thrust the Douglas Aircraft Company into the manufacturing of commercial transport airplanes. The result was an airliner prototype whose descendants – the models which followed it – would change the concept of air travel.

Frye had vision unlimited. So did Donald W. Douglas, President of the Douglas Aircraft Company to whom one of the letters was addressed.

TRANSCONTINENTAL & WESTERN AIR INC.
10 RICHARDS ROAD
MUNICIPAL AIRPORT
KANSAS. CITY. MISSOURI

August 2nd,
19 32

Douglas Aircraft Corporation,
Clover Field,
Santa Monica, California.

Attention: Mr. Donald Douglas

Dear Mr. Douglas:

Transcontinental & Western Air is interested in purchasing ten or more trimotored transport planes. I am attaching our general performance specifications, covering this equipment and would appreciate your advising whether your Company is interested in this manufacturing job.

If so, approximately how long would it take to turn out the first plane for service tests?

Very truly yours,

Jack Frye

Jack Frye
Vice President
In Charge of Operations

JF/GS
Encl.

N.B. Please consider this information confidential and return specifications if you are not interested.

SAVE TIME — USE THE AIR MAIL

Donald W. Douglas, Sr., calls this letter "The Birth Certificate of the Modern Airliner."
(Douglas Aircraft Co. Photo)

The only American-designed combat plane developed during the war, the two-engine Martin bomber, came into use in the early 1920's. Above from left, with the MB-1 is Lawrence Bell, Eric Springer, Glenn Martin, Donald Douglas. (The Smithsonian Institution)

Chapter 2

The New Dimension

Donald Wills Douglas was born in Brooklyn on April 6, 1892, the son of William E. and Dorothy Douglas. An assistant cashier in a bank, Bill Douglas was fond of the sea. It was his wish that young Don would choose the Navy for a career. To encourage his son, they would often walk together down to the big shipyards, where they could see the great Naval vessels born in the drydocks. Young Douglas was fascinated by the ships. He studied hard, passed the necessary examinations, and won himself an appointment to the United States Naval Academy at Annapolis.

Shortly before he entered the service school in the fall of 1909, the seventeen-year-old youth took a trip to nearby Fort Myer, Virginia, where the Army Signal Corps was conducting acceptance trials on the Wright Brothers' flying machine, the first military airplane. Douglas saw Orville Wright put the flimsy, box-kite biplane through its paces, and he never forgot it. He decided that day his future would be with the ships of the sky.

There is a story that Douglas started building model airplanes while at the Academy, launched one from the dorm window one day, and it clipped the plumed hat off a passing admiral. Some accounts claim that as a result of the incident, he was officially asked to leave the school. This is an exaggeration. He did build model airplanes, however, when he wasn't buried in bookwork, or playing on the lacrosse team. And he did leave the Academy, after three years, resigning to enroll at the Massachusetts Institute of Technology and become an engineer.

Graduated from M.I.T. in 1914, after finishing the four year course in 24 months, he was asked to stay on as an Assistant Aeronautical Engineer. The salary was $500 a year.

His days at M.I.T., however, were worth, in experience, many times the dollars he received in pay. There, he worked with wind tunnels, the first aerodynamic research "tools" of their kind and size in the country. He also got to know Commander Jerome Clarke Hunsaker, who had designed the first big wind-tunnel. Hunsaker later was to become head of the National Advisory Committee for Aeronautics (NACA) the first Government-sponsored aeronautical research laboratory. It is now (NASA) National Aeronautics and Space Administration.

The know-how that brushed off on young Douglas enabled him to get a job with the Connecticut Aircraft Company, where he helped design the first dirigible for the Navy. Word of his talent got around, and before long Glenn L. Martin, the pioneer plane builder, hired him to be Chief Engineer of the Martin Company, then located in Los Angeles.

Douglas' reputation grew and about the time that the air war in Europe in 1916 was beginning in earnest, young Don Douglas was offered the job as Chief Civilian Aeronautical Engineer for the Aviation Section of the Signal Corps in Washington, D. C. The challenge was to design better planes than the Fokkers that were Germany's pride of the skies.

Douglas designed planes. He had ideas. But everytime he tried to get them off the ground, red-tape grounded them. Finally, he resigned and went back to Martin, who was building bombers for the Army Air Service. Douglas got right into the swing of things. He designed the Martin Corps d'Armee, which was the forerunner of the Martin bomber, the first order for an American-designed combat airplane. It would be followed by the twin-engined Martin MB-2, the giant biplane bomber that General "Billy" Mitchell used to sink the battleship *Ostrfriesland* in the famous bombing trials off the Virginia Capes in 1921.

If there were any truth to that story about the Admiral dismissing him from the Academy for the model airplane incident, young Douglas had his revenge. The results of the Mitchell bombings changed a lot of admirals' minds about the invincibility of the battleship. From that day to this, seapower has been dominated by airpower.

Donald Douglas was content to be with Martin at Cleveland where he found the work interesting and welcomed the opportunity to design and develop the type of aircraft in which he believed. He liked his working conditions.

But he was ambitious and in the back of his mind, there had long been the wish to establish his own aircraft company. He began giving this project serious thought immediately after the war and during his days at Cleveland, discussed the prospects with factory manager Larry Bell and draftsman "Dutch" Kindelberger.

A day of decision came in early 1920 when he finally went to Glenn Martin and said he would like to leave. Martin attempted to dissuade him but Douglas was firm in his decision and in April of the same year he entrained for Los Angeles.

II

When he arrived in Los Angeles he rented a small office in the back of a barbershop on Pico Boulevard. When he came home at night he hoed potatoes in small gardens back of his dwelling, so the family wouldn't starve.

A friend, Bill Henry, who once had worked for Martin as a public relations man, and now was a Los Angeles sports columnist, introduced Douglas to David R. Davis, a millionaire sportsman and flying enthusiast. Davis had expressed the desire to buy a plane and attempt a coast-to-coast non-stop flight. Don Douglas sold him the idea that the design he was working on could make the proposed 2,500-mile trip from LA to Curtiss Field, Long Island. Davis put up $40,000 to build the craft.

They called it the *Cloudster*. For its time, the ship was big, a wing span of 56 feet, fuselage length of 35 feet and a height of 13 feet. It was a biplane, fabric-covered, and it rested on conventional tractor type — two wheels and a tail-wheel — undercar-

The Douglas-designed "Cloudster" which was the first airplane that could lift a payload equal to its own weight! It was also the first plane that Douglas had designed for other than military purposes. Later it became a passenger transport. (Douglas Aircraft Co. Photo)

riage. The cruising speed was 85 miles per hour and it had a design range of 2,800 miles. The ship was powered with a 400-horsepower Liberty engine. It had one outstanding feature; the *Cloudster* was the first airplane ever built that could *lift a payload equal to its own weight!*

The plane was built in the second story loft of an old planing mill near the Southern Pacific station in downtown Los Angeles. Tools were borrowed from the shop downstairs. As the different sections of the plane were fabricated, they were lowered by block and tackle to a waiting truck, and hauled away to the old Goodyear dirigible hangar and field in East Los Angeles where the final assembly was accomplished.

Ironically, when the ship tried its first test hop in the first part of 1921, it couldn't get off the ground, but it was no fault of the design. Eric Springer, who had been Martin's chief test pilot, had joined the Douglas organization, and Davis had engaged him to pilot the ship on its transcontinental record attempt. When he tried to fly the plane for the first time, Springer simply ran out of take-off distance and had to ground-loop the ship or crash. The Goodyear field wasn't big enough.

On February 24, the ship made its first flight. They had made sure of enough take-off space, making the flight from March Field at nearby Riverside, California. There was a champagne christening with Davis' pretty niece, Jane Pearsall, wielding the bottle, and the plane lifted itself gracefully into the sky. So confident was Davis in the ship's ability, that he accompanied Springer on the initial flight.

Donald W. Douglas, Sr. (left) and David R. Davis. (Douglas Aircraft Co. Photo)

Donald W. Douglas, Sr. (center at front table) with designers and engineers in loft of old planing mill. (Douglas Aircraft Co. Photo)

The second Douglas manufacturing facility in California was a former motion picture studio on Wilshire Boulevard and 24th St. in Santa Monica. (Douglas Aircraft Co. Photo)

The fuselage of the "Cloudster" was fabricated of wooden frame partially covered with veneer. George Strompl, company's first production chief, is holding blueprint. In cockpit is Mr. Douglas wearing business suit and sporting moustache. (Douglas Aircraft Co. Photo)

On June 27, 1921 in the chilly dawn at March Field, Springer and Davis were in the *Cloudster* awaiting the official starter's signal. At 6:00 A.M., on the dot, they were off the ground and roaring eastward.

By noon, they had hurdled the western range of mountains and were zipping along over the Arizona desert near Yuma. At 3:45 P.M. they were over El Paso. The *Cloudster* was eating up the miles. Then, the faithful Liberty motor suddenly sputtered and quit altogether. They were forced down at Fort Bliss, Texas!

Before they got the plane repaired and flew it back to California for a second attempt, the goal was snatched from their grasp. Two Army Lieutenants, Oakley G. Kelley and John A. Macready, in a Fokker T-2 monoplane had spanned the continent – Roosevelt Field, Long Island to Rockwell Field, San Diego – 2,520 miles, non-stop, in 26 hours and 50 minutes! The challenge and the incentive gone, Davis sold the *Cloudster.*

For a while, the first Douglas-built airplane was used as an aerial cruise ship, taking passengers up for sightseeing flights over the California beaches and resort towns. Then, it was sold to T. Claude Ryan, who had started his own aircraft plant and airline in San Diego.

Ryan quickly re-built the *Cloudster* into a luxury passenger transport. The ship became a cabin airliner with plush interior, capable of carrying 12 passengers. Douglas, when he had designed the plane, didn't know that he had built his first commercial airliner.

The truth is, Douglas was more interested in going after the military business. Shortly after he had completed the Davis job, Douglas bought himself a railroad ticket to Washington. With the plans in his brief case for a fast, torpedo-bomber (created basically around the *Cloudster* design) he hounded Navy Department gold braid until he made them listen, and convinced the right authorities his new plane was just what the Navy needed. He came back to the coast with an order to build three of the ships.

The only trouble was, he didn't have any place to build the planes. Neither did he have enough money to buy materials or tools for the job. It was Bill Henry, again, who came to his aid. This time, the "angel" was the publisher of the Los Angeles *Times,* Harry B. Chandler, who with some banker friends put up $15,000, the amount Douglas said he needed. With the money, Douglas moved into the small factory layout in Santa Monica, California. It marked the beginning of the present Douglas Aircraft Company's sprawling empire.

Admittedly, there were some tight moments in those early days. Sometimes,

The "Cloudster" was fabricated in the old planing mill factory and then hauled to the Goodyear dirigible hangar and field in East Los Angeles for final assembly. Note the sign. (Douglas Aircraft Co. Photo)

Douglas M-2 mailplane. It was put into service flying the mail between Los Angeles and Salt Lake City by Western Air Express. Through this contact, probably, Douglas first became acquainted with Jack Frye when WAE merged with Transcontinental Air Transport (TAT) to become Transcontinental & Western Airlines, Inc.. (Western Airlines Photo)

Douglas confessed, he wished he had asked for more capital to start with, but it was against his Scotch grain. It wasn't easy. Workers had to sacrifice a few paydays. Their wives often helped to sew on the fabric covering. They had to beg and borrow for credit to get tools and materials. But they got the torpedo planes built. Everybody got paid, and more orders from the Navy followed. The plant grew.

By 1924, Douglas was building several different types of planes: Navy torpedo bombers, a highly-successful and economical single-engined mailplane, and some observation ships for the Army Air Corps. He was also working on a special project – the DWC – *Douglas World Cruisers.* These Liberty-powered biplanes could be used with either a wheel-type undercarriage, skis or big pontoons. Before the year was out, Army flyers in the DWC's had circumnavigated the globe, the first round-the-world flight in history.

By 1930, the Douglas name was a magic word in aircraft manufacturing circles.

III

Jack Frye followed with keen interest the design genius of the "Flying Scotsman." Indeed, Frye and Richter had seriously considered buying one of the popular Douglas *Dolphin* amphibians and starting a scheduled airline from Los Angeles to fabulous Catalina Island, 25 miles off shore in the blue Pacific, a resorter's paradise. The Hollywood crowd had promised to support the venture. It was the next project on the list for the Aero Corporation of California before the business was sold to "Pop" Hanshue.

Douglas also knew of Frye. They had met at various aviation dinners held around Los Angeles. Both had a profound respect for each other in their particular fields.

Perhaps, this is why Don Douglas looked twice at Jack Frye's letter, which he found

This was the scene in 1924 at Santa Monica when U.S. Army Air Services fliers hopped off on their epoch-making, round-the-world flight. The plane is a Douglas World Cruiser (DWC). (Douglas Aircraft Co. Photo)

in his stack of mail that Monday morning, the fifth day of August, 1932. The letter was marked – *Attention: Donald W. Douglas, President.*

Because Douglas knew of Frye's reputation as an airline operator, he was, naturally, more than just casually interested in the views which the latter set forth in the attached specifications. Consequently, he took the mimeographed page listing TWA's requirements for the super skyliner home with him that night to give it more serious thought.

The TWA specification called for an all-metal, trimotored monoplane. But, it said, that a combination materials structure or a biplane configuration would be considered. The main internal construction, the wings and fuselage, however, must be of metal.

Powerplants recommended were the 500 to 550-horsepower engines equipped with superchargers for high altitude operation, and built by Pratt & Whitney Engine Company of Hartford, Conn. These were the famous *Wasp* engines that powered the Lockheed *Vegas* which were setting all kinds of aviation records.

The plane, the specification set forth, must provide for a crew of two, pilot and co-pilot, with a cabin capable of carrying at least 12 passengers in comfortable seats with ample room, and fully equipped with the miscellaneous fixtures and conveniences generally expected in a commercial passenger plane. The payload should be, at least 2,300 pounds, with full equipment and fuel for maximum range.

The maximum gross weight specified was 14,200 pounds, almost double that of the Ford Trimotors. This must include allowances for radio, the latest flight instruments and navigational aids for night flying, and enough gasoline capacity for a range of 1,080 miles, the specification said.

Other performance requirements were:
Top speed, sea-level (minimum) 185-mph
Cruising speed, sea-level 146-mph
Landing speed, not more than 65-mph
Service ceiling (minimum) 21,000 feet
Rate of climb 1200 feet per minute

There was no doubt about it. Here, was a challenge tempting to any plane designer's ego.

It was 2:00 a.m. when Douglas finally laid the TWA proposal away and decided to turn in. But that night he slept fitfully because his subconscious mind kept going over, and over again, the challenging aspects of the TWA proposal. The mind kept asking questions. . . . *With the depression on, what assurance was there that the military orders, the prime source of Douglas business, would continue? Wouldn't Roosevelt, a former Assistant Secretary of Navy, if he were elected, slash the air appropriations and build more battleships? Moreover, with the whole air transport industry in a state of confusion, might not now be an opportune time to get into the commercial transport field?*

Next morning, the first thing Douglas did when he got to the plant was to call a meeting of his engineering, design and production chiefs. The group, when they gathered in Douglas' office, was comprised of men who had been with him almost from the beginning of the company. Over the ten year period, they had been chiefly responsible for the design and development of the planes which had given the company its spectacular rise to a prestige position in the industry.

The "boss" didn't waste any time getting to the point of the meeting. He got out the Frye letter and read it aloud.

One by one, he took up the requirements set forth in the specifications, pausing after each item, to get the group's opinion. They broke for lunch, but met again right afterwards, and the idea sessions continued all day, and long into the night. There were arguments, pro and con, over specific details and methods of approaching certain problems. But on one point everybody agreed – *In the best interests of the company, they should go after the TWA business, work up a design proposal and submit it to the airline people as soon as possible.*

The meeting finally broke up, when Douglas suggested everybody think about the thing for a couple of days, and they would meet again on Friday. Before he, himself, went home, he wrote a letter in long-hand for his secretary to type up in the morning. The letter addressed to Jack Frye simply said:

> "We are interested in submitting a proposal in answer to your bid invitation for the design of a new

James H. "Dutch" Kindelberger, in 1929, while chief engineer at Douglas Aircraft Co., in front of an early Douglas transport. Later, he became Chairman of the Board of North American Aviation, builders of the Supersonic XB-70. (Douglas Aircraft Co. Photo)

transport plane. When will it be convenient for some of our engineers to get together with your technical people and present our views?"

IV

"Well, what do you think?" Douglas opened the second meeting of the minds with that question.

James H. "Dutch" Kindelberger, Chief Engineer, was the first to answer. "I think, that we're damn fools if we don't shoot for a twin-engined job instead of a tri-motor," he stated. "People are skeptical about the trimotors after the Rockne thing. Why build anything that even looks like a Fokker or Ford?"

Kindelberger seemed enthusiastic as he continued: "Both Pratt & Whitney and Wright-Aeronautical have some new engines on the test blocks that will be available by the time we're ready for them. Lots of horses . . . any two of them will pull more power than any trimotor flying right now."

Douglas was in accord. He favored the bimotored idea, too. Perhaps, he recalled a bit of prophetic writing he had done under his byline in the January 1, 1919 issue of *Aviation* magazine, the leading trade publication. Then, talking about the new Martin bimotored bomber which he had helped to design, he had written – "The Martin twin is easily adaptable to the commercial uses that are now practical. . . . As a mail or express machine, a ton may be carried with comfort not only because of the ability of the machine to handle efficiently this load, but because generous bulk storage is

Arthur E. Raymond. He is now with the Rand Corporation. (Douglas Aircraft Co. Photo)

available. . . . Twelve passengers in addition to the pilot and mechanic can be carried non-stop up to 600 miles. . . . Requirements for safety, so important in air transportation, are especially well fulfilled by this machine because it can fly on one engine only!"

Besides, Douglas had a copy of a *Popular Mechanics* magazine on his desk in front of him. There was a two-page cut-a-way drawing, an artist's conception of the new Boeing 247 transport. "Take a look, in case you haven't seen this," he said holding up the magazine for all to see. "It looks pretty good to me.

Arthur E. Raymond, Kindelberger's assistant, got in his two cents worth with the remark – "There's a bad feature about the Boeing design that bothers me. . . . The main wing spar cuts right through the cabin and almost divides it in half. What's more, I don't like the fuselage cross-section. A tall guy would have to stoop over to walk up and down the aisle. . . ."

Kindelberger butted in – 'For Chris' sake, if we're going to build this thing, let's make it big enough, too, so a body can walk around in it, and stand up and stretch once in a while!"

"Why not use a modified version of Jack Northrop's taper wing?" Raymond continued. "Its airfoil characteristics are good. The taper and slight sweepback will give us some latitude with the center of gravity."

That wing would work, Douglas was thinking. *The internally-braced rib and spar, multicellular aluminum construction was strong enough to support the engines, mounted, say, on a stub-wing center section, one on each side of the fuselage. . . . It might be just the ticket.*

Raymond was way ahead of him – "We could build the wing in three sections," he explained. "A center section integrated right into the fuselage itself, a kind of stub-wing arrangement. That way it will be strong enough to support the engines and we'll have only the assembly. . . . At the same time, it will eliminate the need for the long, main wing spar obstructing the cabin . . ."

". . . We can bolt the outer wing panels to the center section, using a carpenter's butt joint," Douglas picked up the thought. "Then, slap on a piece of aluminum fairing and we've got it made."

Fred Stineman, one of Douglas' most capable designers, had something to add. "Ray's got a good idea," he pointed out. "With that kind of an arrangement we can extend the engine mounts protruding forward out of the wings, and get more direct benefit of the propeller thrust rushing back over the airfoil, building up more lift forces."

"If we wrap the engines themselves in the new NACA cowlings," he went on, "taking advantage of the streamlining, it should give us a big gain in top speed."

"What about a retractable gear?" someone interjected.

"The Boeing's got one," Douglas said. "We'd better plan on it, too. It should cut down on the drag about 20 per cent."

"Just make the engine nacelles bigger," Kindelberger chipped in. "Then, we can hide the wheels in the nacelles."

While this was going on, two other senior design engineers, Ed Burton and Fred Herman, had been listening, but they were talk-

Ed Burton. (Douglas Aircraft Co. Photo)

Fred Herman. (Douglas Aircraft Co. Photo)

ing in low tones to themselves and making some sketches on a note pad.

Burton took the floor.

"The way we're talking, it sounds like we're designing a racing plane," he remarked. "What about this 65-mph landing speed Frye wants?"

Herman was thinking about the same thing. "The way I see it, we're going to have to come up with some kind of an air brake, maybe, a flap deal that will increase the wing area during the critical landing moment and slow the plane down. . . . Conversely, it will give us more lift on take-off, help tote that big payload."

The talk went on like that for hours. Then, it broke up, but they were back at it again the next day. The days dragged into a week before they had kicked all the ideas around and arrived at any firm conclusions as to the direction they would take in finalizing the proposal. But slowly, the thinking was changing into more than theory, the ideas became more realistic, and the plane was shaping up.

Harry Wetzel (left) with unidentified early Air Mail pilot. (Douglas Aircraft Co. Photo)

They all agreed:

(1.) The ship would be a low-wing monoplane.

(2.) They would use a modified version of the Northrop wing.

(3.) It would be powered with two engines, not three.

(4.) The landing gear would be retractable into the engine nacelles.

(5.) They would devise some kind of a wing flap arrangement.

(6.) They would use the NACA cowlings and nacelles.

These were not new ideas. They had been tried before on other planes. But this was the first time, to anyone's knowledge, that all of them had been incorporated into a single airplane.

As the engineers and designers came up with the problems, and the answers, Harry Wetzel, Vice-President and General Manager, who also sat in on the conferences, tried to translate the aeronautical mumble-jumble into production language and factory problems. Some things they could do. Some things they couldn't do with the tools and facilities on hand. It would be a big re-tooling job to build the transport by the numbers. One thing was sure, the first plane would have to be a hand-built job.

They also had a name for the project. They called it the DC-1 – Douglas Commercial Model No. 1.

After the unfortunate Rockne incident TWA, as rapidly as possible, tried to equip their fleet with the all-metal Ford trimotors, an 11-passenger plane popularly called "The Tin Goose." (TWA Photo)

Chapter 3

"There's only one way to find out . . ."

High above the Mojave desert in the night sky, a TWA Ford trimotor droned eastward toward Phoenix. In the cockpit, Paul Richter was at the controls and D. W. "Tommy" Tomlinson was riding co-pilot. Up front it was noisy, and the wind, whistling past the corrugated metal skin, sounded like a howling banshee. It was drafty and cold, and the vibration was unpleasant and nerve-racking.

"How's the new stratosphere project coming?" Richter shouted above the roar of the motors.

Tomlinson, a former Navy flyer, was a special assistant to Jack Frye. There was talk that the airline planned to build a special airplane to explore the problems of flying in the substratosphere altitudes above 20,000 feet. It was Tomlinson's project.

Paul Richter in cockpit of DC-1. (TWA Photo)

D W. "Tommy" Tomlinson and Northrop "Gamma" overweather ship. The wing construction on this plane, designed by Jack Northrop, was one of the secrets of the DC-1 airfoil. Tomlinson worked closely as TWA representative with Douglas in flight-testing the DC-1. (TWA Photo)

Charles A. Lindbergh (center) and TWA officials. (TWA Photo)

"I think we're going to go with the Northrop job," he told Richter.

"*Alpha* or *Gamma*?" Richter laughed. (These were the names of two Northrop plane models.)

"The *Gamma*," Tomlinson said. "The bigger engines with the turbo-superchargers, should be able to boost it way upstairs. . . ."

The plane roared on through the night.

It was a strange coincidence. Up there in the rattling old Ford trimotor, Richter and Tomlinson were talking about Jack Northrop. Far below them, the Santa Fe eastbound train was clickety-clacking over the rails. The lights in its cars gave the appearance of a giant phosphorescent serpent moving across the desert floor. In one of the Pullman compartments, two other men were talking about Northrop. Arthur Raymond and Harry Wetzel were on their way to New York City to present the DC-1 proposal to the TWA people.

"We're lucky to have had the experience with the Northrop wing," Raymond was saying.

"It sure makes the production simpler," Wetzel agreed. "We can use many of the machines and tools we already have for the wing fabrication job."

The outer wing panels shall be demountable from the center wing by means of a continuous flanged bolted joint.

Materials and workmanship shall be in accordance with the Department of Commerce requirements and shall be subject to TWA inspection and approval during construction. Where Department of Commerce requirements do not cover, those of the Army or Navy shall apply.

The fuselage shall be metal monocoque. Fin and stabilizer shall be attached directly to the fuselage and shall be cantilevered from it. Construction of the tail surfaces shall be multicellular, similar to that used on the Northrop "Alpha."

There were notes, drawings, blueprints and photographs scattered all over the compartment for reference; a mass of disassociated facts and figures. Somebody had to put them all together in a presentation that was readable and made sense. Raymond and Wetzel had drawn the assignment.

Douglas had received an answer from Frye setting up a meeting with Lindbergh and Richard W. Robbins, TWA president, in the New York offices of the airline. Things were moving fast. Now, Raymond and Wetzel were writing the final version of the proposal enroute.

The wings shall be of cellular multiweb construction similar to that used on the Northrop "Alpha," Raymond wrote in longhand on a lined tablet. *The center portion of the wing shall be integral with the fuselage and shall mount the nacelles and retractable chassis (landing gear).*

It was dull, technical, engineering writing, a tedious, time-consuming task. Everything had to be absolutely accurate. Details were vitally important. The TWA crowd knew their stuff. They would shoot holes in anything that smacked of impracticability.

At Chicago, where they had to change trains and board the Pennsylvania Railroad Limited, Raymond was just about halfway through with the presentation.

There were so damn many little things:

The arrangement of the lavatory at the rear of the cabin in connection with the cabin entrance door shall be similar to that used on the Fokker F-10, Raymond's almost numb fingers, jotted down. *The toilet unit shall be constructed completely of metal and shall be easily cleaned. The container shall be removable. Design to be approved by TWA.*

A call button shall be provided in the lavatory.

There shall be space of one-inch between the outside of the seat arms and the fuselage wall, and an aisle sixteen-inches wide between the seats.

Semi-sealed space suitable for dry ice shall be provided in the buffet for cooling refreshments.

One hand fire extinguisher shall be located in the cockpit and one at the rear of the cabin.

The clock for the instrument panel shall be a Pioneer-Waltham, Type 543 – with two sets of hands.

Every mile the train clicked off, it seemed, Raymond wrote down another item, 989 in all, and each had to be listed by type, source and weight. Besides, there were the general descriptive paragraphs and the estimated performance figures. By the time he had finished, he had used up five pads of paper. The train was pulling into Penn Station.

Fortunately, the detailed design spec was done in time for them to keep their appointment. When they walked into the TWA offices, Frye was there to meet them. So was Tomlinson, who had flown the eastbound trip in the day before. Walt Hamilton and Richter also were present for the meeting.

Robbins, TWA President, joined them about 10:30 A.M. and brought Lindbergh with him. Harold E. Talbot, Jr., Chairman of North American Aviation which was affiliated at the time with TWA through the General Aviation (General Motors) interests, also dropped in. This was a pleasant surprise for Raymond and Wetzel. They knew Talbot was a close friend of Don Douglas.

II

For more than three weeks there were discussions with Frye and Lindbergh and the airline representatives. At times, there were disagreements over different approaches to specific problems. But, one by one, the differences were ironed out.

Although tired, Raymond and Wetzel were in high spirits. After the first few meetings, they hadn't heard mention about the other designs which, Frye admitted, TWA was considering. Every indication pointed to Douglas getting the contract. A good sign was that the airline lawyers began sitting in on just about every meeting. The technical discussions were being translated into legal, contract terms.

There was just one last point of agreement to be resolved.

Raymond called Douglas long-distance to talk about it.

"It looks like we're in," he said. "But we have to have your decision on a matter Lindbergh insists on."

"What does Lindbergh want?"

"He wants a guarantee that the plane will be able to take-off with a full load from any field along the TWA routes – *on one engine*. It must also be able on one engine to climb and maintain level flight over the highest mountains along the way."

For a moment, Douglas' thoughts went back to the Martin Twin. But that was like comparing *Old Ironsides* with Germany's *Bremen* luxury liner.

"How do you feel about it?" he asked Raymond.

"I did some slide-rule estimates. . . . It comes out 90 per cent YES, and 10 per cent NO. The ten per cent is keeping me awake nights. One thing is sure, it's never been done before with an aircraft in the weight class we're talking about. . . ."

"Let's wait till I check with Kindelberger," Douglas said. "I'll call you back."

When Douglas put the question to Kindelberger, "Dutch" made the Lindbergh demand sound almost too simple.

"There's only one way to find out," he declared, "Build the thing and try it."

On September 20, 1932, the contract was signed in Dick Robbin's office. The price agreed upon for the service test airplane was $125,000 to be paid in gold bullion. If the costs of the service test model went over that figure, Douglas would have to stand the difference. An option clause in the contract gave TWA the right (and there was the intent) to buy all, or part of sixty additional airplanes in lots of ten, fifteen or twenty at $58,000 apiece. This figure did not include the cost of the powerplants.

The same day Douglas signed the work order to start the DC-1 project and sent it

Ford Trimotor interior. Seats were wicker back chairs, six along one side and five along the other side of a narrow aisle. Note lamp fixtures on walls. (TWA Photo)

down to the shops.

Talking with Raymond in New York, he made the comment – "It will probably cost us two or three times that figure to build the airplane, but the future looks bright."

That night, he was also pleased at the Douglas stock close in market reports he read in the paper. Inwardly, it tickled him.

Raymond had told him that from the very beginning, Frye and Lindbergh and the other technical people, had "bought" the DC-1 proposal. Their main reason for hesitating had been, "trying to convince the bankers that a plane with this kind of performance can be built."

Apparently, the bankers were convinced. The meetings in New York and the whole program were supposed to have been very secret and confidential so as not to tip off the competition on what TWA was doing. But somewhere along the line, it must have leaked out. On the day he had received the invitational bid from Frye, Douglas Aircraft closed at $7.12 per share. The day after the contract for the DC-1 was signed, it was up to $16.00!

III

Wetzel stayed in New York for a few days to complete the contractual arrangements. But Raymond and Frye headed back to Kansas City to iron out some of the fine points in the revised design specs. They made the trip by air. The discussions lasted for several days. Then, Raymond boarded another TWA plane and flew to Los Angeles.

It was the first time that he ever had flown coast-to-coast. He, frankly, didn't like flying. But he decided it would be good business to see first-hand the good and bad points of the then, in-service airliners. It would certainly help in avoiding the same mistakes in the DC-1.

"That trip was an experience I'll never forget," Raymond described it. "They gave us cotton to stuff in our ears, the 'Tin Goose' was so noisy. The thing vibrated so much it shook the eye glasses right off your nose. In order to talk with the guy across the aisle, you had to shout at the top of your lungs.

"The higher we went, to get over the mountains, the colder it got inside the cabin. My feet nearly froze.

"The lavatory in the tail was so small that you could barely squeeze through the door. It wasn't even a good Chic Sale.

"The leather-upholstered, wicker-back chairs were about as comfortable as lawn furniture, and they were so narrow they pinched your fanny.

"When the plane landed on a puddle-splotched runway, a spray of mud, sucked in by the cabin air vents, splattered everybody.!"

The first opportunity he had to get with Douglas, Raymond described the flight in disgust. "We've got to build comfort, and put wings on it," he emphasized. "Our big problem is far more than just building a satisfactory performing transport airplane."

His philosophical attitude on the subject, started everybody thinking seriously about such things as soundproofing, cabin temperature control, improved plumbing, more comfortable seats – and no mud baths! All of these innovations were to be engineered and built into the DC-1 transport.

Designers, engineers and draftsmen were already at work on the first drawings and blueprints. They had started even before Raymond and Wetzel left for New York. Don Douglas really had made up his mind all along that they would build a commer-

Will Rogers and "Slim" Lindbergh in cockpit of Ford Trimotor. Note the external control cables running alongside the corrugated skin. (TWA Photo)

Amelia Earhart with unidentified passenger riding as passengers in Ford Trimotor. The famous aviatrix flew one of first TAT Fords when these planes pioneered air-rail transcontinental route in 1929, forerunner of TWA. (TWA Photo)

cial transport, whether TWA bought it or not.

Here and there in the shops, things began to look different. Something big was going on, and a visitor could sense it in the workers' attitude, and see it by the glint in their eyes.

IV

There is a pattern that follows true to form in the design and building of any new airplane. It was the formula used by the Wright Brothers, when they built the

The Ford Trimotors were also in use by other airlines, as is evidenced by this American Airways Ford, (forerunner of American Airlines, Inc.) which brought FDR, the Democratic nominee for President, to the 1932 convention in Chicago. FDR would become first president to use the airplane as mode of travel. (American Airlines, Inc. Photo)

When Douglas decided to build the DC-1, the Douglas Aircraft Company plant, located at Santa Monica with adjacent Clover Field, looked like this: about 350,000 square feet of factory space, approximately 900 employees. (Douglas Aircraft Co. Photo)

Wright Flyer which was the first successful, heavier-than-air, power-driven, man-carrying, flying machine. The same process also applies to the DC-8, the Douglas titan of the skies in the Jet Age.

This development process, not unlike the practices used in ship-building, breaks down into four major operations. (1) The blueprint and design stage, where the action takes place over the drafting boards, turning ideas into workable plans. (2) The construction of a reduced-scale model for wind tunnel testing to determine if the design is aerodynamically sound. Can it fly by all standards of aerodynamic law? (3) Building of a full-scale mock-up to determine the best location for the installation of necessary accessories, systems and fixtures. (4) The fabrication of the plane itself.

When work started on the DC-1, the Douglas Aircraft Company in Santa Monica covered about eight acres of land adjacent to an excellent, all-paved-surface airport named Clover Field. Office buildings and factory provided about 350,000 feet of floor space. There were some 900 people employed at the plant.

In the jigs, and moving along the assembly line, when George Strompl, shop superintendant got the order to "make room for the new transport," were some Army observation planes, the Navy torpedo bombers, and a new twin-engined amphibian which had just been adopted as a standard type for Army, Navy and Coast Guard squadrons.

There was also, the Douglas subsidiary, the Northrop Corporation, with a factory of some 140,000 square feet of floor space located at the Los Angeles Municipal Airport near El Segundo, California. Northrop employed another 1,000 persons whose skills could be called upon. It was producing an all-metal, low-wing, mail plane, popularly called the *Alpha*. Another design, along the same lines, but bigger and with many new innovations, called the *Gamma*, was in the experimental stages. Both these planes were headline makers, and the plant was famous for its pioneering efforts in the design and development of high-speed, high-altitude performance aircraft.

The DC-1 was to be built in the Santa Monica plant. Even when they started just thinking about the project, it began to shove other things out of the way.

The blueprint stage began in a corner of the factory in a little cubicle about the size of a double hotel room. There was the usual,

George Strompl, who was shop superintendent during the DC-1 project. (Douglas Aircraft Co. Photo)

Two views of DC-1 scale model in California Institute of Technology Wind Tunnel. (Douglas Aircraft Co. Photo)

and expected, engineering wit's sign on the door – FRANKENSTEIN'S WORK SHOP. The men who designed the DC-1, turning the concept into a reality, practically lived there for the next six months.

Other factory workers, who didn't take much heed of the more serious sign that said – SECRET PROJECT – KEEP OUT – peeked in whenever possible, and saw strange hieroglyphics taking shape in the lines on the drafting boards. They saw, too, the cut-a-way drawing of the Boeing 247 pasted on the wall and the admonishment under it which read – *Don't copy it! Do it better!* There was another reminder sign – *When you design it . . . think about how you would feel if you had to fly it! Safety first!*

Dr. W. B. Oswald. (Douglas Aircraft Co. Photo)

Engineers, too, have their weaker moments. Probably they will never change. One sees the same signs today in any big aircraft or missile plant.

Perhaps, that is why – as someone has said – airplanes are born, not made. They are hatched in men's minds, and they grow because their creators approach the problems of flight with the human touch, as well as the cold, scientific facts.

V

Out of "Frankenstein's Work Shop," back in the fall of 1932, there came first, the drawings for a Lilliputian version of the new transport – an 11th-scale model. These were followed by hundreds of full-scale drawings, the patterns and instructions for building the wings, fuselage, empennage, and every part, system and accessory thereof, for the DC-1. Turned into blueprints by the yard, they could cover the playing field in a dozen football stadiums.

Meanwhile, the small model was undergoing hundreds of tests in the 200-mile-an-hour wind tunnel at the California Institute of Technology. Supervising these findings was Cal Tech physicist and aerodynamicist, Dr. W. B. Oswald, who had been hired as a consultant on the project.

"Meanwhile, these investigations included tests on three complete wings with various modifications," Oswald explains. "We also tried out various tail surfaces, landing gears and tail wheels of different sizes, several sets of ailerons of special types, six arrangements of high-lift wing flap devices and other aerodynamic features.

"We learned a lot. Early configurations, for example, showed instability characteristics, and it forced design changes of a hitherto untried arrangements, affecting the center of gravity of the airplane.

"The result was we increased the sweepback of the outer wing panels, creating a sharper frontal wedge-like effect for the whole wing, which offered the advantage of moving the engine nacelles further forward, and having the center of gravity come well ahead of the wing for stability.

"If the wind tunnel tests had not been made, it is very possible that the airplane would have been unstable, because all the previous engineering estimates and normal investigations, had indicated that the original arrangement was satisfactory."

When the wind tunnel tests were finished and the final aerodynamic configurations firmed up, the fabrication process began simultaneously on two airplanes. One was a full-scale mock-up made of wooden frame work and covered with heavy paper to simulate the aluminum skin of the real airplane. The other, was the DC-1 itself. Both jobs posed new problems. The first, because man is never satisfied, and kept changing things around to determine the best location and proportions of all structural details and installations. The second, because the metal skeleton and stressed skin construction was new, applied to an aircraft of this size, and the work was, in many respects, trial-and-error operation.

George Strompl, one of those loyal friends who had left Martin to cast his lot with Douglas in the beginning, recaptured some of the DC-1 construction scenes in a vivid word picture.

"We called the mock-up, the *fun house* because so many bodies kept going in and coming out of it," George says. "This procession never seemed to stop. One day, for example, a group of men would bring in a dozen or so wooden boxes of odd shapes and sizes – dummy fixtures – and they would disappear inside the mock-up for hours. Then, out they would come, bringing the boxes with them. The next day, it would be the same thing over again, only the boxes would be different shapes and sizes from the ones of the previous day.

"I remember, I'd be passing by the thing, and I'd peek in for a look – there would be two or three seats along one side, and it began to look like the interior of a passenger plane. The next day, I'd look in again, and the seats would be different type seats entirely.

"One day the cabin would be trimmed with a certain kind of material, in a bright attractive color scheme, with curtains, carpeting and chair upholstering blending nicely – a sight we didn't expect to see in an airplane in those days. But, the next time you looked at it, the 'wall-papering' was of a different material, so was the carpet, and colors looked like some tattoo artist had gone berserk.

"We began to think the interior decorators had blown their stacks. Nothing like this had ever gone on before in the plant. It was a lot different from building a fuselage with an open cockpit, slapping a pair of wings on it, and rolling it out of the factory – which was standard operating procedure with the Army observation jobs and the Navy planes."

Jack Frye, in another interview in 1952 when he was President of the General Analine Corporation, also remembered the DC-1 mock-up.

"Tommy Tomlinson and I spent days in the mock-up, in the pilots' compartment, trying out every possible arrangement of the various items," Frye explained. "A complete control system with wooden dummy members made to exact size and in working order, was installed with strings in place of the control cables.

"Every lever, knob and handle, even such minor things as the remote control handle for the radio and the auxiliary heat control for the cabin, were actually installed in a countless variety of positions to determine the most practical arrangement.

"The instrument board was complete with full-scale dummies of all the flight, fuel and powerplant dials and controls."

"Trying out the cockpit lighting and the radiumized dials on gauges and indicators, sometimes, we sat in that 'hot box' for hours, in total darkness except for the instrument lights. Then, to test the instrument panel lighting against any possible reflections from ground lights, we had workmen outside, throw flashlight beams into the cockpit.

"The cockpit seats just about drove us nuts. Naturally, we wanted the seats to be comfortable, so at first, we put arm rests on both sides of the seat. But the cockpit was so narrow, and the space in between the two seats was so cluttered up with throttle controls and other gimmicks, including the auto pilot, that it required a contortionist to get up out of either seat and go back into the cabin. When you tried to climb out of the seat, you had to straddle the control column, and that could have proved dangerous.

"In the final arrangement, the seats were designed so that the arm facing the aisle could be folded back out of the way to facilitate getting in and out. It could be quickly locked back in place, when the pilot was seated. The problem of the control column was solved with a yoke type control, mounted on a U-shaped frame, so that each pilot had a wheel, but the movement of the controls was as one unit."

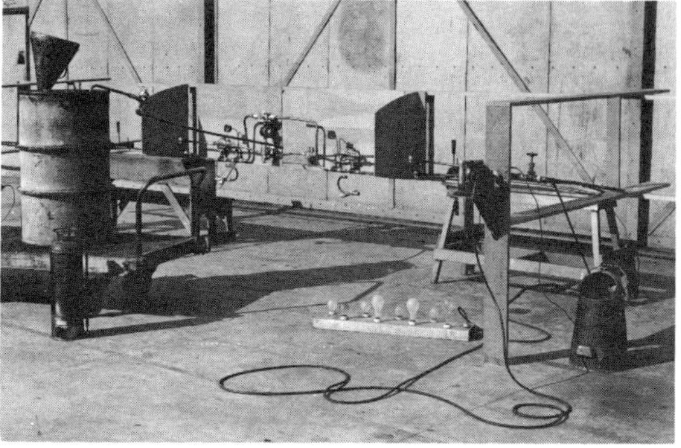

Jerry-rigged test installation for trying out gasoline and oil feed systems for the DC-1. (Douglas Aircraft Company Photo)

VI

There were a number of other working model set-ups made for test purposes. A complete brake system was built up with cylinders, oil lines, handles, hand brake lever and all component parts. Similarly, they duplicated the hydraulic retracting system for the landing gear and wing flaps. The fuel system also was duplicated, with

DC-1 Cockpit. (Douglas Aircraft Co. Photo)

The DC-1 wing structure, adapted from the Northrop multi-cellular design, showing the "honeycomb" rib construction. (Douglas Aircraft Co. Photo)

all gasoline and oil lines of actual size and length, and all valves and controls installed.

The construction problems on the plane itself are illustrated by this further description of Strompl's – "We didn't have any big hydraulic presses for stamping out cowlings, fairings and the odd-ball shaped aluminum parts that an airplane requires, like they have today. The work on the DC-1 of this nature was all done by hand. It required craftsmanship, not just the operation of a machine.

"The sheet-metal worker studied the plan carefully. Then, he went over and took a sheet of aluminum, the right size and gauge from the stockroom, scratched out the pattern he desired onto this raw stock, and went to work with his tin snips. After that, he found the right shaping blocks and tapped the thing with mallet blows until it took the proper form.

"Sometimes, an operation of this kind took several days. Today, the same thing takes a fraction of a minute."

There was trouble right from the start,

One of the wing tests with shot bags piled on the DC-1's aileron to subject it to extreme pressures. (Douglas Aircraft Co. Photo)

too, in the fabrication of the DC-1's wing. The Northrop multi-cellular construction consisted of a flat skin, re-inforced by numerous logitudinal members and ribs. The skin carried the stress loads and torsion, with the ribs preserving the contour (airfoil) and dividing the internal structure up into a number of small, rigid boxes or cells, a honeycomb effect. This type of construction provided very small unsupported areas, extreme lightness for its strength and rigidity, and at the same time simplified inspection, maintenance and repair.

It had proved highly satisfactory in the Northrop *Alpha* design, but in this case, the total wing area was comparatively small. When the principle was carried out on a larger scale for the big transport wing, it was necessary, while maintaining the advantages of the honeycomb structure, to redesign and enlarge the structural members.

Because a wing of this magnitude and area never had been built using this type of structure before, a test wing section was fabricated and subjected to extreme strength tests.

"We not only had to design the plane itself, piece by piece, assembly by assembly," Douglas points out, "but we had to devise testing techniques, and design and build the machines to carry them out.

"One of the sights I'll never forget is looking out the window and seeing Fred Herman, perched up on the seat of a steam roller, and driving the thing back and forth, up and over that wing test section. The structure never gave an inch. It was almost unbelievable, and I was tempted to go down and drive that steam roller myself."

About the same time, Douglas would have seen another sight worthy of remembering, had he been standing on the ramp at Boeing Field up in Seattle, Washington. On February 8, 1933, bright and shiny in its coat of silver, the Model 247 roared into the sky on its initial test flight.

It is likely, though, that Douglas would have chuckled a little bit to himself at the

They didn't know how to test the wing for strength, but man will find a way. That's Fred Herman up on the steamroller. The wing didn't even wrinkle! (Douglas Aircraft Co. Photo)

Boeing Model 247 (United Air Lines Photo)

remark one of the Boeing engineers made as he watched the sleek, twin-engined transport wing its way, a thing of grace and beauty, out over Puget Sound.

"They'll never build 'em any bigger," the engineer said in a moment of exuberance over the occasion.

The DC-1 was bigger.

Moreover, some 1300 miles to the south, it was beginning to take shape in the transformation process from drawing board to blueprint . . . to model . . . to mock up . . . to plane of tomorrow.

VII

For the uninitiated, the terms of aircraft nomenclature, the airframe – fuselage, wings, tail-surfaces and under-carriage – are the aircraft manufacturer's prime concern and responsibility. It is true, he has to design and build this airframe based on the power plants available, whether that is a piston-engine-propeller combination, turbo-prop, pure jet or a rocket motor. But these propulsion units, he buys from the engine manufacturer "off the shelf," like the boating enthusiast goes down to the hardware store and buys the outboard motor for the rowboat he built in his backyard. Only, it must be pointed out, the airframe builder doesn't pay for the powerplants; this is a separate contract between the customer and the engine manufacturer.

Consequently, $125,000 for the DC-1, or the $58,000 for any one of production planes, did not include the price of the engines. The powerplants would be furnished by TWA. But, as the airframe neared completion, the airline people still hadn't decided definitely on the engines. It was a toss up between the Pratt & Whitney *Hornet* or the Wright Aeronautical *Cyclone*, aircooled, radial engines.

Naturally, both engine companies wanted the contract. Both the big engine concerns sent field engineers and mechanics to the Douglas plant with their latest engine models. It was essential that the airframe and engine people work closely together. In this case, the plane had been designed so that either of the two engine types was adaptable. The competition for the engine contract was fierce.

"It looked like there was a war going on down in the hangar area where the engine boys had set up shops," Douglas described the scene. "The Wright gang had set up their own camp on one side of the ramp, and the P&W crowd had done the same thing across the way. There was a kind of *no-man's land* in between.

"Workers from neither faction never crossed the big white line which had been painted between the two camps. Nor did the two groups ever fraternize; they didn't even talk to each other. Work went on in each camp with the respective engines hidden from the opposition by giant screens and tent shelters.

"It was a standing joke, that if you walked from one camp to the other, you were running the risk of being shot as a spy.

"After things had been going on like that for a while, I called in Ivar Shogran, Chief of our Powerplant Section, and told him we should try to get the groups together. The situation was getting unhealthy, and disrupting other workers. Besides, there wasn't any reason for feud anymore.

"Back at the main Wright plant in Paterson, N. J., they had developed a new cooling fin and cylinder design which showed great promise. Both we and TWA had decided to go with the Wright *Cyclones* in the DC-1.

Ivar Shogran. (Douglas Aircraft Co. Photo)

"I'll never forget Ivar's expression when I told him. He threw up his arms in disgust, and practically shouted – *Don't tell those guys down on the line anything. We might get a helluva good engine outta this war yet!*

"Our little private, 'war of the horses,' as we called it, kept right on, even after the participants learned, via the grapevine, that the Wright engines had gotten the nod.

"As it finally developed, we tried both powerplants before the airline placed any production order."

By the time the DC-1 was ready to accept the engines, another development cast a shadow over the whole operation. The em-

By mid-May 1933 the fuselage of the DC-1 was beginning to take shape. This was the only DC-1 ever built. (Douglas Aircraft Co. Photo)

phasis on comfortization and all the plush and plumbing, had added a lot of weight to the basic design. Before the engines were even installed, the ship was half a ton overweight!

It was a serious turn of events. There were some raised eyebrows in engineering. The minds behind the eyebrows said the ship had grown too heavy; that the wind tunnel tests didn't mean anything, and neither did all the hopes and prayers. The plane was just too much metal for the known powerplants available to lift off the ground.

"She won't get off the ground with both engines running wide open," one skeptic declared, and offered to bet on it. "How the hell can we ever expect to pass the single engine test?"

"What about it?" Douglas asked Raymond.

"I've been talking with Al French, the West Coast representative for the Hamilton Standard Propeller people," Raymond assured the boss. "French says the new adjustable pitch propellers have been perfected, and that Frank Caldwell's gear box idea will greatly increase propeller efficiency. They'll be ready by the time we're ready to fly the ship."

All along, they had known what was happening, and what to do about it. They had been banking on the new props to bail them out of trouble.

With the new adjustable pitch prop, it meant that pilots could automatically adjust the blade angles so that they would take bigger "bites" of air at take-off power, providing increased thrustpower which would pull the heavier loads, beat up bigger cushions of air to support the wings. Likewise, the "bite" could be dampened for cruising speeds so the engines wouldn't eat up all the gasoline too quickly or burn themselves out.

If it worked, they had it made.

But as Kindelberger had said – *There was only one way to find out.*

Chapter 4

"Old Three Hundred"

Douglas Commercial Model No. 1 was given the license number X-223Y and Company Plane No. 300. In this photo taken minutes before her maiden flight she was on the flight line at Clover Field. Note the vintage cars in background. She was big for her day and weighed more than six tons, even without her cabin furnishings. (Douglas Aircraft Co. Photo)

The last week of June, 1933, little more than ten months after Don Douglas had opened Jack Frye's letter and bid invitation, the plane TWA wanted was rolled out of the factory hangar and onto the ramp at Clover Field. She was a thing of precision and promise. Bright and shiny, her aluminum skin glistened in the sun's rays. Although her lines were sleek and trim she was a giant; more than six tons of metallic machine.

According to Douglas, the ship had cost more than $307,000 to build, including the design and engineering hours.

"That figure loomed mighty big everytime I thought about the $125,000 price tag we had put on the ship for TWA," Douglas admits. "The odds, however, were in our favor. The TWA people had just about made up their minds, even at this stage, to place a mass order for the ship. Frye, himself, had given us this intelligence. Actually, even before the DC-1 first flew, the production model DC-2's, were beyond the drawing and blueprint stages.

"About the only thing that might cause the whole deal to blow up, would be if something were radically wrong with the design, which the wind-tunnel and design studies certainly didn't indicate was the remotest possiblity. Then, too, there was the single-engine take-off requirement."

Out in the open, the DC-1 looked like she could do anything that she might be called upon to perform. The fuselage was sixty feet in length from nose to tail, half again as long as a Greyhound bus. In profile it was fish-shaped, oval-like in cross-section, with six square windows along each side. The ship rested on the conventional aircraft undercarriage. The nose was high in the air.

Walking forward, up the cabin aisle to the pilots' compartment in the nose, was like walking up an inclined ramp – about a 30-degree angle. There was a large arch-like door on the left side of the fuselage just behind the last rearward window. Two smaller doors, one forward of the cabin and the other in the tail, provided access to mail and baggage compartments. Pilots entered the airplane through the main cabin door.

The wing of the DC-1, tip to tip, measured 85 feet, and in plan form it was shaped like a wide-angle inverted "V",

Carl A. Cover. (Douglas Aircraft Co. Photo)

about seven feet wide at the blunt-nosed apex (center section) with the outer panels tapering off to about three feet in width at their half-moon-shaped tips. The airfoil, or cross-section of the wing was an elliptical plane, some two-feet in thickness, allowing for internal gas tanks. Total wing area was 789 feet, and the wing was designed to lift and support about 22 pounds per square inch!

The DC-1's engines were the latest Wright, 710-horse-power, nine-cylinder, air-cooled radials. Propellers were three-bladed, nine-foot diameter, Hamilton Standard's incorporating the adjustable pitch mechanism.

The plane, as it stood there in the hot June sunshine, was still far from complete, although it was ready to make its test flight within a few days. Inside, the cabin was still raw frame and skin with no insulation or sound-proofing of any kind on the walls. No comfortable chairs been installed, only a couple of bucket-type seats for test equipment. The "plushing-up" would come later.

Don Douglas had informed Frye that they were planning to fly the airplane for the first time on July 1, weather permitting.

There were some skeptics, including one TWA pilot, who had stopped by to look at the ship. He commented — "too damn big. It will never get off the ground."

II

There was plenty of excitement in aviation circles around Los Angeles on Saturday, July 1, 1933. It was opening day for the Thirteenth Annual National Air Races. Some 50,000 persons had gathered to see the show. The events got off to a record-breaking start when the crowd saw Roscoe Turner, in his golden Gilmore Oil Company Special racing plane, come roaring out of the eastern sky to win the Transcontinental Bendix Trophy Race. He had set a new cross-country speed mark — 11 hours, 40 minutes!

Almost at the same moment the wheels of Turner's racer touched the ground, the DC-1 was roaring into the sky before the anxious eyes of the hundreds of Douglas workers, who took their lunch hour to watch the transport they had built test its wings. This was the scene at Clover Field, and nobody who saw it cared much about the Air Races. They had their own air show.

All morning long Carl A. Cover, Douglas Company Chief Test Pilot and Vice-President Sales, had been taxiing the ship back and forth across the field, but the wheels never left the ground. As it drew near noon and Cover saw the crowd gathering, he pulled up in front of the Flight Operations office at Clover Field for a last word with Don Douglas, who had come down to see the take-off.

"How's she handle?" Douglas asked.

"Like a dream," Cover answered. Then, in one of his rare nostalgic moments, he added — "She's born to fly and belongs up there with the angels!"

After that, he and Fred Herman, the project engineer who went along as a test observer, climbed aboard the plane and started the engines. The next few minutes would tell the story.

This is the way Douglas remembers what happened:

"It was a bright, clear day and a slight breeze was blowing in off the ocean.

"Cover taxiied the plane out to the far end of the runway at the east end of the field. He gunned the motors for a minute and then she came roaring back.

"The DC-1 was airborne at exactly 12:36 P.M. by my watch. Looking up, we saw the plane's nose dip sharply."

"Half a minute later, the port engine sputtered, then quit.

"But, somehow, Cover pulled her up a few hundred feet, and I thought by the thunderous roar that the remaining engine would tear itself loose. What happened was almost eerie. There wasn't any sound. Both engines had sputtered out.

"This time the nose dropped at a precarious angle. *She's going to crash!*" somebody yelled.

"But the engines came to life again, and the ship began to gain a little altitude. She climbed only a couple of hundred feet, however, and the engines suddenly quit again. Down at a rakish angle came the plane's nose. There was that deafening roar again, but Cover had stopped the dive and started to climb.

"It was uncanny. We couldn't figure out what was going on. Yet we knew something was radically wrong.

"For the next ten minutes we saw a demonstration of flying that would put even the best aerial circus performer to shame."

"Carl would gun the engines. There was the roar and the plane would climb sluggishly. Then, the roar would die out and, momentarily, the ship would drop a little. Up and down, up and down in a saw-tooth pattern, Carl jockeyed the ship, somehow always managing to gain a little more altitude.

The DC-1 started to climb, but seconds after this photo was made the port engine sputtered and quit. It was Saturday, July 1, 1933, and before her maiden flight was over, they almost lost the airplane. (Douglas Aircraft Co. Photo)

"When he finally got the plane up to about 1,500 feet, Carl executed a graceful bank and, virtually without any power at all, coaxed it down to a rough, *but safe landing.*"

On the ground, Cover told Douglas – 'It's beyond me . . . Everytime I'd try to pull some power and start a climb, there wasn't any power. But, whenever we'd start dropping with the nose in a downward position, the engines would pick-up automatically. I didn't even have to touch the throttles. All I could do was pray she'd hang together and stay up long enough to get some altitude, so we could turn around and try to get back down . . ."

With her specially-designed Douglas "air brakes" (the wing flaps) almost fully extended, the DC-1 is about to touch down after her maiden flight. Cover is credited with pilotage that saved the airplane. (Douglas Aircraft Co. Photo)

"How did she react to the controls?" Douglas wanted to know.

"Good response," Cover said unhesitatingly. "Doug, I honestly don't think there's anything wrong with the engines."

They walked on out to the plane to watch the mechanics as they began pulling out the engines. It was obvious they weren't going to find the trouble in a minute. Later that afternoon Douglas went sailing. The sea was a good place to try and fathom the sky's secrets.

III

It was Ivar Shogran's turn to sweat. He thought, perhaps, that, maybe, they should have listened to the Pratt & Whitney guys who had maintained all along their *Hornet* engines were better than the Wright *Cyclones.* Now, he and the power plant technicians had to yank out the DC-1's engines and start tearing them down, part by part, until they located the trouble.

"For the next five days, I think we took those engines apart and put 'em back together again a dozen times," Shogran explained, looking back on the problem.

"The trouble was, we couldn't find anything wrong. On the test blocks, the engines would run for hours on end without a sputter."

It was during this period that a surprise visitor dropped in to look at the DC-1. His sudden appearance created quite a bit of excitement.

Wetzel and Shogran were out on the flight line, just standing there, talking about the problem with the engines. The DC-1, its engines out and the nacelles, empty open-mouthed cones, was sitting on the paved ramp in front of the big hangar. Workers were installing some new test equipment.

Suddenly, out of nowhere, a sleek brilliantly-painted biplane appeared overhead. It darted downward, flipped over on its back, flying up-side-down, and zipped by the hangars only a few feet off the ground. Everybody ducked, and the ship missed the DC-1 by a scant 10 feet.

Wetzel was furious. He picked himself up and shook his fist in the direction of the fast-climbing and disappearing aircraft. "That damn fool!" he shouted. "If he dares land here, I'll get him grounded for life."

"Here he comes again, duck!" Shogran yelled.

Several times, the pilot swooped low over the field. Then, he would climb up into the blue and perform a series of acrobatics the like of which the observers never had seen before. Finally, as a climax, the stunter cut his plane's engine completely, and glided the ship down to a perfect "dead-stick" landing, letting the plane roll to a stop right beside the DC-1.

Wetzel rushed out to the ship, and started to yank the pilot out of the cockpit, until he saw who it was. Ernst Udet, one of the most famous German aces of World War I, and a renowned stunt flyer, had decided to accept Don Douglas' invitation and come over to see the new transport plane. Over at the National Air Races, still going on, his act was one of the featured attractions. He hadn't meant to cause any furor – "just wanted to give the boys a show!"

All was forgiven. They invited Udet to lunch in the executive dining room, still a ritual at Douglas for all VIP's. After lunch, they showed him the DC-1 and the man, who was to become Hermann Goering's foremost lieutenant in the *Luftwaffe,* was highly impressed and enthusiastic. Commenting on the details of the multi-cellular wing, he said – "If Junkers had used this principle, they would have been far ahead of everybody. It is just one step better than ours." As it was the Germans were not far behind. The German aircraft industry, inspite of the terms of the Versailles Armistice restrictions, was again beginning to grow. The time was not too far distant when the name Junkers (the JU-88's) would write a bloody page of history across the skies over Poland and France.

Udet went back to the Air Races, after a final acrobatic salute which this time, even Harry Wetzel enjoyed. Shogran went back to his problem – finding out what was wrong with the DC-1's engines.

"We found the trouble in the carburetors," Shogran recalled. "They had been designed with the floats hinged in the rear with the fuel lines feeding gas from the same direction. Every time the plane would climb, the gasoline couldn't flow uphill, so the fuel was automatically shut off. We didn't have pressure fuel systems, then.

All we did was reverse the floats and feed lines; there never was any more trouble."

IV

When she was ready to fly again, the DC-1 was subjected to one of the most rugged, extensive flight test programs ever required of any previous airplane. Since Carl Cover's other duties as sales executive kept him out of the cockpit a goodly part of the time, most of the flight testing of the new transport was turned over to a freelance test pilot named Edmund T. Allen. The program was in capable hands for Allen was regarded by many in aviation circles as the dean of all test pilots.

Allen's test flying began during World War I when the Army sent him to England to test warplanes and study flight testing methods. Returning to this country, he brought his knowledge to Wilbur Wright Field near Dayton, Ohio, the early Army Air Service's experimental test center, where he tested many of the World War One pursuits and bombers. After the war, he was hired as chief test pilot for the National Advisory Committee for Aeronautics (NACA) at Langley Field, Virginia. It was there that Eddie decided that test flying was more than "seat-of-the-pants stick jockeying and courage." He resigned to attend the University of Illinois and the Massachusetts Institute of Technology specializing in aeronautical engineering.

Back in the sky again, Allen became known as the first of the "engineer-test pilots." Once he told an audience – "If you're looking for a swashbuckling movie hero test pilot, you've picked the wrong speaker. This business today is a science. You fly the big ones with a slide rule."

To make ends meet and further his education Allen took his turn flying the air mail – the tough route over the Rockies from Salt Lake City to Cheyenne. He had plenty of time and numerous narrow escapes to learn the difference between theory and fact, science and skill. Dedicated to improving the ships he was flying, Allen heard of the experiments Northrop was running with a new design at Cal Tech, a fast, sleek high-flying mailplane, the Northrop *Gamma*. Seeking to learn more about what was going on, Allen contacted "Doc" Baily Oswald who was in charge of the experiments. It was a highly successful mental marriage.

Test Pilot "Eddie" Allen. (Boeing Airplane Co. Photo)

Eddie Allen went to work for Douglas as a test pilot and engineer. His first big assignment was the DC-1 flight test program. Allen took the ship up almost every day when it wasn't in the shops and "wrung it out."

First, they ran some stress analysis tests to find out if certain structures, in actual flight attitudes, were as strong as they were when you ran a steam roller over them. There was some little concern over the butt-joint attachment of the outer wing panels to the center wing section. Such a wing mounting principle was still highly experimental on a plane of any size.

To "see" what actually happened, engineers mounted a 35-mm. motion picture camera with a built-in-the-lens cross-hair for use as a horizontal reference line in the cabin, and focused it on two vertical scales mounted out on the wing tip. In addition, a 16-mm. motion picture camera was mounted in the cockpit and sighted along the top surface of the outer and center wing panels. Thus, they had full coverage of any flutter or flapping motion which might occur.

With this unique test equipment aboard, Allen took the plane up and ran through

During the flight tests of the DC-1, movie cameras were mounted in the cockpit and back in the fuselage to study the "flexing," ornithropic action of the wing. There was concern over the butt-joint arrangement attaching the outer wing panels to the stub-wing faired to the fuselage. They wanted to be sure no signs of weakness showed up. (Douglas Aircraft Co. Photo)

a series of maneuvers, sharp climbs, dives, banks, turns and horizontal wiggle-waggles. Sometimes, he exerted forces of 3G's and more on the wings, producing loads three times the plane's gross weight. On film, later, the experts learned that the deflection of the wing was negligible.

Next, they loaded the plane to about 18, 000 pounds gross with dummy weights – sand-bags and lead ingots simulating a full payload of fuel, passengers, crew and mail – and took it up to an altitude of 22,000 feet, far above the TWA specification requirement.

The only thing that happened was that one of the test observers who went along, "passed out" when he was so busy taking notes, that he forgot to put on his oxygen mask. Allen reported she handled beautifully in the thinner air regions.

There followed a whole series of landing and take-off trials with astounding results. The ship actually got airborne with a full simulated load in less than 1,000 feet of runway. The new wing flaps, increasing the lift area during take-off, helped make it possible. Likewise, the flaps slowed the plane down to below the 65-mph prescribed landing speed.

One time, while they were shooting the take-offs and landings at old Mines Field, Allen had to make a wheels up landing. It was a "freak" accident.

Franklin R. Collbohm, who today is Chairman of the Board of the Rand Corporation, remembers the incident of the plane as though it happened only yesterday. At the time, Collbohm was Chief of Flight Research for Douglas.

"Allen was flying the plane," Collbohm says, "and Tommy Tomlinson was the co-pilot. I went along to make some notes and observations. 'Doc' Oswald was also aboard.

"During several of the landings I was standing right behind Eddie and Tommy up front, and at the critical let down point, I would operate the hand pump which raised and lowered the landing gear.

"Then, I decided to go back in the cabin and look out the door to ascertain the landing impact sequence of contact, whether the main wheels or the tail wheel hit first. Eddie had been shooting for three-point landings, but there seemed to be a tendency for the ship to be a little tail heavy.

"We had removed the door purposely for this observation, and I was lying flat on the floor with my head stretched out as far as possible trying to keep the main wheels and the tail wheel in view, all in the same spectrum.

Franklin R. Collbohm. (North Central Airlines Photo)

During one test the DC-1 landed on its belly when no one cranked the wheels down. She suffered some scrapes and a couple of bent props, but was back in the air again in a few days. (Douglas Company Photo)

"The tail wheel hit first, all right, but I felt the ship was settling awfully fast. The next instant, I got a face full of tar and rocks and I knew, instinctively, what had happened. The wheels were still up, and the propeller tips were chewing up the runway.

"Allen and Tomlinson told me later they were equally surprised. Oswald had gone up front and was standing there in my place and both pilots thought I was still working the gear. Nobody had told 'Doc' anything about pumping the lever."

Except for a couple of bent propellers the ship was undamaged. When they got a new set of props, they took the plane back to Clover Field.

"When I informed Douglas of what happened," Collbohm adds, "Doug fussed a little bit because things like this are always expensive. But, then, he remarked sarcastically – *"It's a wonder Lindbergh or Frye didn't think about making that one of the requirements."*

Following the wheels-up incident, came the speed trials. Back and forth over a measured course at various altitudes they flew the ship. On one run the DC-1 hit 227 m.p.h., racing plane performance.

During these speed runs Allen's engineering genius and background paid big dividends. For sometime, he and Oswald had been working on a method for finding the exact power output of an engine at any given moment of flight. It was an intricate, complex formula. They talked Douglas into letting them try to prove that it worked with the DC-1. Collbohm was assigned to help them.

"They really had something," Collbohm explains. "As a result, they were able to devise cruise-power tables that would let pilots take advantage of the most efficient power-rating settings at different altitudes. Within the cruise-speed range, it increased the efficiency and economics of the airplane by about 20 per cent.

"Translated into airline operational costs it meant a sharp reduction in costs per plane mile. The DC-1 was the fastest transport ever built up to that time – and the most economical."

They burned up more than 10,000 gallons of gasoline on this series of tests alone, but it was worth it ten times fold to the customer. Frye put it this way – "That 20 per cent gain looked like a mighty nice profitable dollar-sign. Maybe, for the first time, we had an airplane that could make money just carrying passengers. We wouldn't have to rely on mail pay."

V

It was almost World Series time before they finished the major part of the test program, and time for the most critical test of them all – the single-engined take-off with a full load.

"Allen flew the plane over to Winslow, Arizona to make the tests," Collbohm, who was in charge of the trials, reminisces. "This was the highest airport along the entire TWA system, elevation, 4,500 feet. The engines would have to work over-time in the thinner air even for normal operations. Expecting one engine to pull the load was asking a lot. TWA was making us play with the blue chips.

"We had worked out quite a systematic procedure to be followed for the test. Allen and Tomlinson would fly the plane and I would work the gear.

"With the plane loaded to maximum – about 18,000 pounds – we were to start a normal take-off run. The minute the landing gear struts were fully extended, which would indicate the wings were supporting the ship and it was airborne, Tomlinson would reduce the power about one half on the starboard engine. At the same instant, no matter what happened, I was to start raising the wheels up.

"We had decided to try it like that first, a kind of dry run. Then, the next time Tomlinson would cut the switch on the engine and we'd try it on one engine, alone.

"Everything was set and agreed upon. The plane started down the runway eating up the concrete like a drag racer on the freeway. The high altitude and the heavy load necessitated an abnormally long run, as was to be expected.

"She used up three-fourths of the strip before I felt the struts relax. Then it happened...

"Tomlinson didn't reach for the throttles. Instead, he reached up and cut the switch on the right engine.

"Allen, taken by surprise, jammed forward hard on the throttle, pouring the coal to the remaining engine.

"The plane shook and staggered, but it continued to climb. At about 8,000 feet, well above the mountain tops, Allen leveled off. The ship was maintaining altitude and performing normally on the one engine.

"I remember Allen glancing at Tomlinson with a 'what-the-hell-did-you-do-that-for' look in his eye.

"Tommy answered him – *'It's this way – you work for the manufacturer. I work for the customer. I just wanted to see if the old girl is as good as you guys claim she is!*

"*'Next time,'* Allen said, *'let me in on the gag. It's my neck you're risking, too, you know.'*"

"Since they had plenty of fuel aboard, Allen flew the ship across the high peaks around Winslow and all the way to Albuquerque, New Mexico – 280 miles away. He never once used the port engine," Collbohm concluded his story.

One of the TWA's scheduled flights, a Ford trimotor, had taken off before them. They were on the ground and ready to start back by the time the Ford landed at Albuquerque.

A few days later, on the strength of the performance reports in every category of the manufacturers' tests, TWA placed an order for 25 of the planes. The Douglas beach-head into the commercial transport field was secure.

VI

Back at theDouglas plant the DC-1 underwent a major face-lifting job. In a few short weeks, it emerged the luxurious transport airliner that Frye had wanted all along, and not just a metallic tube with wings, whose interior looked like a cluttered-up machine shop.

Even George Strompl, when he looked inside, had to admit that, maybe, those guys who had been "fiddle-faddling" around in the mock-up had known all along what they were doing.

The main cabin of the DC-1 was 23-feet, six-inches long, six feet, 4-inches high (tall enough for Kindelberger to stand up to full height with plenty to spare) and five-and-a-half-feet from wall to wall. There was thick carpeting on the floor, and the walls and ceiling were heavily insulated with sound-proofing material, covered with a leatherette-type outer finish in a cream and bluish-grey decor. Inside, it was quieter than a Pullman car.

Douglas had heard about a young acoustical engineer, Dr. Stephen J. Zand, who had done an excellent job of deadening the noise in the slow Curtiss *Condor* biplanes used by Eastern Air Transport, and he had hired him to work on the DC-1. Zand, who flew on most of the test flights taking hundreds of "soundings" with delicate noise-level measuring instruments, had done wonders with the airplane.

Between the fuselage skin and the inner cabin wall, compressed Kapok fiber sheets

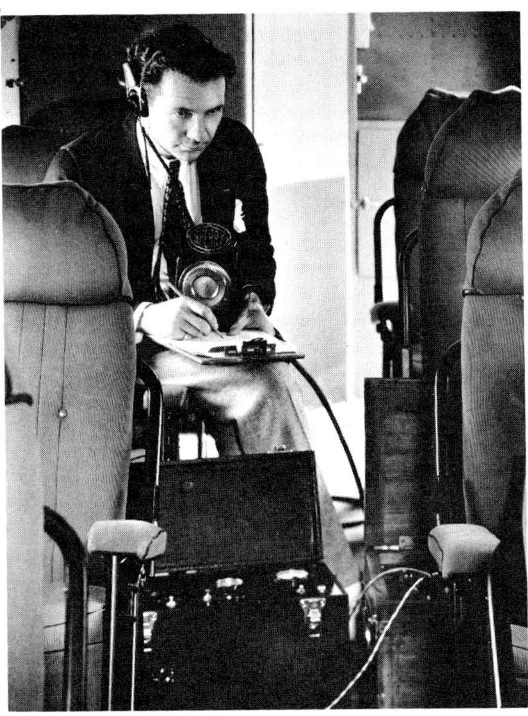

Dr. Stephen J. Zand, acoustics expert, took hundreds of sound tests aboard DC-1 in flight and on the ground. Plane was as quiet inside as a Pullman car. (Douglas Aircraft Co. Photo)

were placed to absorb the high frequency sounds. A sound-deadening bulkhead – two-and-a-half inches thick – was built to separate the forward mail and baggage compartments and the cockpit from the passenger cabin. It made the cabin 12 to 14 decibels quieter than the pilot's compartment.

To prevent noises from entering the cabin through the ventilating or heating systems, the ventilators and heat intake ducts were treated with a special sound-deadening cement, and sound filters were provided at critical points. At major structural joints, rubber spacers were applied with a high sound dampening effect.

Furthermore, each piece of cabin furniture was designed so that it would contribute its part to the absorption of sound. Chairs, for instance, were mounted on rubber supports, and the metal hand rail on each wall was stuffed with sound-proofing material.

Engines were mounted flexibly on special rubber insulators. Exhaust noises were reduced by carrying the blasts of hot gases below the wing, so that the wing itself blanketed the noise and deflected it away from the cabin. Likewise, stress carrying structural members in the wings were designed so as not to transmit vibration to the passenger compartment.

All of this produced a remarkably silent airplane. Before the sound-proofing, the noise level inside the fuselage was in the range of 98 decibels, only 25 decibels quieter than the sound people on the outside heard, when they watched the plane take-off with engines roaring at full power. When Zand had finished his work, the DC-1's cabin had a sound-level of 72 decibels even when the ship was zipping along at better than 200 m.p.h.

One engineering report summed it up this way – "For the first time in aeronautics and, perhaps, in any moving vehicle, the principle of balanced accoustics had been successfully accomplished. This airplane is not only the most quiet airplane flying, but also has a noise spectrum which seems to be less fatiguing to passengers."

Of all the advantages the DC-1 had to offer, from the passenger standpoint, this was one of its most important contributions to air transportation.

Another was comfortable seating and a roomy cabin. The seats they finally decided upon were of aluminum alloy frame, so designed that the back was adjustable for reclining at a low angle and the occupant could stretch out and cat-nap. There was plenty of leg room – 40-inches between seats. Heavily upholstered with leather and mohair, the seats were wide and comfortable and they were also reversible so that passengers could face forward or rear-ward, which-ever the individual desired.

Each seat also had its individual small reading lamp on the wall above it. Running the full length of the cabin along the ceiling above each row of seats, was a stowage trough for hats and other miscellaneous items of apparel. There were also foot rests and safety belts provided.

To the rear of the cabin was a small buffet or galley consisting of a serving shelf with enclosed cupboard beneath. The cupboard contained space for thermos jugs and an electric hotplate for keeping soups warm. There was also space for box lunches, and a container for refuse.

Beyond the buffet to the rear was the lavatory, about the size of 4 phone booths complete with toilet unit and wash basin.

In addition, the ship had a system for supplying fresh air inside the cabin at all times. The cabin, cockpit and lavatory were also heated, with the temperatures thermostatically controlled. Passengers could ride in

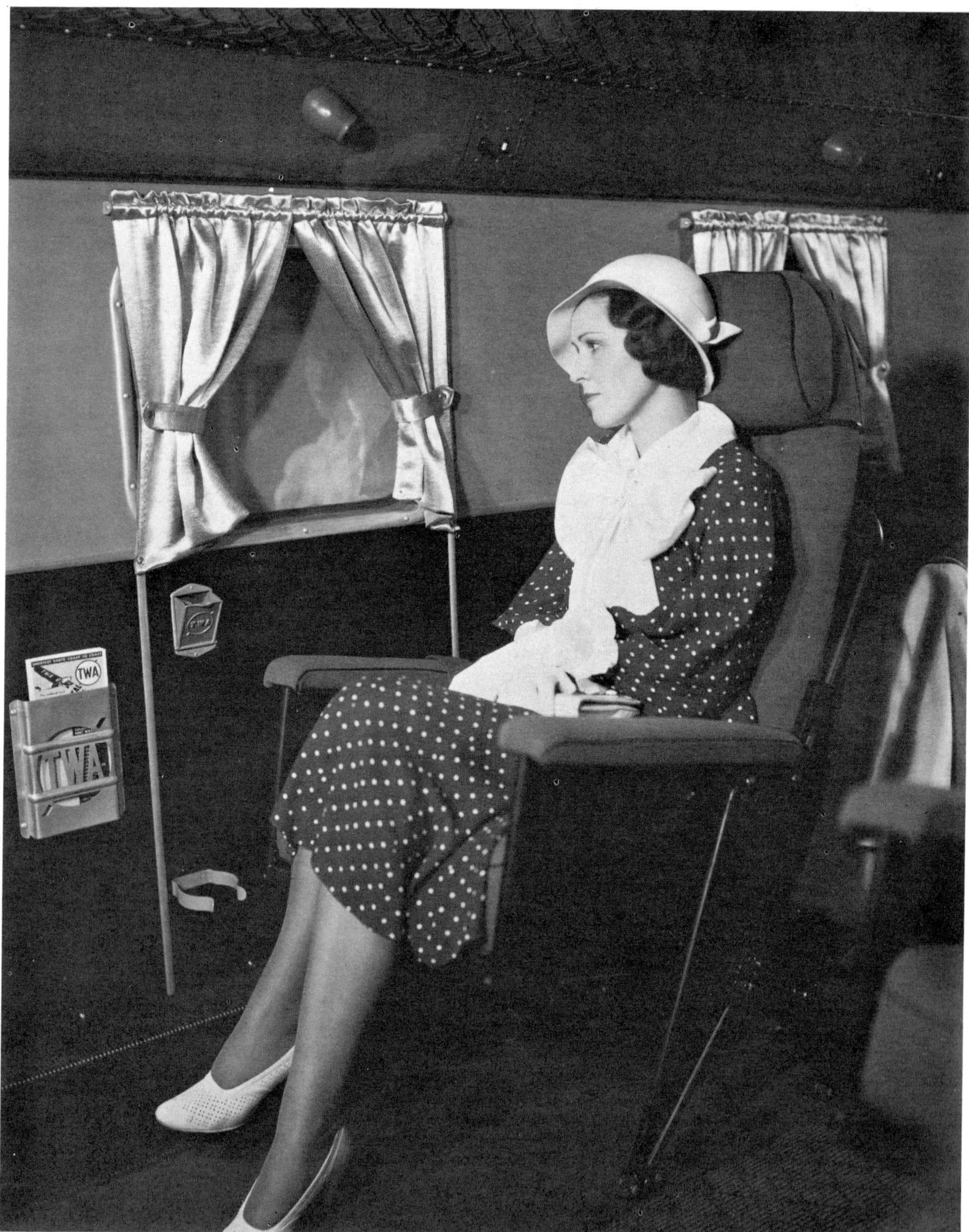

DC-1 had comfortable, upholstered seats, the largest of any airliner to date and there was plenty of leg room. Note air vent in luggage rack, ash tray and obvious omission of the cup for "air sickness." They didn't forget the time-table, though. (Douglas Aircraft Co. Photo)

comfort at 70-degrees F. temperatures inside, even when the outside temperature was 20-degrees F. below zero!

Such was the interior of the luxury transport that TWA was about to introduce to the air traveling public. They had done well adhering to Raymond's device – "build comfort, and put wings on it."

With all its plush the DC-1 flew even better than it did when it was a working test airplane.

But there were still some more performance test flying ahead. After the Douglas pilots and TWA pilots had finished their tests, Les Holloceck and "Colonel" Joe Marriott, Bureau of Air Commerce inpectors took over. The airplane passed its qualifying tests as a transport, meeting all the government's standards, with flying colors. It was given a blue ticket, the right to serve as a common carrier and a license number – X-223Y.

TWA had its own serial number to assign to the aircraft – No. 300 – and for years, even to this day, those who remember the ship refer to her fondly as "Old Three Hundred."

VII

The plane was officially delivered to TWA in December of 1933. There was an appropriate ceremony at the Los Angeles Municipal Airport and Tomlinson, representing the airline, handed Don Douglas the check for $125,000.

It was the beginning of a new era for the Douglas Aircraft Company which was to become the largest producer of commercial airliners in the world. And TWA was coming down the stretch, a sure winner in the race with United, and other competitors.

Douglas had gambled on the DC-1 and won. He even upped the price per airplane to TWA from $58,000 to $65,000. How he got the increase proved Douglas had an eye for business as well as a keen engineering mind.

Reading over the original contract one day, he noted the clause – *to be paid in gold bullion.* But months had passed since the contract had been drawn up, and in between, FDR had taken the country off the gold standard. The agreed-upon figure ($58,000), Douglas thought, should be adjusted to compensate for the change in the silver certificates. He decided to do something about it.

Early in November, before the delivery date, Tomlinson was flying the DC-1 on a demonstration flight, coast-to-coast. Douglas, who had never ridden in the plane before, decided to go along.

"It was a wonderful trip," he told friends later. "I felt as much at home in the cabin as I do on my yacht."

The trip, however, was not without incident.

Flying over the mountain passes near Albuquerque, one of the engines conked out. This time it was for real. "I didn't even notice it back in the cabin," Douglas remembers. "Neither did anybody else until Tomlinson came back and explained the situation. Just to be on the safe side, we turned around and went back to Albuquerque. But the plane never seemed to lose any altitude. It was under perfect control all the time. For all it mattered, back in the cabin, everything was normal."

They found the trouble with the engine, fixed it, and the plane flew on to New York.

There, Douglas took up the matter of the declining dollar with Dick Robbins, TWA President and the legal eagles. The original contract – since gold was no longer legal tender – was null and void, he pointed out.

There were some arguments, pro and con, but TWA finally agreed to pay $1,625,000 for the initial order of 25 DC-2's. That was an increase of $7,000 per ship.

Actually, Douglas Company records show, taking into consideration the original design, engineering and fabrication, the DC-1 prototype had cost, finally, $307,000. The first twenty-five ships resulted in a net loss of $266,000 to the company. But, they built an extra twenty-five planes to sell to other customers (Douglas had no airline affiliation) while completing the TWA order, and it soon took the company out of the red.

"This airplane," Douglas was to tell a Chamber of Commerce group at an Anniversary of Flight dinner at a future date, "was to lead the company and the American commercial aviation into new horizons."

This was a familiar scene at the Grand Central Air Terminal, Glendale, California, BEFORE the DC-1 came into existence. (TWA Photo)

The scene changed at Grand Central Air Terminal when TWA put its new DC-1 transport into the picture. Even when she still had the "X" number, TWA flew the ship up and down its route taking up passengers on demonstration rides. Later the plane went into regular scheduled service for a time. (Douglas Aircraft Co. Photo)

Chapter 5

Up There With The Angels!

History tells us the new transport design was to change many things and many lives in many lands. It has been said "Old Three Hundred" is the airplane that *sold* air travel and gave millions of land-lubbers the confidence to try their wings. Perhaps, in all fairness and for accuracy's sake, this distinction belongs more to the first and second generation descendants of the original prototype – the DC-2's and DC-3's. But one thing is certain, there would never have been the long line of famous DC ships in the world's skies if it hadn't been for the DC-1.

The ship was destined for a long and illustrious career. And she made many invaluable contributions to the science of aerostation.

For the next sixty days after TWA took delivery of the plane in September, 1933, it flew up and down the trans-continental airway, a preview of wings to come.

At every stop along TWA's route, the plane was on display and made demonstration flights to show off its many new features, and acquaint the air traveler with the comfort and speed and safety that would be his when the airline started regular scheduled service with this type of ship.

This public-acceptance campaign over, the airplane one day in February, 1934, was to make headlines with an unprecedented transcontinental dash that had far more purpose behind it than merely to set a new speed record.

In Washington, for months a special Senate investigations group, The Black Committee, (Chairman, Senator Hugo L. Black of Alabama) had been scrutinizing the Air Mail contract situation. They had uncovered what appeared to be some shocking scandals, alleged favoritism and fraud in the manner that the Post Office Department had awarded the mail contracts to the private airline companies.

In the White House, Roosevelt decided to squelch the scandal mongering in the Post Office Department, if there were any, before it had a chance to smear his New Deal program. His course of action, after hearing all the evidence and upon the advice of his "brain trusters," was the cancellation of all the civilian-airline mail contracts.

On Friday, February 9, 1934, FDR signed an Executive Order (No. 6591) which said the airlines would cease carrying the mail at mid-night on February 19th. The Army Air Corps would take over.

II

Back in Kansas City when Jack Frye heard about the cancellation order, he picked up the telephone and called his friend E. V. "Eddie" Rickenbacker, America's ace of aces in the first World War. Rickenbaker at the time, was vice-president of Eastern Air Lines, "The Great Silver Fleet."

"Rick," Frye said, "we've got to do something to show the public that we're better qualified to fly the mail than the Army fliers. This muck-raking down in Washington has gone far enough. I don't mind the insinuations of scandal so much – maybe, there have been some deals, – but I see by the papers, they're pointing the finger at our pilots, operational procedures, and our equipment. Let's show 'em they don't know what they're talking about."

"It's a noble thought," Rickenbaker mused. "Just what the hell have you got in mind?"

Frye had been thinking. He had a plan. Over the phone he unfolded it to Rickenbaker. The latter jumped at the idea.

When he hung up, Frye called Tommy Tomlinson into his office. "Wherever the DC-1 is, get it back here fast," he said. "We've got a job for her."

It was 10:00 P.M., February 18, 1934, two hours before the air mail contract cancellation order went into effect. The DC-1 was poised at the end of the runway at the Burbank Air Terminal in California. Her

Interior of cabin of United Air Lines' Boeing Model 247 transport. Note the narrow aisle and the obstructive wing spar that dissected the cabin. (United Air Lines' Photo)

The DC-1 interior of cabin. By comparison with other planes of the era, the new airliner was by far the roomiest. Reversible seats on the left-hand side permitted 12-passenger configuration. Crew member in rear is not steward, but one of pilots. (TWA Photo)

mail compartments were filled with sacks of letters, the last load of eastbound private-contractor transcontinental mail. In the cockpit Jack Frye was at the controls and "Eddie" Rickenbaker was co-pilot. A crowd had gathered to see the take-off. The flight had been well publicized, Frye and Rickenbaker had seen to that.

Jack Frye waved to the on-lookers, released the brakes, gave her the gun, and the plane was airborne and climbing in the direction of Cajon Pass. Their destination was Newark, New Jersey – the airport serving New York City – almost 3,000 miles away.

High over the Rockies the plane streaked through the night sky flying on automatic pilot. They were free to work on navigational problems, and they "XXX-ed off" the checkpoints along the route, which took them almost in a straight line to Kansas City where they planned to refuel.

When they landed at KC a light snow was falling. The weatherman warned that a blizzard was roaring down from the Great Lakes and would cross their path.

In the air again, the plane headed for Columbus, Ohio. It was daylight now, but the sky was grey and a cold front was closing in all around them. By the time they landed at Ohio's capital city, the ceiling was down to about 1,000 feet. Mechanics hurried to get the plane in the sky again because the stuff was dropping fast. It was not a minute too soon when the plane lifted off the runway; ten minutes later, the field was socked-in. The blizzard had struck.

With Jack Frye as pilot and Capt. "Eddie" Rickenbacker as co-pilot, DC-1 approaches Kansas City airport on record-breaking flight when it carried last load of Air Mail before Army fliers took over by FDR's order. The flight did much to prove airlines' capability to fly the mail, undoubtedly helped in the ultimate decision to turn the job back to the privately-owned commercial air carriers. (TWA Photo)

Spotting land-marks was hopeless now. The swirling snow blotted out everything. They were "on instruments" and sucking oxygen from the tubes, as Frye climbed the ship up to 19,000 feet to get above the stinking weather. Up there, the DC-1 broke out into bright sunshine, smooth air. Picking up a tail-wind, it was cruising along at better than 225-mph!

Over the "Hell Stretch" of the Alleghenies they flew. Then, down to the lower altitudes, sailing along above the picturesque Quaker farmhouses, until, finally, there, beneath the wings, was Newark.

When the DC-1 landed, shortly before noon, February 19th, the plane had set a new transcontinental record for transports – thirteen hours and 4 minutes.

The two airline executives had proved their point.

"This plane," editorialized one New York newspaper, "has made obsolete all other air transport equipment in this country or any other."

III

For the next year, little is recorded of the DC-1's activities except for notations, correspondence and clippings in a scrapbook which Paul Richter kept. From these, we learn that the plane went back to the factory for a short time. Pratt & Whitney *Hornet* engines, latest of their line, were installed in place of the Wright *Cyclones*. A series of performance tests were run, and then the ship was refitted again with the Wright engines of a slightly increased horsepower.

According to Richter's files the plane was also used for some tests with de-icing "boots" on the wings and propellers, and as a test-bed for experimental night flying equipment and new air navigational aids. In the press, there appeared items, now and then, which referred to it as "TWA's flying laboratory airplane."

As such, the plane was used for high altitude tests in developing new equipment for use of passengers and crew in the regions of the sub-stratosphere. Similarly, it was used to try out devices for increasing engine horsepower at the high altitudes. It was also fitted with various equipment applicable to the development of super-charged cabins.

Early in 1935 the plane was loaned to the Department of Commerce and the U.S. Army Air Corps to test a new Sperry automatic pilot linked to the Kreusi radio compass. Not much importance was placed on the tests, but this was the beginning of a long-range attempt to develop the automatic flight control systems in aircraft.

The year 1935 also saw the DC-1 make big headlines again. It was to demonstrate to the world its superior performance.

In April, for example, Tomlinson with pilots, H. B. Snead and Pete Redpath aboard, set a new coast-to-coast mark of 11 hours and five minutes. The transport plane actually had beaten the time set by Roscoe Turner in his specially-built racer on July 1, 1933, the day the DC-1 had made its first flight.

But this was just the beginning.

It must be remembered, that this was the period in aviation history that a nation's air strength was measured by the number of world's records for speed, endurance, altitude, payload and other performance characteristics, that its pilots and planes were able to claim. There was no such thing as superior air power, as we know it today. At the time, France was first in the air. The U.S. was a poor third behind Italy in the number of world marks that our fliers could claim.

One man deserves credit above others for his effort to do something about the situation and raise the prestige of American aviation in the world's eyes. He was Senator William G. McAdoo, who had just been made president of the National Aeronautical Association, the agency responsible for setting the rules and keeping the official times for any airplane record attempts in this country. When he took the job, McAdoo announced the N.A.A. was going to sponsor and promote an all out assault by American flyers on the world records, put the U.S. in the lead. TWA put the DC-1 at the disposal of the N.A.A. to try for a number of new records.

Thus, on May 16, 1935, we find Tomlinson and Joe Bartels, another veteran TWA pilot, in the cockpit of the DC-1 at Floyd Bennett Field, Long Island, ready to start on an attempt to set a long distance, non-stop record. They were to fly a triangular course from Floyd Bennett Field

"Tommy" Tomlinson and pilots H. B. Snead and Pete Redpath set Transcontinental record with DC-1 in April, 1935. Note plane has different number on tail, R-233Y. It was no longer considered an experimental aircraft. (TWA Photo)

to Bolling Field, near Washington, D.C., thence to Willoughby Spit at Norfolk, Virginia and back to Floyd Bennett. N.A.A. had marked the course, and official timers were stationed at the points of the triangle to clock the plane as it passed overhead. The record would be official over the 5,000 kilometer course.

The plane took off at 7:00 A.M., climbed up to 10,000 feet and headed toward Bolling Field. Around and around the triangle – New York-Washington-Norfolk-New York – Tomlinson and Bartels flew the ship until 1:50 A.M. the next morning, when they had covered the required distance. Timers clocked them at 18 hours, 22 minutes, 49 seconds. Their average speed was 169.03 miles per hour, far in excess of any previous performance for this distance.

The DC-1's performance during the N.A.A. sanctioned record attempts was spectacular, almost phenomenal. Altogether, between May 16-19 it broke three former American records; established eight new records; set two world records in new categories, and finally broke five former world's records. The U.S. had moved up into second place with 39 world's records to its credit as against France's 40.

IV

"Old 300 has served its time and completed its job for the airline and now has been sold to private interests," said a TWA news release in the spring of 1936.

"The big airplane, the only Douglas DC-1 ever constructed," the story continued, "was delivered by TWA to Howard Hughes, well known motion picture director and an individual who is becoming even more widely-known as one who is interested deeply in aviation. The delivery was made at the company's headquarters plant at Kansas City and Mr. Hughes left a few hours later for New York with Harlan Hull, TWA's chief pilot, acting as pilot for the flight. Also aboard at the time was Ed Lund, mechanic for the air going movie director.

"Hughes did not inform the company as to his plans for the machine at the time of the sale," the announcement concluded.

When Hughes got the DC-1, he immediately installed more gas tanks in the wings and fuselage, increasing the ship's potential range to more than 6,000 miles. The engines were changed, putting in the latest Wright 875-horsepower *Cyclones*. Then, for months afterwards, the plane underwent another series of gruelling tests. Hughes planned to fly around the world in the DC-1.

The DC-1, however, missed her date with destiny and the opportunity to follow the trail, blazed by her famous ancestors, the Douglas World Cruisers. Hughes, at the last minute, switched to a newer and faster plane, a modified Lockheed 14-passenger *Lodestar*. Christened *The World's Fair 1939*, the plane wrote its name indelibly in the pages of aviation history.

At 7:26 P.M. on Sunday evening July 10, the plane, carrying a total load of more than 25,000 pounds, lifted off the runway at Floyd Bennett Field and headed eastward across the Ocean. It landed at Le Bourget Field at 2:47 P.M., EST.

Off the ground again at 8:24 P.M., after Lund had made some engine repairs and adjustments, it headed across Europe for Moscow, Russia, landing at 4:15 A.M., Tuesday. It was quickly off again and by 2:00 P.M. the same day settled to earth at Omsk, Siberia. At 6:37 P.M. it departed across the frozen land for Yakutsk and completed the 2,456-mile flight in 10 hours, 31 minutes. Taking off at 8:01 A.M., it roared across the vastness of Russia's Arctic Circle Domain, and a little more than 12 hours later it was back on American soil again, landing at Fairbanks, Alaska. Departing at 9:36 P.M. (Wednesday) it made the trip to Minneapolis, Minnesota in record time and, after a quick refuelling stop, headed for Floyd Bennett Field.

The wheels touched the ground at 2:34.10 P.M. Thursday, July 14, after the ship had flown a total of 14,824 miles, circumnavigating the globe in a total elapsed time of three days, 8 minutes and 10 seconds.

"Old 300" probably could have made the flight, but she couldn't have made it so fast because she simply didn't have the speed. Significantly, however, as this is written, anybody can board a Douglas-built DC-8 Jetliner and fly around the world via Pan American World Airways and connecting carriers, virtually at the earth's equatorial middle (25,000 miles) in just about half the length of time that Hughes required to cover little more than half the distance.

Today's route, which takes the passenger – New York to Paris, Rome, Istanbul, Teheran, Karachi, Calcutta, Rangoon, Bangkok, Hong Kong, Toyko, Honolulu, Los Angeles and New York – runs on timetable schedules, and the whole distance can be traversed in Douglas intercontinental DC-8's, all direct descendants of the DC-1.

Donald Douglas, in addressing the members of the famous Newcomen Society would declare – "Our rugged off-spring, free to roam over the oceans and continents of the earth and the limitless horizons of the sky, are scattered around the globe. They move about like the four winds and make their homes in strange and far-way places."

V

After Hughes decided in favor of the Lockheed, the DC-1 for a time just sat there on the ground at the Burbank Air Terminal. Nobody paid much attention to the historic airplane.

In fact, the story goes, that the plane sat there so long, the airport manager called Howard Hughes and wanted to know – "What are you going to do with that airplane out here?"

"What airplane?" Hughes asked.

"The one parked out here at Burbank?"

"Hell, I wondered where I parked that ship," Hughes is reported to have replied, and hung up.

Finally, he sold the DC-1 to an Englishman, Viscount Forbes (The Earl of Granard) who planned a flight across the Atlantic. Later he decided against the hop.

But the DC-1 finally did get to make the ocean voyage. Forbes shipped it across on a freighter bound for the Port of London in June 1938. Hughes may well have flown over it on his way to Paris and around the world.

The DC-1, on arrival, it was soon found out, was too big to pass through the London dock gates and the plane had to be loaded on a barge and shipped down the Thames to Dagenham, where it was unloaded at the Ford Works pier. There, on Dageham Common, a public park, visitors were agog to see workman assembling the airplane. When it was ready, they also witnessed an unusual event. Imperial Airways pilot, Captain W. Rogers, who the plane's owner had hired for a personal pilot, took off from the grassy lawns and flew the ship to famous Croydon Air Field. For about three months after that, the DC-1, operating under a new license number (G-AFIF, a British certification) flew around Europe wherever the Earl's whims took him.

Later, Forbes sold the ship to a French company, and for a long time, nothing was heard about her whereabouts. Then one day in 1939, the name of the DC-1 turned up in the news dispatches, datelined Barcelona, Spain. It was "Old 300," her shiny metal skin in war-paint and camouflage and bearing Spanish registration markings, which flew the members of the Republican Government out of Barcelona to Toulouse, as the Nationalists took over the former capital.

The ship had been purchased by the Republican Government for L.A.P.E. (*Lineas Aeros Postales Espanoles*) the Spanish airline. During the Civil War in Spain, it was used as a reconnaissance warplane and as a personnel transport for important government leaders.

It made the headlines again in April, 1939, when the Republican Government collapsed and, once more, the leaders escaped in "Old 300," flying over the Pyranees into France and exile. That time she was even shot at by Nationalist planes, who were tipped off to the escape route. But the DC-1 outsped them, and delivered her cargo of high officials and documents safely.

The war over, the DC-1 was turned over by the Nationalists who had taken it as a prize of war, to the *Sociedad Anonima de Transportes,* the forerunner of today's Iberia Air Lines. Back in civilian colors again and re-named – *Negron* – after a famous Nationalist pilot killed in combat, the plane was used in regular service flying the route between Seville-Malaga-Tetuan.

Then, one day in December, 1940, it happened.

On this fateful morning, the plane came in right on schedule from Tetuan, landing at the air field near Malaga, a seaport city in Southern Spain. It took on several passengers and some mail. The door was slammed shut and it taxied out to the end of the runway for a take-off.

According to an Iberian Airlines' pilot, who saw what happened in the next few minutes – "The plane came roaring toward us. Then, suddenly, when her wheels were only inches off the ground, one engine sputtered and quit. The next instant, she was mushing down on her belly in a cloud of dust. When the dust cleared away, the plane was a pile of junk at the end of the runway."

Her passengers and crew, a bit shaken up, but otherwise uninjured, walked away from the wreckage. "Old 300" had never killed anybody. She had never cracked up before, even. Her luck had run out, that was all.

Wreckage of the DC-1 on the plains of Malaga, Spain. It was the end of a long, long journey, but she left a high heritage. (Douglas Aircraft Co. Photo)

Later, Spanish Air Force mechanics were sent to Malaga to dismantle the wreck and salvage spare parts. They took what was useable and left the skeleton to die.

There is a legend that picks up from here, according to Mike Oliveau, Douglas Company Vice-president in charge of the European Operations, who has visited the site many times. Oliveau says that monks from the nearby Cathedral of Malaga took pieces of the metal frame and used it to fashion an Andas, a symbolic stretcher-like affair. They claim the metal came from the DC-1. And this Andas still is part of the church treasury. On church festival days it is used to carry the image of the Blessed Virgin through the streets.

Perhaps, Carl Cover, who was first to fly the DC-1 more than a quarter of a century ago, was right, when he remarked — *she belongs up there with the angels!*

Chapter 6

"There Goes a Dooglas, Dooglas!"

George Strompl saw Douglas coming down the hall and stopped him. "Just thought I'd remind you, Doug, my hat size is 7¼ and, if you don't mind, make it one of those wide-brimmed, western-style Stetsons."

He was pulling Don Douglas' leg. They had made a bargain a short time before. Douglas had called Strompl into his office and told him things were going from bad to worse in the shops with the DC-2 program. He wanted an explanation.

During that meeting, at which Bob Berghell, the company's auditor was present, Douglas showed Strompl some figures on the production costs of the new airliner.

"George, we've got to do something about this," Douglas began, "Berghell, here, tells me the first batch of DC-2's has been taking about 58,000 man hours per airplane. At that rate we'll have the sheriff at our door in another thirty days. What the hell is the lag?"

Strompl had to admit he also was a little concerned. "Those big presses from Mt. Gilead, Ohio haven't arrived yet," he informed Douglas. "The first twenty ships have been practically hand-made."

"When will the presses be here?" asked Douglas.

"Within the next ten days. They've had labor troubles back at the plant according to the latest excuses."

"Well, when they get here, how much do you think we can cut down on the number of man hours per airplane?"

"Forty per cent, give or take a little. . . ."

"Okay, you do that, George, and I'll buy you a new Stetson hat."

The meeting broke up on that note.

Now, a week later, Strompl was reminding Douglas about the bargain. "The big hammers are here," he said. "We'll have them tripping in a few days."

"Good. . . . Let me know how it goes. I want to see some better figures. . . ."

Douglas went on his way. He would liked to have stopped longer and told George the news Carl Cover had brought back from Wright Field about the new bomber competition coming up. But, maybe, it was a little premature.

He'll forget all about that hat, Strompl thought to himself as he saw Douglas disappear into the Design Room. He smiled, and turned to walk through the factory out to the loading platform by the spur siding where workmen were unloading the huge presses.

II

Walking through the plant, Strompl couldn't help but notice how the new DC-1 transport design had changed things. He stopped and reflected for a moment about the events of the past two years which suddenly and unexpectedly had taken the company out of the doldrums and thrust it once more into a new path of progress. You could see it in the expressions on the workers' faces. It was a thing called pride coupled with the desire to work and the bright promise of a new future. It electrified the whole atmosphere. Strompl lived it, being closer to the work force than Douglas. It was the stuff that makes good airplanes, great airplanes. Things hadn't been going too well. The year 1932 was one of the worst years in the company's existence. They only sold 70 airplanes. Sales barely hit the $2,000,000 mark. The TWA order, alone, was more than half that amount of business.

From where he stood, Strompl could take in a panoramic view of the entire factory. It didn't look like there was any depression on here. Douglas was building planes for everybody, planes of all kinds. There was the *Dolphin*, an eight-passenger amphibian moving down the line, 51 on order for the Army, Navy and Coast Guard. The *Dolphin* also had suddenly become very popular for millionaire sportsmen like Powell Crosley,

Overnight with production of the DC-2's for TWA, the whole complexion of the Douglas plant changed. The new transport took over. Note Army trainers and Dolphin amphibian in left of picture. (Douglas Aircraft Co. Photo)

Plane No. 301, the first DC-2 for TWA went into final assembly in the latter part of April, 1934. Frye and Rickenbacker had wanted to hurry this ship into the sky to make the historic mail flight, but the plane was not ready in time. It has been reported erroneously that the DC-2 made the flight. (Douglas Aircraft Co. Photo)

The first DC-2, Plane No. 301, bearing license Number NC-13711, was delivered to TWA in mid-May of 1934. It went into scheduled service between Columbus, Ohio, Pittsburgh, Pa., and Newark, N.J., serving New York City on May 18th the same year. (Douglas Aircraft Co. Photo)

Jr., and the Vanderbilts. In another section of the plant were the 0-2MC-4's, improved basic trainers for the Army Air Corps. Here and there in the line popped up a specially-built 0-38P ordered for the Peruvian Navy. But all of these were in the shadow of the transport assembly line.

Such was the scene in mid February 1934, about the time that Frye and Rickenbacker were showing the world the DC-1 with their record-breaking, cross-country flight. Actually, Frye had wanted to make the flight in a brand new DC-2, but the delay in getting the presses on time, and other mass production problems made it impossible to have the first of the production transports ready in time. Target date for the first delivery was set for sometime in May or June.

With the DC-2, it wasn't just a matter of mass producing the DC-1. In a way it was like starting all over again – planning, blueprint, model, mock-up, fabrication. This machinery had actually been set in motion *before* "Old Three Hundred" ever spread its wings.

One day in June, 1933, Douglas, Kindelberger, Raymond, Wetzel, Frye, Tomlinson and the others were huddled together looking over the wind tunnel results and the indicated performance figures of the DC-1. There was no doubt in their minds – if the plane proved up to the performance figures they had before them – they had a sure winner. In truth it was a pretty smug group. There was even an air of over-zealousness in the room.

Maybe, it was because they were all thinking the same thing. *With such a performance potential, why not stretch the design a little in the production model DC-2?*

Nobody of the group alive today will take credit for the initial suggestion. But it was probably one of the TWA people, with an eye on the profit potential of selling more tickets, who proposed they put two more seats in the cabin and make the ship a 14-passenger transport.

The result was that they made the production model DC-2 a bigger airplane by lengthening the fuselage two feet, adding another window on each side. The first plane was delivered to the airline on Monday, May 14, 1934.

Clancy Dayhoff, veteran newsman and TWA west-coast public relations representative, described the new "queen of the skies" in an official press release:

"The silver ship is a low-wing cantilever monoplane. The entire external appearance of the transport is remarkable for its complete freedom from struts and control system parts. In harmony with clean design, the wheels retract into the engine nacelles but are so arranged that emergency landings are possible while the gear is in the retracted position.

"The passenger salon is twenty-six (26) feet, four (4) inches long, five (5) feet six

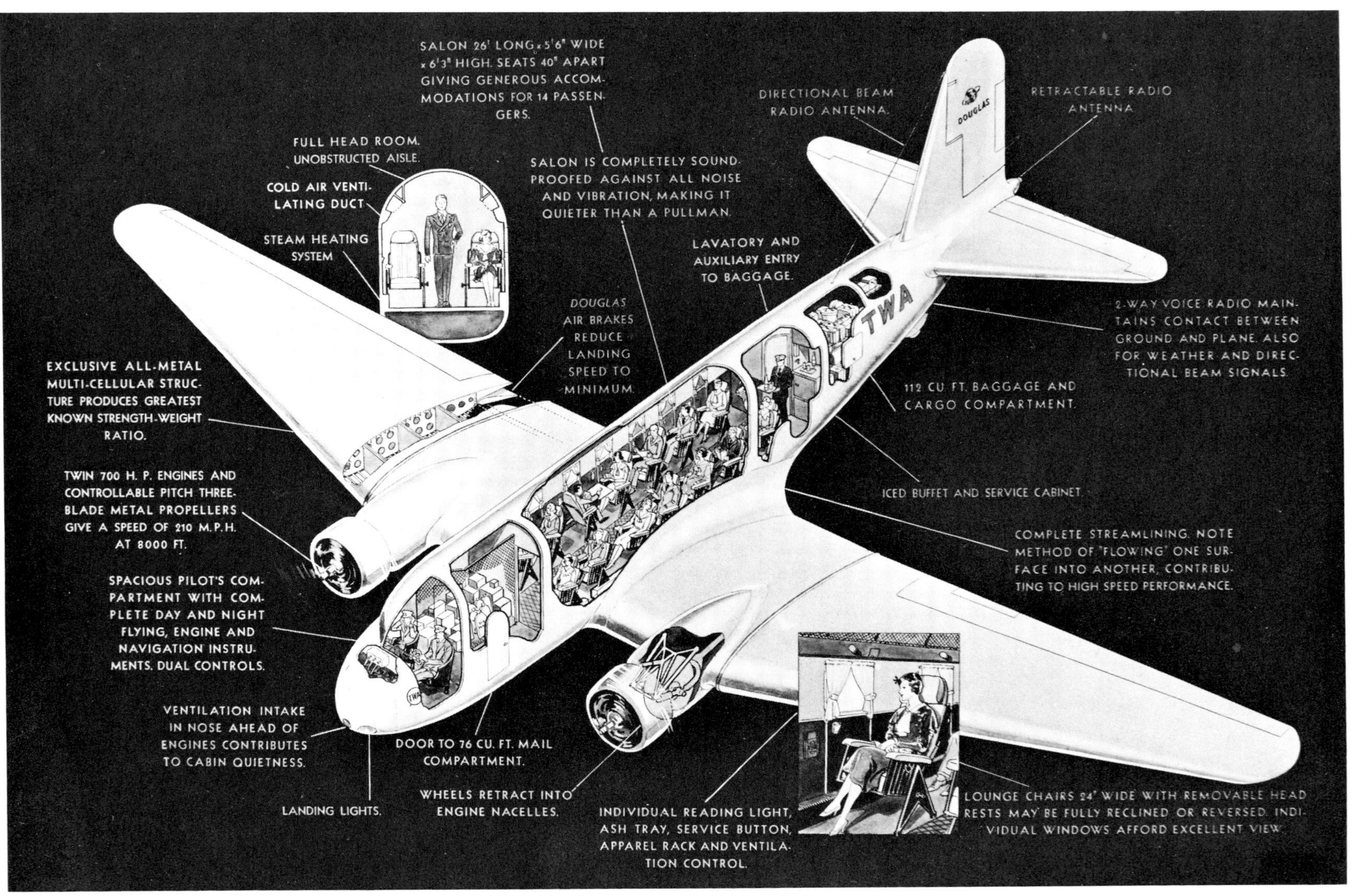

Cut-a-way Drawing of DC-2 (Douglas Aircraft Co. Photo)

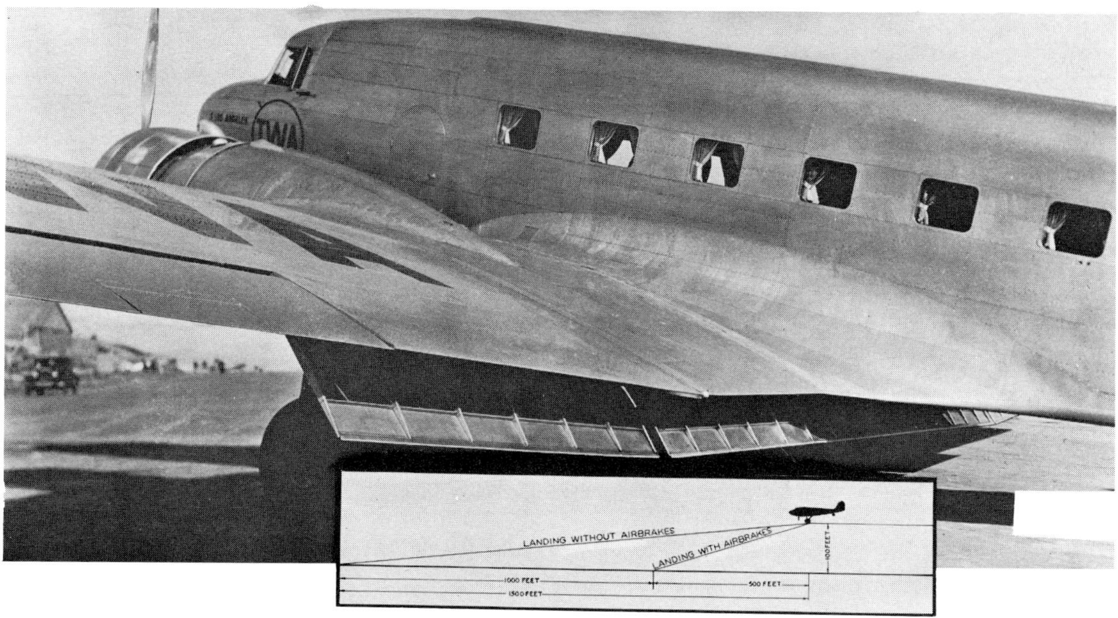

The Douglas "Air Brakes," flap-like panels that slip off the under-side of the wing, pioneered in the DC-1, gave the DC-2 the capability to land in short fields. They were a feature of the basic design carried on into the DC-3's which gave the planes great versatility during wartime operations and as peacetime wings serving smaller airports. (Douglas Aircraft Co. Photo)

(6) inches wide, and six (6) feet three (3) inches high. The great height of the passenger salon permits even the tallest person to walk fully erect in the cabin for its entire length. The (passenger) compartment is fitted to accommodate fourteen passengers in two rows of specially-designed lounge chairs 40 inches wide and separated by a central aisle 16 inches wide. Chairs are deeply upholstered and fully adjustable for reclining or reversing to face the passenger behind. Each seat has a private window and because of the height of the seat above the wing, there is excellent vision from all chairs.

"The transport is equipped with two 710-horsepower Wright *Cyclone* motors, which are supercharged to insure a fast cruising speed at high altitudes. Two controllable-pitch, three-bladed, two-position, hydro-controllable, Hamilton Standard propellers pull the 12,000-pound plane through the air. The propeller pitch is controlled by the pilot and is changed by oil pressure for climb and cruising speed.

"There are two main fuel tanks of 180 gallons capacity each and two auxiliary tanks of 75 gallons each, making a total of 510 gallons maximum fuel supply, enough to fly non-stop 1200 miles.

"The fuselage is of semi-monocoque construction with smooth riveted skin. The material used is a new extra light aluminum alloy having a thin coating of pure aluminum to give it high resistance to corrosion. The entire (fuselage) interior is accessible from nose to tail. The empannage is built integral with the fuselage to insure absolute rigidity.

"The Douglas *air brakes* – split trailing edge flaps – are built into the lower side of the wing to increase the lift and drag for slow, restricted landings. The flaps when hinged full-down cause a gain in lift of 35 per cent and a slow-down increase of 300 per cent. They are operated by a hydraulic system controlled from the cockpit."

Later, after he had flown in the ship, Dayhoff, wrote – "Flying in the new luxury liner transport is like putting wings on a luxurious living room and soaring in complete security and comfort. The Douglas transport is the crowning achievement in commercial transportation, creating a new ideal in luxurious travel combined with high speed and high performance characteristics coupled with great security."

At that time, TWA, also released officially its claims for the new airplane: "Maximum speed of the plane is 213 miles an hour at

14,000 feet altitude . . . but at 18,000 feet the speed jumps to 225 miles an hour because engines operate more efficiently at that altitude. With the *air brakes*, a new innovation for heavy transport planes, the landing speed is reduced to 58 miles an hour. Under single-engine power the airplane easily rises from takeoff to a ceiling of 9,000 feet without exceeding the engine's normal operation limits.

"The ship will climb at the rate of 1050 feet per minute. It has a service ceiling of 23,600 feet, but it will climb to an absolute ceiling of 25,400 feet."

III

TWA inaugurated scheduled service with the DC-2 on May 18, 1934, between Columbus, Pittsburgh and Newark, N. J. A week later the ship was flying between Newark and Chicago. Within the span of eight days it broke the speed record (New York to Chicago) four times. There was nothing in the skies that could match it for speed and comfort.

After that, as fast as the planes rolled out of the Santa Monica plant, they were flown to Kansas City for acceptance by the airline.

By August 1, TWA proudly announced in its advertising – "Coast-to-coast in 18 hours via 200-mile-an-hour luxury Airliners." Called *The Sky Chief*, the through plane left New York (Newark) at 4:00 P.M. daily. Landing in Chicago shortly after the dinner hour, the plane was in the air again Kansas City-bound at 8:25 P.M. Departing from KC at 11:30 P.M. the ship made the non-stop jump to Albuquerque, New Mexico. On the ground briefly for refuelling it took off again at 3:20 A.M. arriving in Los Angeles at 7:00 A.M.

For the first time the air traveler could fly from New York to Los Angeles without losing any part of the normal business day!

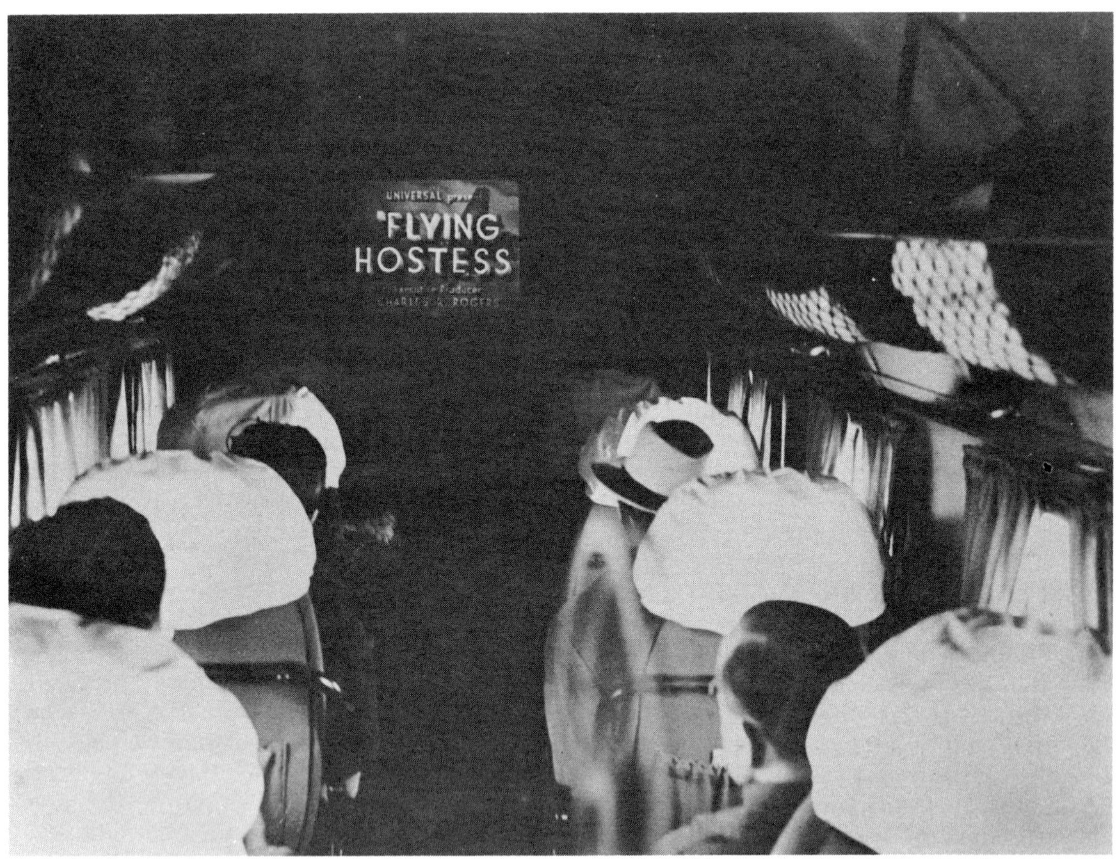

TWA in its Jet Age advertising boasted of pioneering in-flight movies and here's proof. Passengers riding in one of the first DC-2's enjoyed a picture called "Flying Hostess"—in 1934! ***(Douglas Aircraft Co. Photo)***

By mid-April, 1934, DC-2 fuselage sections were moving down the assembly line by the numbers. (Douglas Aircraft Co. Photo)

DC-2 center wing section and nacelles waiting to move onto the fuselage assembly line. (Douglas Aircraft Co. Photo)

Public acceptance of the super skyliner was even greater than TWA had imagined or hoped for. Passenger load factors – number of seats sold and occupied – skyrocketed. The TWA-Douglas team had taken the lead in air transport.

Orders for the new transport piled up.

Douglas, himself, was pleasantly surprised. "I remember early in the program," he reminisces, "I told Frye that I felt we might build fifty of the planes, but that would just about saturate the market. Then, when we passed that mark, I remember telling Raymond one day that it looked like we might make 100 of the ships. But, honestly, I couldn't see going beyond that figure.

"Now, looking back, it was never nicer to have been wrong."

Altogether they built 138 of the DC-2's.

Ironically, it was not Don Douglas, nor was it entirely the efforts of his fine sales organization that took the DC-2 program out of the red. Rightfully, much of the credit must go to one of the most famous of all aircraft designers – Anthony Hermann Gerhard Fokker. The man who had designed the plane in which Knute Rockne was killed – the unfortunate accident that had forced TWA to turn to Douglas for the DC-1 transport design – played a major role in building up the sales of the DC-2's.

Fokker and Douglas first met in 1933 when the "Flying Dutchman" came to Santa Monica to look at the new DC-1 transport. It was the beginning of a close relationship.

Both were "dreamers of the drawing board" and during the middle thirties when Fokker spent a lot of time at the Douglas plant, it was not uncommon to see them huddled together discussing their views on aerodynamic laws and "pencilizing the planes of tomorrow." When they weren't challenging each other in a duel of the slide rules, they were matching yachting skills, or in more relaxed moments, competing for the biggest catch of marlin or sailfish.

Someone once remarked – "Though they were miles apart in background and in personality characteristics, they were cast from the same aerodynamic mold. The world will never know which of these two famous plane designers contributed the most to the furtherance of air transportation. The Fokker planes and the DC-ships blazed the trails of aerial commerce across the world's skies."

When he saw the DC-1 for the first time and flew it (Fokker was an expert pilot, had taught himself to fly in his own plane which he had designed and built himself before he was out of his teens.) Tony Fokker admitted he didn't have words that could adequately describe his delight with the ship.

But he did have a checkbook.

Right then and there, Fokker placed an order for one of the DC-2's – "as soon as you can make delivery." He also made a deal with Douglas to obtain European sales and manufacturing rights for the

This DC-2, one of the first sold to K.L.M. (Koninklyke Luchtvaart Maatschappy) named the "Uiver," flying in the famous London-to-Melbourne Air Derby in 1934, came in second. Flying time was 90 hours, 13 minutes and 36 seconds. (K.L.M. Aerocarto N.V. Luchthaven Schipol)

Douglas transport. At the time some fifty commercial airlines the world over were using Fokker planes as standard equipment. "I'm convinced every one of them who can afford it will buy the DC-2," Fokker told Douglas.

He was that kind of man.

When Tony Fokker died in New York at the age of 49, Douglas wrote – "He was a pioneer in aviation, who grew with the industry and helped shape its destiny. His urge to improve and perfect was never-ending, and recognized no limitations, admitted no impossibilities.

"His mind was prolific of suggestions of a creative sort, covering many things other than aviation. We saw at first-hand his inventive genius and his brilliant business acumen, and learned many aspects of a truly dynamic personality.

"To the Douglas organization, Fokker's passing is a keen personal loss, for we knew him and loved him."

It was quite natural in view of Fokker's close association with the Dutch airline, K.L.M., that they should be his first customers for the DC-2. Initially KLM bought two of the planes which, like their famous prototype, the DC-1, made the trip across the Atlantic via freighter on the fall-storm swept decks of the *S. S. Staendam,* a Dutch ship.

IV

One of the oldest commercial airlines in the world, KLM, founded in 1919, almost immediately started service with the DC-2's over its 9,000-mile route from Amsterdam to Batavia. Within a few short weeks after the ships began regular scheduled service, one of them which had been christened, *Uiver,* (stork in Dutch) made headlines with its spectacular performance in the famous London to Melbourne Air Derby.

On October 20, 1934 at the airfield in Mildenhall, England, near London, twenty planes were lined up for the start of the 11123 mile race from England to Australia. The stakes were high – the $2,000 Sir MacPherson Robertson Gold Trophy and $75,000 to the winner. There were entries from France, England, Holland, United States, Germany and Italy. Some of the entries were biplanes and specially-built racing ships with built-in range for the long overwater hops.

When it was announced that the DC-2, a commercial transport, would compete against the souped-up "specials", most of the aviation world felt that it was like putting a limousine up against a racing car. *"American propaganda,"* one London newspaper headlined, *"an audacious assumption that such a ship could expect to compete with the fastest planes and designs on the continent."*

Actually, the DC-2 was flying under the Dutch flag, piloted by KLM pilots K. D. Parmentier and J. J. Moll. What made its appearance in the race even more incredible is that KLM had announced the plane would fly its regular route – 1,000 miles farther than the prescribed course. The only requirement in the rules was that the planes make stops at Bagdad, Allahabad, Darwin, Charlesville and Melbourne.

The DC-2 *Uiver*, when it took off on the first leg of its journey carried a crew of four – pilot, co-pilot, navigator and mechanic – three paying passengers and 30,000 letters.

Back in Santa Monica Don Douglas followed reports of the ship's progress. He had a particular interest in the race because the Douglas design was competing with two other U. S.-built planes both of which were in commercial service. One of them was a Boeing 247-D, piloted by Colonel Roscoe Turner and Clyde Pangborn. The other was a Lockheed. In effect, the three major builders of commercial airliners in the U. S. were putting their reputations on the line with obvious prestige and selling powers in favor of the best performer.

The DC-2 didn't win. But it came in second in both the speed and handicap divisions. Top honors went to British pilots, C. W. Scott and T. Campbell Black flying in a sleek, two-place deHavilland *Comet* biplane. The winner's time was – 70 hours, 54 minutes, 15 seconds.

Parmentier and Moll landed the *Uiver* 90 hours, 13 minutes and 36 seconds after

Capt. E. V. "Eddie" Rickenbacker, then Vice-President of Eastern Airlines, was one of the first customers to buy DC-2's. Eastern pioneered New York to Miami run with Florida Flyer. (Douglas Aircraft Co. Photo)

Pan American Grace Airways introduced the DC-2 over the Andes mountains of South America, proof of the new airliners' high altitude performance capabilities. (Douglas Aircraft Co. Photo)

they had left London. They had made five more stops and had flown most of the way as a scheduled airline operation.

One of the KLM pilots told Douglas — "During the regular stop-over at Bagdad, we used to see small street urchins point up to the sky every time one of our ships would lumber overhead and the youngsters would shout — *there goes a Dooglas, Dooglas!*"

The DC-2 meets some Lamas and Gauchos on the Pampas plains of Argentina. (Douglas Aircraft Co. Photo)

Years later, in 1940, Major Mahmoud al Hindi, Arabian army officer, on a visit to the Douglas plant, also told the designer of the DC-ships that the name "Douglas" was uniformly applied to all airplanes in his country shortly after KLM's DC-2 flew over the country for the first time on its way to Melbourne.

Future sales of the DC-2 were assured. Early in 1935, Captain Eddie Rickenbacker, who had recently become General Manager of Eastern Airlines, placed an order for fourteen of the ships, put them in service on the New York-Miami run.

To promote the operation Rickenbacker staged a one-day VIP flight in a DC-2 between the two cities making the round-trip in little more than sixteen hours. Guests took off from N. Y. in the morning, had dinner in Miami, returned the same evening.

It was the beginning of the "Great Silver Fleet."

Other domestic airlines, Western, Braniff, Northwest, as rapidly as possible, converted their fleets to the Douglas DC-2 aircraft. Likewise, Pan American World Airways introduced the ships over its Latin American and South American routes.

V

It was more than speed, built-in safety and luxury that put the fabulous DC-2's into the aviation spotlight. These factors, of course, won public acclaim. But to the airline operators the ships meant something else. They were money-makers. For the first time, the airlines had a vehicle that didn't eat up its payload/profit potential in fuel, operational and maintenance costs.

When the DC-2's in service, flying under the flags of 21 different countries reached their 20,000,000-mile mark, little more than a year after TWA's No. 301 inaugural flight, Douglas made a survey of the different air transport lines and private operators to see how the DC-ships were doing.

Here, in part, is that report:

"With 108 silver-winged transports in service in the eastern and western hemispheres, flying approximately 75,000 miles every 24 hours on night and day schedules in all kinds of weather, operators claim that the skyliners are performing work

Flying under the flag of Ceskoslovenska Letecka Spolecnost, the pre-communist days Czechoslovakia, the DC-2 quickly became the prime mover of the country's air transport system. (Douglas Aircraft Co. Photo)

DC-2's showed up in China (China National Airways Corporation) C.N.A.C., a Pan American Airways affiliate. Later these planes performed miracles in World War II. (Douglas Aircraft Co. Photo)

under variable operating conditions not possible heretofore.

"United States operators and Pan American Airways in South America report 15,000,000 miles flown in the first eight months at an efficiency of 98.8 per cent. Douglas planes owned by foreign operators and private individuals in America and Europe made up the remaining 5,000,000 miles.

"TWA, American Airlines, Eastern Air Lines and Pan American Airways report their fleets of Douglas ships are negotiating 52,289 miles a day with 21,499 miles flown at night and 20,790 miles of daylight flying. Of the 26,259,665 miles flown in the U. S. during the first six months this year, 7,286,437 miles were flown by Douglas transports or 27.7 per cent. However, the 42 Douglas planes "available for service" constituted only 7.6 per cent of the total planes in service in the U. S., a remarkable tribute to the Douglas operating ability.

"Operating efficiency increased on the airlines using the Douglas luxury liners from the first month the planes were placed in service. Airlines report that operational efficiency – planes in the air not on the ground for mechanical delays – jumped 20 to 25 per cent. In some cases, there was reported a 66 per cent gain in average "air time," per day."

The fact is some of the airlines were facing bankruptcy before the advent of the DC-2 ships. But with the new airliner's demonstrative performance economy and reliability there was new hope for the whole industry. As one airline vice-president declared in an interview – "There was pie in the sky."

VI

Development of the DC-2 brought many honors to designer and plane builder Donald W. Douglas. The ships had been in service less than a full year when Douglas was invited to deliver the annual Wright Memorial Lecture before the Royal Aeronautical Society in London. Founded in 1866, the society, oldest of its kind in the world, was recognized as aviation's foremost scientific organization. It was with great pride that Douglas accepted the invitation.

In London, Douglas, as he prepared his lecture notes, was also proud to read this advertisement in one of the British aviation publications:

> "DOUGLAS DC-2, 210-m.p.h. Transport. The speed of the Douglas DC-2 is combined with a useful load of 5,880 pounds and a range of 1225 miles. . . . This useful combination offers world supremacy for both commercial and military purposes . . . a fact evidenced by the more than 100 Douglas Transports now in service under the flags of 12 nations."

It was typical of Douglas' nature, however, that in his lecture he should pay tribute to so many others for the combined effort which made development of the new airliner a reality.

Quoting from his paper:

"An alert and ambitious military technical personnel played its part in accelerating the use of brains by our designers. Growing competition among the airlines spurred the development of faster and safer airliners. . . .

"All agencies concerned in and contributing to aviation have been most alert,

In 1936 Donald W. Douglas was awarded the Robert J. Collier Trophy, aviation's highest honor, for his design and development of the DC-2. Here he is shown being congratulated by President Franklin D. Roosevelt in ceremonies at the White House. (Douglas Aircraft Co. Photo)

cooperative and constructive. . . . Our engines have been developing at a pace to permit the airplane designer to raise his sights. . . . Our instrument and radio people have aided tremendously by furnishing us with means to fly in bad weather. . . . Propeller makers have been most helpful, and, in fact, I can say that the development of the variable pitch propeller to the point it has reached today, is probably the most fundamentally important development of this period.

"Comfort was studied with care, and sound engineers developed efficient and practical methods of eliminating the formerly disagreeable and tiring noise of the air transport. . . . Heating and ventilation comparable to that found in modern buildings was affected after the aid of related industries was combined."

Concluding his talk Douglas said – "A glorious future lies before aviation. . . . Its development has only just commenced."

Returning to his homeland, Douglas was received with another high honor in recognition for his work on the DC-2 airliner.

On Wednesday, July 1, 1936, three years to the day after the DC-1 made its initial flight, Douglas stood before the President of the United States to receive the Robert J. Collier Trophy, aviation's highest award.

He heard Franklin D. Roosevelt say, reading from the citation – "This airplane by reason of its high speed, economy, and quiet passenger comfort, has been generally adopted by transport lines throughout the United States. Its merits have been further recognized by its adoption abroad and its influence on foreign design is already apparent."

There was a bigger, better DC-ship already in the skies – the fabulous DC-3.

Coming out of the White House after receiving the Collier award, Douglas read about the new plane in the headlines. An American Airlines DC-3 "Flagship" had just flown non-stop from Newark, New Jersey to Chicago and return – a distance of 1,472 miles in 8 hours and five minutes. There was also the announcement that American fliers would begin non-stop service with these planes within the week between New York and Chicago.

Don Douglas looked forward to riding the new DC-3 skyliner back to Santa Monica.

Chapter 7

Please Do Not Disturb!

The first DC-2 airplane had been in service less than a month when an upheaval occurred in the whole commercial aviation picture. On June 12, 1934, Congress passed a law that was to have far-reaching effects on the aircraft manufacturing industry and the future of America's air transport system. Known as the Black-McKellar Bill (The Air Mail Act of 1934) the measure put all civil aviation under three branches of the federal government.

Under the new law the Post Office Department was made responsible for awarding all air mail contracts and determining routes and schedules. The Interstate Commerce Commission fixed the mail rates and payments. The Bureau of Air Commerce had the authority to regulate the airways and license all pilots and machines. At the same time, the Act separated the aircraft manufacturing concerns and big holding company combines from their air transport operations because of the trend toward monopolistic empires. In short, it was illegal for an aircraft builder to own any part of an airline operation.

Some of the smaller operators were knocked out of the picture when the Post Office took away their mail routes. Others merged to produce a whole new pattern of airline networks criss-crossing the nation.

Of all the aircraft manufacturers, Douglas stood to benefit the most. The Douglas Aircraft Company never had had any affiliation with an air transport operation. Moreover, in the new DC-2, the company had an airliner that was far ahead of any other. Naturally, the new, financially stronger and larger airline companies rushed to buy the DC-2 in order to stay abreast of the competition. Overnight, Douglas had more business than he ever had anticipated from the transport field. Many of the air carriers which previously had been bound to buy the products (planes) manufactured by their parent companies, were free to do business with the Scotsman.

II

With the passage of the Black-McKellar Bill, there emerged a new airline operation that was to zoom into power,and prestige. In time, it would become the biggest trunk line in the country – American Airlines, Inc.

The man chiefly responsible for what happened was a tall, soft-spoken, but stern-faced and determined Texan named Cyrus Rowlett Smith. A student of law, economics and business administration at the University of Texas, Smith had worked in a bank, had been an office manager, an accountant and auditor in an office specializing in receiverships, and treasurer of a power company which owned an airline.

Cyrus Rowlett "CR" Smith.
(American Airlines, Inc. Photo)

It has been said of Smith that he took air transportation out of the hangar, put it in the terminal building and moved it to Wall Street where it belonged. There is little question that "CR," through the years, has demonstrated conclusively he knows how to make an airline make money. Ever since he took over the helm of American Airlines in 1934, the line began to climb like a rocket.

Basically, the Smith success formula was quite simple: (1) Give the air traveler a transport plane fast, safe, luxurious, yet operationally economical enough to keep the ticket within the price of anybody's pocketbook. (2) Get out and *sell* that airplane not just as a vehicle of the air, but as a transportation medium the same as you would sell tickets on an ocean liner, a crack New York Central Limited or a Greyhound bus.

The vehicle to implement this philosophy, Smith didn't design or build, but he provided the spark and the incentive to bring it into being. So far as the airliner is concerned it was an evolution; an equipment improvement program that made flying safer and more attractive to the traveler. With an eye on passenger appeal he took a good airplane (the DC-2) and excited men's minds and productive know-how to make it a great airplane.

The result was a new member of the DC-family of skyships came into the picture, the DST – Douglas Sleeper Transport.

III

Smith, who became chairman of the board of American Airlines and guided its course in the Jet Age, got into the aviation picture at the age of 29 when he was made treasurer of Texas Air Transport, a small air mail operation. When Texas Air merged with Southern Air Transport, Smith became Vice-President Operations of the new organization and built himself a reputation as a leader in the development of air passenger service throughout Texas and the southland.

Right from the start, Smith brought something to the airline operation that it had been sadly lacking – business background. He disproved an old axiom among aviators that an airline should be run by fliers.

No man to tackle something without knowing what it is all about, Smith learned how to fly, and he learned the airline business from the ground up. With Smith running the show, Southern won recognition and was absorbed into the fold of the big and powerful Aviation Corporation (AVCO, a holding company) to become an important route segment of American Airways, Inc. Soon, Smith was running the airline's

Curtiss "Condor" which American Airways, predecessor to American Airlines, Inc., introduced as first sleeper plane. (American Airlines, Inc. Photo)

Stinson Model "A" Trimotor. (American Airlines, Inc. Photo)

flight operations, southern division, and later was made head of the entire system's operation.

At the time, he didn't have much to work with.

By the company's own admission, according to an official press release, – "There were four things wrong: its route pattern made no sense; it owned a weird collection of aircraft; service was spotty; financial losses were running high.

"The route sprawled from coast to coast, but not in a straight line. A slogan – *from coast to coast and from Canada to Mexico* – was whimsically misquoted by employees – *from coast to coast via Canada and. Mexico!*"

The whimsy could have been carried further. The line operated just about every type of transport plane then on the market – the trimotor Fords, Fokkers, Lockheeds, Stinsons, Bellancas and the big bi-motored, lumbering Curtiss *Condors*. Pilots said it was called "American" because its equipment policy was – "so damned democratic – you can fly anywhere in anything!"

Smith was shackled by other things, too. Aviation Corporation which owned American Airways, Inc. was one of the prime targets of the Black-McKellar Bill. The Act

This is one of the Stinson tri-motored high-wing monoplanes used by American Airways prior to the introduction of the DC-2 and DC-3 airliners. The planes were 12-passenger, fabric-covered so-called "luxury" ships. Speed —about 125 mph! (American Airlines, Inc. Photo)

William (Bill) Littlewood.
(American Airlines, Inc. Photo)

took the infant from its parent and American Airways became American Airlines, Inc. On May 13, 1934, Smith was made president of the new company.

His first act was to fight for a new mail contract and he won. The Post Office Department awarded American Airlines a third airway, coast-to-coast, across America. He was in the ring with the heavy-weights – United and TWA.

Ironically, "CR" was in the same position that Jack Frye had found himself in two years before. He didn't have any planes that could possibly compete with TWA's new DC-2's or United's 247 Boeings.

Fortunately, the Douglas Company had an "open door" policy with regard to its popular DC-2 transports. New customers were always welcome. Smith promptly ordered 15 ships and the famous American Airlines "Flagship Fleet" was born.

IV

It was the summer of 1934. Smith, with his Chief Engineer, William (Bill) Littlewood were on the ramp at Love Field, the Municipal Airport serving Dallas, Texas. They were going to board an American Airlines' plane and fly westward to Los Angeles. It was a different kind of plane than the DC-2, a big red and blue Curtiss *Condor* biplane, a twin-engined, cloth-covered, 12-passenger airliner. The *Con-*

When "CR" Smith took over as President of American Airlines, Inc., he immediately ordered DC-2's, the start of the famous American Airlines' "Flagship Fleet." (American Airlines, Inc. Photo)

dor had something the DC-2 didn't have. It was a "sleeper" plane. Passengers could climb aboard and get into a pullman-sized bunk and sleep all the way to the West Coast. American had pioneered "sleeper plane" service on May 5, 1934 between Los Angeles and Dallas.

When they climbed aboard the *Condor,* a pretty stewardess was already making up the bunks.

Smith, almost subconsciously, remarked to Littlewood – "Bill, what we need is a DC-2 sleeper plane!

Neither slept that night though the flight was smooth.

They were both thinking the same thing – *Why not make the DC-2 a sleeper transport? It was big enough. It had the power.*

Littlewood, the engineer, was thinking it could be done. He was roughing it out in his own mind, how it might be done. He had some strong ideas on the subject. He knew the story of the DC-2, how they had stretched it from a 12-passenger into a 14-passenger airliner. With a little more wing and a fatter fuselage the "rubber airplane" could be stretched again.

Smith was thinking, too. If he could put a DC-2 sleeper on the line, he could throw a hot curve at United and TWA. It would be a strong point for his sales people. The "hard sell" was on. In the next round in the battle of the giants for the transcontinental business, he was determined to come out slugging.

When they disembarked at Glendale Terminal, "CR" told Littlewood about his thoughts. They were a good team. Littlewood already had caught the signal. He said he would work up some preliminary specifications.

Smith didn't waste any time. Back in Chicago, American's home base, again, he called Don Douglas on the telephone.

Could Douglas make the DC-2 into a sleeper plane?

If so, American was interested.

Douglas was a little cold to the idea. His first reaction was – "we can't even keep up with the orders for the DC-2's!"

That was what he told "CR" on the telephone.

Smith, however, wouldn't take NO for an answer. The long distance bill mounted into hundreds of dollars. Finally, he broke through Douglas' obstinacy by virtually promising he would buy, sight unseen, twenty of the sleeper planes if Douglas would build them for American.

Douglas agreed to have his people work up a design study.

Smith said he would send Bill Littlewood out to Santa Monica to help.

When he hung up, "CR" was almost in a cold sweat.

He had virtually committed American Airlines to a multi-million dollar order for an airplane that wasn't even on paper yet and he didn't have any idea where he could get that kind of money.

Littlewood headed west.

Smith went to Washington to see his old friend and Texan, Jesse Jones, who was the head of the New Deal's Reconstruction Finance Corporation. FDR had set up the alphabetical agency to help keep business in business. There had been a lot of talk about the RFC. The publicity had been superb. Congress had even justified it, an organization to "ward off financial disaster."

Smith believed what he read. When he walked into Jones' office to present his case, he came right to the point.

"Jesse," he said, "American Airlines *is* a disaster if you don't make us a loan."

He got the money – *a $4,500,000 loan.* But he still didn't have the plane.

The project – DST – Douglas Sleeper Transport, however, was moving along at a rapid pace.

V

The 200-mile-an-hour wind tunnel at the California Institute of Technology was roaring like a man-made hurricane. In the test section was an eleventh-scale model of the proposed DST. There was nothing strikingly different about the model. Outwardly, it looked like the DC-2, but there were big differences. They had widened the fuselage and lengthened it. The wing span was greater. There was a different shaped rudder and vertical stabilizer.

To the layman these things would not be evident nor important. But to the small group of Douglas engineers and Littlewood of American, as they watched the various recording instruments tell the story, the

A. L. Klein. (Douglas Aircraft Co. Photo)

changes they had made became big question marks.

This was test No. 267.

A. L. Klein, the Cal Tech physicist and "Doc" Oswald were in charge of the tests. They had called Littlewood and asked him to come over to see their latest design modification. Admittedly everybody had been quite concerned with the aerodynamic characteristics of the model up to this point.

Klein summed it up this way – "The bigger plane with its change in center of gravity had produced the stability of a drunk trying to walk a straight line."

"We had tried everything," he explained, "but the results fell far below the expected performance. In the back of our minds we couldn't be sure that, maybe, we hadn't stretched the airplane too much in trying to meet the sleeper version requirements."

Oswald was talking to Littlewood:

"Bill, if this thing doesn't work we might as well forget about the whole project. This instability we're getting wouldn't rock a passenger to sleep; it would rock him right out of the berth."

They watched the test with anxious eyes.

Littlewood could see the model. But, admittedly, he couldn't see that it was much different from the others which he had seen in the tunnel. He was pleased, however, when the test results began to show positive stability characteristics.

Finally, they shut off the wind.

Klein and Oswald were all smiles. "Well, I think we hit on the answer," said Oswald.

By modifying the wing and changing the airfoil section slightly they had shifted the plane's center gravity. In layman's terms they had changed the position of the fulcrum for the teeter-totter. It was an aerodynamic secret that was to make the DST one of the most stable aircraft ever to spread its wings.

Littlewood was pleased as punch. He knew now he could report to "CR" that they had a fundamentally sound aerodynamic airplane. It was a great relief to him personally, too, because now he could go ahead with his own ideas to make the plane the most luxurious transport ever built. Results of the wind tunnel tests indicated he could do just about anything he wanted with the DST interior – and Littlewood is credited with being directly responsible for many of the service features and innovations in passenger comfort that the new airliner was soon to introduce to the air traveling public.

He went directly from the wind tunnel over to the DST mock-up.

According to Douglas, the "mock-up" of the DST probably was the most thorough ever made, including some 15,000 hours of engineering and labor. Much of this was virgin research.

They had long before worked out the arrangement of the berths and the seats. Now, they were concerned with something else – physical and mental reaction of air travelers to the environment.

When Littlewood and "CR" had roughed up the general specifications for the DST they had interjected a new psychological approach to the problem. They called it "human engineering."

"One phase of it," Littlewood explained, "was color and decoration. We ran an entirely new study relative to various color combinations and their effects on passengers.

"Some of the things we learned changed a lot of thinking . . . We found, for example, that color was closely tied in with uneasiness, and this human reaction had to be played down in air travel, for it is associated with balance and air-sickness. Certain shades of green work on some travellers in a very unpleasant way. Too much red promotes excitement. Patterns or designs in color, while the color itself may not be objectionable, will assist in unbalancing a person or even aggravate air-sickness."

The result was evident in the DST. Its interior colors were subdued and blended, giving a quiet, restful feeling. Carpets and lower walls were done in darker tones to give the feeling of strength and security underfoot. The upper walls and ceiling were light in color to minimize any uncomfortable feeling of confinement.

There were other problems, other improvements.

Up front in the cockpit American wanted a duplicate set of all instruments for pilot and co-pilot, an added safety feature. They also introduced a new system of cockpit and instrument panel lighting for night flying.

American pilots, flying the DC-2's, had made some complaints about the planes' "stiff-leggedness." The landing gear was shock absorbing, all right, but somehow the ships landed like "they were afraid to bend at the knee joints." Couldn't this be remedied in the DST?

Douglas engineers came up with the answer. It consisted of a "pork-chop" joint in the landing gear struts and a whole new hydraulic landing gear system. More important, they eliminated the hand-pump for lowering and raising the gear. In the DST it was fully automatic. The hand pump was still there, but for emergency only.

A young hydraulics engineer, Hal Adams, had been chiefly responsible for loosening up the limbs, a boon to sleeping passengers, who often times never even woke up during landings and take-offs. He came up with something else, too – the introduction of foot brakes.

Previously the DC-2 had brakes, but the pilot applied them with a hand lever. Adams drew the assignment and put automobile type brakes on the DST. He got the idea from the old Pierce Arrow brake system. When it was finally adapted to the airplane, the pilot could brake the ship on the ground by applying pressure to foot brake mechanisms in connection with the rudder pedals.

The "pork chop" joint produced a whole new gear system. Later it was adapted for the DC-3, as shown above. (Douglas Aircraft Co. Photo)

"I'll never forget the day we tried it out," Hal Adams recalls. "One of our test pilots climbed into the cockpit and taxied the ship out on the ramp. He hit the pedals and the plane stopped so sharply that the tail whipped up and the props made the sparks fly as they nicked the concrete runway."

One by one the problems were solved.

There emerged from the factory cocoon an airplane that made Douglas' eyes sparkle with pride.

"CR" Smith felt it, too, and there were dollar signs in front of his eyes. This plane, his sales people could sell to the traveling public. He already had set in motion a different kind of sales organization and promotion campaign that would revolutionize air transportation market-wise with the same kind of impact that the new plane would have on the equipment program.

By the time the plane was ready, the program would be in full swing.

VI

Work on the new sleeper plane had begun almost immediately after Smith had convinced Douglas that American wanted the bigger plane and Littlewood had drawn up the specifications and recommendations of the airline. That was in the fall of 1934. The project overshadowed anything Douglas had previously attempted including the DC-1 venture.

A Douglas company historical record reveals that a staff of 400 engineers and draftsmen were assigned to the project. Some 3500 drawings later the finalized design began to take shape. Then, in December of the same year, after more than 300 wind tunnel tests, the "keel was laid."

The DST itself did not roll out of the hangar until December 17, 1935 – thirty-two years to the day after Orville Wright made the first heavier-than-air, man-carrying flight in a power-driven airplane at Kitty Hawk, North Carolina. The airplane had come a long way.

The wing span of the DST was 95 feet – almost equal to the entire distance that Orville Wright had flown during those 12 seconds that changed man's concept of the flying machine. The big, silvery airliner weighed a hundred times as much as the first Wright machine. Its engines were fifty times as powerful.

Yet, there was one striking similarity. Aerodynamically, the new airliner used the same principle to lift itself off the ground that was the secret the Wright Brothers had given to the world in their frail, box-kite machine of wooden frame covered with cloth. The formulae of flight, clean aerodynamic design to permit wings to take advantage of the airflow and generate lift, plus a combination of elevator, rudder and aileron control, was the heritage that the Wrights left to men like Douglas, Kindelberger, Raymond, Oswald and all the others who turned the principle of flight into machines of majestic wonder and performance.

Remarkably, the DST made its initial test flight the same day that it made its public debut. Carl Cover was at the controls. He reported the ship "handled beautifully."

The plane itself was a thing of beauty and perfection.

"In tradition which the DC-2 has established for luxury, security and economical high performance, Douglas now presents the DST Sky Sleeper," said an expensive four-color company brochure announcing the new plane. "The Douglas Sky Sleeper is America's first air transport specifically designed for night travel and provides sleeping accommodations for 14 passengers.

"The planes offer 200-mile-an-hour flights from coast to coast with only two refueling stops enroute and with a large fuel reserve. Their two engines, developing a total of 2,000 horsepower, will take off the 24,000-pound transports after a ground run of 980 feet, and with full load the airplanes will climb to an altitude of 23,100 feet. With

First American Airlines' DST (Douglas Skysleeper Transport) made its public debut on the 32nd anniversary of man's first powered flight, December 17, 1935. Note door on left-side of aircraft. The plane had an experimental number X-14988. Small windows are for upper berths! (Douglas Aircraft Co. Photo)

First flight of new DST. Wing was same plan-form as the DC-2 but 10 feet longer, tip to tip. (Douglas Aircraft Co. Photo)

only one engine in operation, level flight at 9,500 feet can be maintained. Refinements in streamlining, a new development in shock-absorbing landing gear, and far-reaching improvements in luxurious appointments characterize the advancements which the DST introduces to commercial air travel."

Describing the plane's interior, the brochure explained – "The main cabin, measuring 7 feet, 8 inches in width, 19 feet, 5½ inches in length and 6 feet, 4½ inches in height, comfortably accommodates twelve of the 14 passengers. Ceiling-height partitions divide the cabin into six sections, three on each side of a wide aisle. The Sky Room, forward of the main cabin on the right hand side of the fuselage, accommodates the other two passengers in secluded quarters. (American stewardesses dubbed it the "honeymoon hut.") In each section, two 36-inch wide deeply upholstered seats face each other for daytime travel and make up into a lower berth at night. These seats are of ample width for two persons, making possible a daytime passenger capacity of twenty-eight. Space is provided for hand luggage under the seats.

"An upper berth 30 inches wide folds up into the ceiling when not in use. Made up for sleeping, the upper and lower berths are 6 feet 5 inches in length. Separate dressing rooms for men and women and separate lavatories, one adjoining each dressing room, are provided at the rear of the cabin.

"Private accommodations for passengers who desire complete seclusion on their air journeys are incorporated in the Sky Room, a completely enclosed compartment in the forward part of the fuselage. It provides sleeping accommodations for two and seating for four. It is equipped with an upper and lower berth, wash basin, mirror and other conveniences."

The brochure also revealed these performance characteristics:

Maximum speed . . . . . . 212 mph.
Cruise speed . . . . 180 mph.
Landing speed . . . . 64 mph.
Service ceiling . . . . 20,800 ft.
Absolute ceiling . . . . 23,100 ft.

It wasn't the fact that the DST was so much faster than the DC-2 that made it a boon to air travel. The important thing was the DST was bigger and could carry more payload. Moreover, it had the built-in range (fuel capacity) for longer hops – New York - Chicago, non-stop, for example. At the same time it was almost as economical to operate as the smaller DC-2.

Douglas, making his annual report (1935) to the Board of Directors told them – "The DST's payload is one third more than that of any other previous airliner. Its gross weight of about 25,000 pounds is half again as great as any airliner now in service!"

"More important," he emphasized, "our estimates show that it costs about 69 cents per mile to operate the plane, which is just about on a par with the cost of operating the Ford trimotors. On a ton-mile basis (the capability of lifting one ton of payload and carrying it one mile) it can carry 6,000 pounds in passengers, mail and freight – more than double the capacity of the Ford trimotors.

"On a typical flight, non-stop, New York to Chicago, for example, the cost of operating a DST is roughly $800. It costs about the same to operate the Ford trimotors between these cities with stopovers at Pittsburgh and Cleveland, because of limited range. The difference is the DST can carry almost three times as much in payload."

He had other encouraging news to report as well. They had a modified version

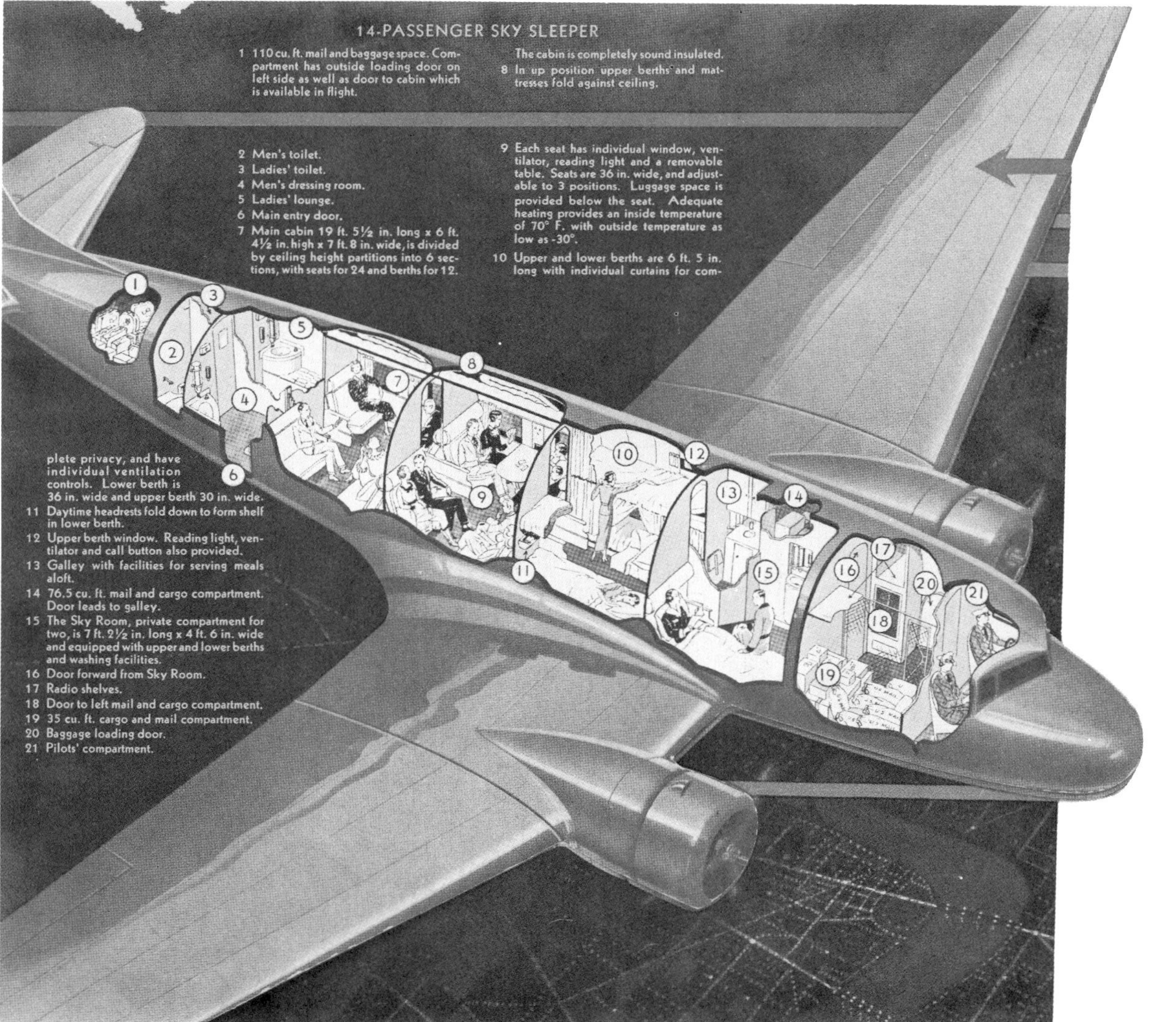

Cut-A-Way Drawing of DST. (Douglas Aircraft Co. Photo)

of the DST (the DC-3) already moving down the line – a 21-passenger luxury plane. And just about all the DC-2 customers were already "signing-up" to buy the newer and larger ships.

VII

The first time the mass public got a preview of the DST and the kind of luxury it brought to air travel occasioned a bit of humor. It was in the spring of 1936. The DST was put on display at the Pan-Pacific Auditorium during an aviation exhibition in progress. The first DST was undergoing a rigid flight test program and confirming all the expectations of the engineers and builders. Already other ships were rolling off the assembly line. One of them made a strange journey.

"It was the slowest trip the plane ever made," Bill Littlewood explains, "We put a DST on a trailer and hauled it from Santa Monica to the auditorium in downtown LA. We got up at 3 A.M. to make the trip in order to avoid traffic. The plane was so big we had a helluva time negotiating the turns. Sometimes I think it was a tougher job than designing the airplane. It was something we couldn't work out with the slide rules."

That night Don Douglas came down to see the show. He wanted to hear first hand some of the comments the layman had to say about the new airliner. The DST was the center of attraction. Hundreds of people walked through the "Skysleeper" and marvelled at its super deluxe interior.

When Douglas saw the plane, however, he frowned. The fact is, he took one look at the exhibit and, as Arthur Raymond said – "got that look on his face he gets when he's going to give somebody hell." He had detected a detail that nobody else noticed.

The explanatory sign read: 14 BIRTHS, 21 SEATS.!

First of the sleeper planes was delivered to American Airlines on June 8, 1936. The ship was flown non-stop from Los Angeles to Chicago and "CR" Smith was on the line at the Chicago terminal to welcome its arrival. So was Ed Doherty, a young reporter who later was to join American Airline's public relations staff.

"I was just a kid about to make my first flight from Chicago to New York," Ed recalls the event. "My grandmother had accompanied me to the airport. She was carrying a rosary and muttering prayers to herself.

"When she saw the plane her face went through a transformation and she said – *Jesus, Mary and Joseph, I didn't know they were so big. Nothing could happen to you in a strong iron contraption like that!*"

American inaugurated skysleeper service, coast-to-coast, beginning September 18, 1936. The first eastbound plane was christened the *Flagship California* by Louise Hepburn, niece of Admiral A. J. Hepburn, amid fanfare and ceremonies at Los Angeles Municipal Airport. The idol of millions, child movie actress Shirley Temple, was on hand to receive the first ticket.

Designated the *American Mercury* on the Airline's time-tables, the flight permitted a passenger at New York to board the skysleeper at 5:10 P.M. and arrive in Los Angeles early the next morning. Eastbound and Westbound trips were flown daily.

Air transportation had a "new look." The airplane, like the railroad Pullman car, had a PLEASE DO NOT DISTURB sign hung on it.

Less than nine months after the first DST was flown, the DC-3 production line at Douglas, Santa Monica, was in high-gear. Not counting the wartime cargo versions, the company would build a total of 803 commercial airliners of the DC-3 type. (Douglas Aircraft Co. Photo)

Chapter 8

Aviation's Model T

When American Airlines' "CR" Smith "talked" Don Douglas into building the deluxe skysleeper transports, something happened to the Douglas Company that had only one parallel in the annals of U. S. transportation. Before the ink was dry on the initial drawings for the DST the plane already had evolved into another configuration – the twenty-one passenger DC-3 airliner which, without doubt, was to become the best-known aircraft in the world, the most versatile and the hardest-working flying machine ever made. In this respect, it has been rightly called – "The Model-T of Aviation."

Therein lies the parallel. What happened to the Ford Motor Car Company when Old Henry came out with the fabulous *Tin Lizzie*, occurred on a smaller scale to the Douglas Aircraft Company of Santa Monica, California.

Overnight, Douglas couldn't produce the new model fast enough. The machine itself became standard equipment on virtually every airline in the world. Don Douglas was to the world of wings what Henry Ford was to the world of wheels.

Before production of the basic model DC-3 and its variations would cease, 803 had been built as commercial airliners and 10,123 as military versions. Although exact figures are not available, it has been roughly estimated that these ships, alone grossed the Douglas company "in excess of *one billion* dollars." No single aircraft ever made such a universal name for its designers and builders, a symbol of "wings for the world" which became the Douglas slogan. No other airplane ever had such an impact on trade and economy the world over. It also would help to decide a war.

"One thing seems certain," Douglas declares, "the DC-3 converted millions of ground lubbers to the acceptance of air travel as a safe and practical means of transportation."

An understatement!

Statistics worked up by Douglas researchers claim that all-told the DC-3 commercial airliners, alone, have carried more than 500-million passengers approximately 100-billion passenger miles, while logging an aggregate of more than 80-million flying hours.

That anything such as this would happen was the farthest from the wildest notions of designer Douglas when he told C. R. Smith he would build the DST back in the summer of 1934.

The truth is, when he hung up the telephone after talking to "CR" when the latter convinced Douglas he should "take a crack" at American's proposed sleeper plane, Don Douglas still wasn't sure he was doing the right thing. According to one source, Douglas turned to his secretary after Smith's call and remarked – "I had to tell him YES, or he would have run up such a long distance telephone bill they couldn't afford to pay for the DC-2's they've got on order."

That same day, talking to Arthur Raymond about the American deal, Douglas confided – "So, they buy twenty of the ships. We'll be lucky if we break even. Remember what happened with the DC-2? We didn't get off the hook until we were well into the second batch of 25 . . . What's more, who the hell is going to buy a sleeper plane? Night flying is about as popular as silent movies."

There was much truth in what he said.

Douglas also had some other reasons for being "a little cold" toward the project. The DC-2 business was booming and he was more than satisfied. He also had a new bomber design, the XB-18, which looked like a sure winner in the upcoming Air Corps competition to be held at Wright Field, Dayton, Ohio in the near future. If the bomber design won, it would mean turning the plant inside out.

Furthermore, Douglas honestly felt at the time that the commercial airliner market was reaching its saturation point.

Unfortunately, the public marveled at the DC-2 airliners, but the man on the street wasn't rushing to airline ticket counters to fly in the ships. To be sure, the airlines had a secure and stable airplane in the DC-2. But the air transportation business was anything but secure and stable. The sheriff was at the door of most airline companies. The airlines, face it, were really starting all over again under the new Air Mail Act. There was sure to be rough weather ahead.

II

Things didn't get much better to change Douglas' attitude as the DC-3 program moved along through the design, engineering and development stages. Troubles started right from the beginning – the first time, in fact, that engineers put the scale model in the Cal Tech wind tunnel. It was not until more than 250 tests had been completed that Klein and Oswald, the aerodynamicists, began to feel they were getting satisfactory performance indications from the new design. It wasn't as easy as it looked to stretch the basic DC-1 design again.

The late Fred Stineman, who was Chief Project Engineer on the DC-3 (he also was one of the design engineers who worked on Old 300 once told a reporter – "The original plans for the DC-3 called for a bigger fuselage, but essentially the same old DC-1 and DC-2 wing. Of course, we added five feet more wing on each side of the fuselage, but in plan form and in airfoil it was the same wing. We soon found out, however, just putting on more wing didn't give us the lift and stability we needed.

"It was really a case of redesigning the wing. In aerodynamicists' terms, we changed the aspect ratio – a thinner airfoil (thickness and cross-section) and narrowed the chord (width) of the outer wing tip panels. Not until this was done did we begin to get satisfactory test results."

As this work progressed, trouble was brewing in another direction. Before actual construction of the airplane itself was started, the preliminary work, alone – design, engineering, mock-up, individual systems and assemblies test machines – more than $400,000 had been expended. Douglas was looking at the dollar sign and not through any rose colored glasses.

"Wetzel and I and Berghell, the auditor were checking over the costs one day,' Douglas reminisces, "and it suddenly dawned on us that with the engineering costs, plus materials and labor, we were building an airplane with a price tag on it that would cost in excess of *half a million dollars!*

"As fast as we were turning out DC-2's, the new model was eating up the profits."

It was small wonder the Scotsman's blood was a little riled. Perhaps, it was just what the doctor ordered. The pressure was on, and the same gang that had turned the trick with the DC-2 put their heads together and came up with a triple play combination that changed the whole complexion of things.

What happened gives us an in sight into the way the Douglas organization works, which, to a great extent, has been responsible through the years for its phenomenal record and growth. It marks the men behind the planes as more than just good designers, engineers, aerodynamicists, production experts. They also had a eye for business.

This attitude is best summed up, perhaps, by a remark attributed to the late Dr. Charles F. Kettering, head of General Motors research laboratories. "The real secret of success is to invent and manufacture *utilization*," Kettering said. "It doesn't mean much if you invent something and manufacture it and nobody can use it."

Essentially, this is what the Douglas gang did when they gave birth to the DC-3. They knew they could make the design and that it would fly. Somehow, they would whip all the aerodynamic problems. But that wasn't enough. They also had to design and develop utility in the new transport; the sleeper version (DST) could easily sleep itself out in short order.

Douglas explained it this way – "In the new design we actually had three airplanes. Initially, it started out to be a sleeper, the first airplane specifically designed as an aerial Pullman. But during the mock-up stages, it became apparent that the larger fuselage, increased wing area and the more powerful engines available made the basic design a very flexible airplane."

Shortly, a Douglas sales brochure proudly announced:

THE DC-3, 21-PASSENGER DAY PLANE – wider, longer and higher than the famous DC-2, with 21 lounge seats provided in the cabin in two rows; double seats on one side of the aisle and a row of single seats on the other.

THE DC-3, 14-PASSENGER SKY CLUB – offering luxury and comfort of railroad club car appointments, being equipped with 14 deeply upholstered swivel chairs.

THE DC-3 CUSTOM MODEL – living room or parlor furnishing in a roomy cabin; and "office aloft" for the traveling executive.

The future for the new design looked a little brighter.

III

Almost immediately, orders began to pour in for the new transport plane. Smith wanted some of the 21-passenger DC-3s to augment American Airlines' fleet of sleeper planes. Jack Frye and the TWA people started negotiations for a $2,000,000 order for a 23-passenger version of the Day Plane. Rickenbacker followed suit to bolster the growing numbers of "The Great Silver Fleet." United Air Lines also got on the band wagon of progress.

When United "bought," it was a deal that gave marked personal satisfaction to Don Douglas. In a way it was like the capitulation of a strong competitor. The advent of the DC-3 ships sounded the death knell for the Boeing 247 airliners, backbones of the United Air Lines Fleet. Plane builder Douglas couldn't help but think back, and perhaps chuckle a little, over the turn of events.

Little more than three years before, he had entered the transport field with an "on-paper design" (The DC-1) at a time when United's Boeing 247s were being acclaimed as the "aboslute ultimate in air transport design." There is no question, that the low-wing, high-speed Boeing 10-passenger airliners were revolutionary. The best ships of their day. But the DC-1 outperformed them in every respect. United did everything possible to "soup-up" the 247's to meet the competition. It was hopeless. TWA with its DC-2s left the Boeing far behind. When American Airlines en-

W. A. "Pat" Patterson of United Air Lines. They would never stop buying Douglas planes. (Douglas Aircraft Co. Photo)

tered the transcontinental race with its DSTs and DC-3s it all but made the Boeings obsolete.

As a result, in the spring of 1936, W. A. ("Pat") Patterson, United's fiery and dynamic President, paid a visit to the Douglas plant and he had a blank check in his pocket to buy some DC-3s. United was going to get rid of the Boeings and get back into the cross-country competition. Things had reached a point where the "Mainline Airway" faced an equipment and economic strangulation.

Douglas likes to recall that first meeting with Patterson:

"It seems Pat had some difficulty getting in to see me. Somehow, word had got around that he was closely affiliated with that plant up north (Boeing) and nobody put themselves out too much to find out just what he wanted. The fact is, he never did get into my office to talk things over. We got together the first time at a luncheon meeting of the Aviation Committee of the Chamber of Commerce held at the old Del Mar Club on the ocean front.

"I was sitting between Patterson and Harry Wetzel, when Mister Patterson leaned over and told me he had been trying to see me for a couple of days. Pat explained, almost in a whisper, that all he wanted was to *buy some airplanes!*

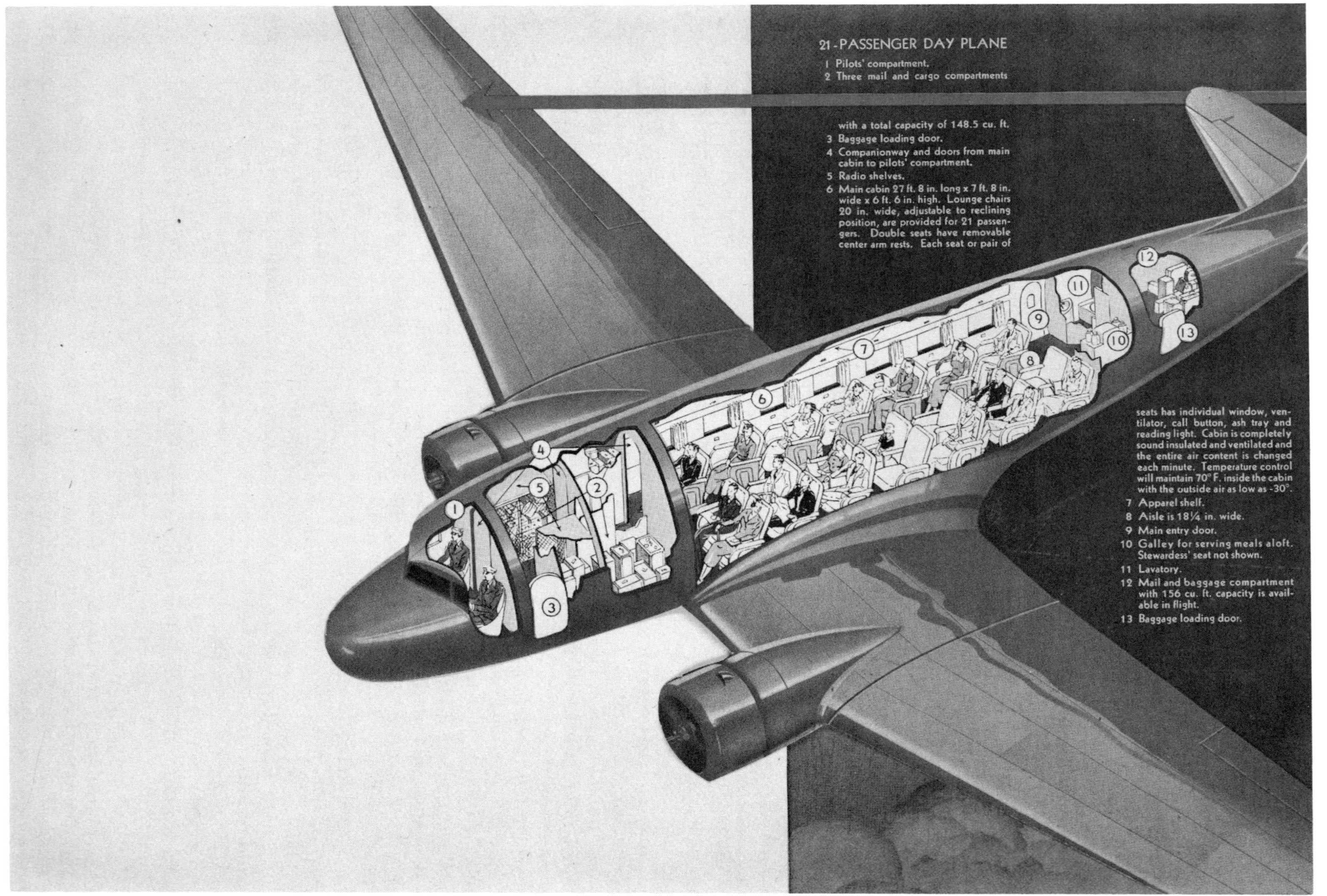

Cut-A-Way Drawing of 21-passenger DC-3 Dayplane. (Douglas Aircraft Co. Photo)

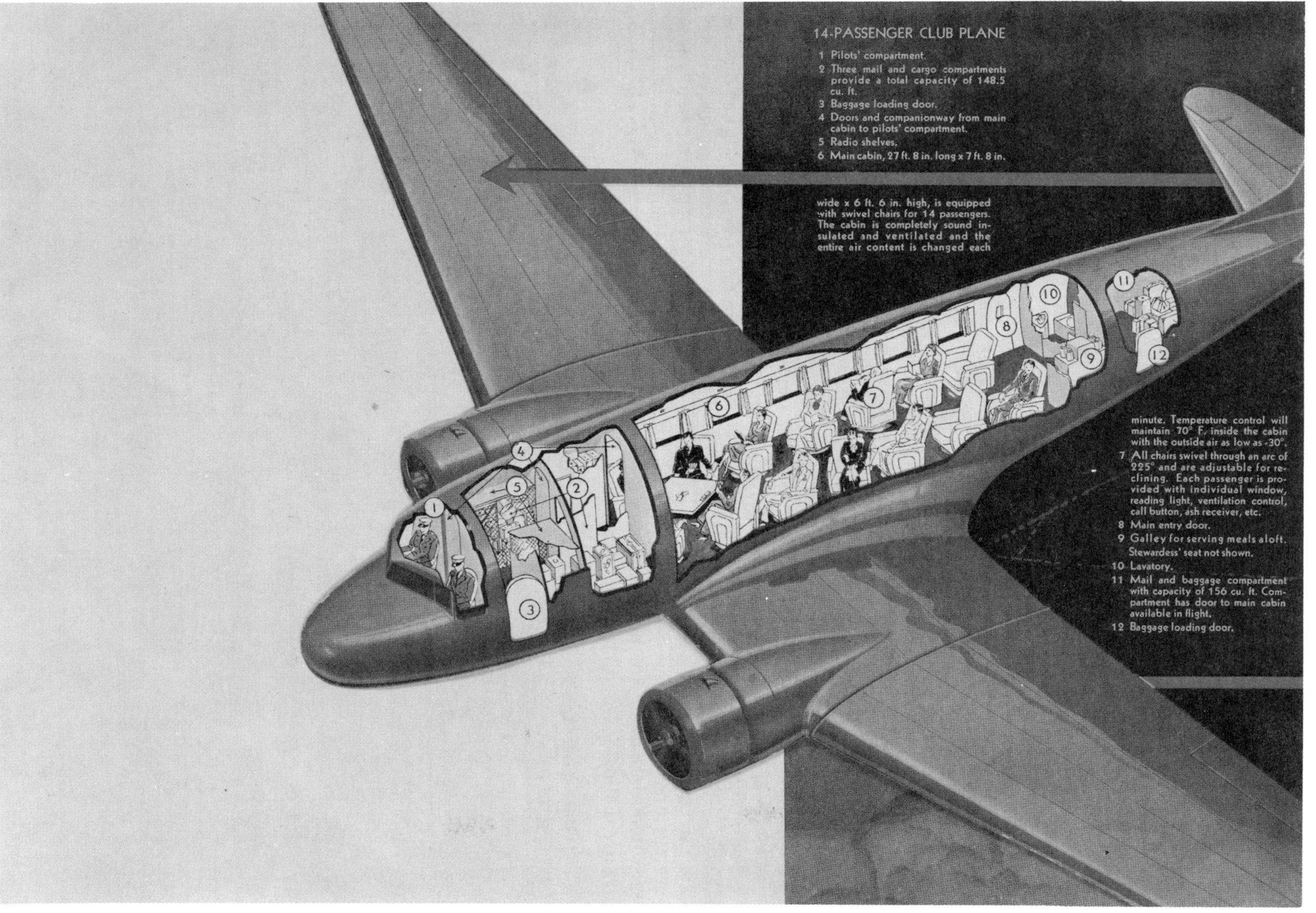

Cut-A-Way Drawing 14-passenger Club Plane. (Douglas Aircraft Co. Photo)

"After the meeting we went back to the office to talk contract details and I'll never forget a remark Harry Wetzel made.

"Patterson asked Harry if he (Patterson) could go out and take a flight in one of the DC-3s to get an idea of the ship first-hand before he signed the papers.

"Wetzel thought a minute and then told him – *"I'm sorry, but we don't have one of the ships here at the plant for demonstration purposes; it costs too damn much to operate them!*

"It was a helluva way to talk a customer into buying an airplane.

"Later, however, we borrowed a DC-3 from one of the airlines and gave Pat his ride. United within a short time placed an order for twenty of the ships."

Many years later, in the late of spring of 1959 when United took delivery of its first DC-8 jetliner, Patterson was reminded of the incident. He remembered it. "The truth is," Pat confided, "Harry Wetzel really did them a big favor. When he blurted it out about the operating cost, I decided right then and there that this was the most honest damn company in the world and I wanted to do business with them."

The United order had several implications. Patterson wanted something different. The UAL ships would be powered with the 14-cylinder Pratt & Whitney *Hornet* engines instead of the Wright *Cyclones.* These ships cost more than the Wright-powered planes because of the newer engines. But the new engines would make Patterson's DC-3s about 14 miles per hour faster, and they could pull the planes up to a higher maximum altitude – 24,300 feet, ideal for United's route over the highest peaks of the Rockies.

Simultaneously with the announcement that they were buying the DC-3s, Patterson also announced United's plans for "Skylounge" Flights, an extra fare plane in a bid for the "blue ribbon" New York-Chicago business. For an extra $2.00 a ticket, United's users could have plenty of leg room and Club Car comfort. It was Patterson's answer to "CR" Smith's deluxe sleeper service. The dog-eat-dog race was on for the transcontinental airline business. The advent of the DC-3 was like a blood transfusion for the same reason. The winner would be decided only by operational and management skills.

United's planes not only had the more powerful engines, but Patterson also went for the DST version. Here a UAL "Mainliner" demonstrates its capability to fly on one engine. The DST introduced first full-feathering propeller. (Douglas Aircraft Co. Photo)

United's answer to the competition was this "Chair-Car" version of the DC-3. It was beginning of company's "extra-care," "extra-fare" Red Carpet service philosophy. (Douglas Aircraft Co. Photo)

The standard DC-3 interior was this American Airlines' version, 21-passengers—seven rows of two seats on the left side and a single row of seats on the right side of the airliner. (American Airlines, Inc. Photo)

Douglas' worries were over as the orders for the DC-3s piled up. He hadn't pressed his luck, after all. The old saw about building a better mousetrap, held true in the aircraft manufacturing business as well as anywhere else. The impact of the DC-3 design on the Douglas company had an electrifying effect.

In December 1937, only two years after the first DC-3 (it was really the DST) made its initial flight, Harry Wetzel could tell Douglas that the company had set an all-time high in production. That month, alone, they had produced 36 planes and parts totalling $2,700,000 worth of business. The Douglas luxury liners made up the bulk of the orders. There was a backlog of $5,250,000 in foreign orders for DC-3s and $2,000,000 more on the books for the domestic airlines.

Likewise, the military business was booming, and as we shall see the DC-designs also had their effect in this direction. The over-all picture was bright. By comparison in 1932, at the time Douglas and Frye got together over the DC-1 design, the Douglas Aircraft Company employed a total of 902 workers; the payroll was $1,514,785 per annum. In 1939 – seven years later – with the DC-airliners in service all over the world, and the company building a "front-line" bomber (B-18) based on the DC-designs, the plant force numbered 9,000 and the yearly payroll was $12,000,000.

IV

Writing in Collier's National Weekly, James H. Winchester declared – "The affection of the nation's airlines for the DC-3 is akin to the distressed heroine's love for the guy who paid off the mortgage on the old homestead. Just as the Model-T brought fame and fortune to Henry Ford, so the DC-3 brought prosperity and honor to the air lines." Acceptance of the new machine was automatic. But there were, as is true with every new development,

After World War II, DC-3's pioneered "air coach" service and some planes were fitted as 28-passenger versions—seven rows of four seats. The plane had proven its ability to carry greater payloads during the war years. (Douglas Aircraft Co. Photo)

especially in aeronautical design, the usual "bugs" to be worked out and the normal period of growing pains. The DC-3 had its share."

One day, for instance, during the flight test program on the first DC-3 Frank Collbohm, still in charge of Flight Research the same as he was on the DC-1, came into Douglas' office with some disturbing news.

"Doug, this is a beautiful flying airplane," he said, "but she's got a critical performance area. We might have to red-tag it."

Collbohm proceeded to tell Douglas what was wrong.

"Under certain speed and altitude conditions, she 'fish-tails' like a big shark making turns in an aquarium tank. Sometimes, it gets violent, like a crack-the-whip at a carnival."

They went to work on the problem down in Engineering.

There was a way pilots could counteract the effect by certain actions on the controls. That's what Collbohm meant by "red-tagging it" – put the responsibility on the pilot, make him take corrective measures when the ship started acting up. Douglas frowned on the idea. If there was something wrong, his philosophy was to "get at the core of the problem and correct it in the basic aerodynamic design."

Consequently, there were more wind tunnel tests. Engineers rode along as observers on test flights and actually experienced the strange "fish-tailing" maneuver. One young design engineer, Eugene Root, thought he had a possible answer. He suggested they add more moveable rudder surface and change the airfoil shape on the horizontal tail. (Actually, it amounted to using flat surfaces instead of curved ones.) The idea worked and Douglas patented it in Root's name. It was and still is one of the secrets of the whole family of planes that sprang from the DC-3 giving the ships superior controllability and stability.

There were other problems, too. Pilots complained about the ship's heating system. The windshield leaked. Raincoats were prescribed as standard operating equipment. Pilots used to report on the radio – "Light rain outside; heavy rain inside!"

Initially, too, the plane acquired a nasty

For her size the DC-3 had a large rudder. This photo shows one of first ships to be delivered to KLM. (Douglas Aircraft Co. Photo)

name. They called her "The Flying Whore" – no visible means of support. Pilots would take one look at her thin, tapered wing and shake their heads. She was too big. The wing wouldn't support her. Moreover, in flight, the wing had a tendency to flap. Sometimes, pilots said, they would look out at the wing tips and "see them flapping like a bird's." The pilots were accustomed to rigid wings, big strong "I"-beam spars and ribs, not this "honey-comb" structure butt-jointed at the fuselage that made it like an ornithopter.

The trouble was they didn't understand, and they had to be told. The flexibility was engineered into the wing purposely so that the plane could "roll with the punches." That's the way a good fighter might describe it. According to the aerodynamicist, it means that the wing was built to absorb updrafts or downdrafts of tremendous forces. With the loads they were calling upon the wing to lift and support, it would snap off like a telephone pole in a tornado if it didn't have this inherent flexibility.

That could have been what killed Knute Rockne. The Fokker had lost a wing.

The word got around, however, that the flapping wing was a blessing and not a blight. Veteran pilot Joe Hammer, for instance, was flying his DC-3 with a full load of passengers from Chicago to Detroit. Just beyond South Bend, he ran into an innocent layer of clouds. But right in the middle of the cloud bank the plane was hit by a downdraft so severe that some of the passenger seats were ripped from the floor. Safety belts snapped like paper bands. Yet, the ship kept right on flying. It was still intact and he managed to pull out, level off, and fly into Detroit.

On the ground inspectors swarmed over the ship. But they couldn't find even a loosened rivet. After that, there were no more complaints about the flapping tendency of the DC-3 wing. Pilots accepted it without question as the eccentric trait of a loved one.

Looking back on some of the troubles they had with the DC-3, Douglas likes to recall a remark that "Dutch" Kindelberger made. "Don't fret about these things, Doug," Kindelberger used to say," "There never has been an airplane built that wasn't full of bugs. And you can't delouse 'em with insecticide. You gotta pick 'em out the hard way like hunting fleas on a Saint Bernard. Then, when you finally get one that's making his nose itch, there's another one biting him under the tail."

The DC-3 had an itchy tail, and she had "bugs" biting her all over for a while. But when all was said and done, pilots and passengers alike grew to love her and trust her more than any airplane ever built. Even today when you ask pilots what they like about her, they will tell you – "She's an honest and straightforward plane to fly. She handles well. She is fairly simple for a new pilot to "check out" and become adjusted to on the ground and in the air. Her inherent stability is good. She has good response to the controls. She has good cockpit visibility which facilitates ground maneuvering. The DC-3 is a pilot's airplane."

V

The impact of the DC-3 on the air transport industry released growth cells that suddenly transformed a nervous, immature, almost sickly infant into a calculating, husky, independent member of the transportation family. For all its little faults and whims, the DC-3 brought to air transportation a vehicle which put air travel on a common carrier basis for the first time. Whereas the DC-1 and the DC-2s were revolutionary in their design and pioneered many innovations, the DC-3 was evolutionary. Because of its size and improved design it was better able to utilize the benefits of technological progress in such things as the auto-pilot, higher horsepower engines, the controllable-pitch propellers, braking systems, wing flaps, cockpit and radio aids.

"The DC-3 itself was the agent of standardization that accounted for much of the growth," "CR" Smith once declared. "It was uneconomical and unsightly to have a system full of mismated aircraft. What was needed was one attractive type capable of carrying a sizeable load a good distance in jig time and at a low cost. The DC-3, at that time, we considered the perfect airplane."

There were many reasons for the "degree of perfection" that the DC-3 achieved. Basically, its design, construction and performance were factors which greatly contributed to the reduction in operating costs and helped the airlines to get on their feet and provide a fast, safe and reliable air transport service.

A good summation of what happened when the DC-3 entered airline service came from Orville Wright, co-inventor of the airplane. The day that TWA inaugurated DC-3 service into Dayton, Ohio, where Orville lived and was born, and the first heavier-than-air flying machine was built, Orville, himself, came out to the airport to inspect the new airliner and take part in the inaugural ceremonies.

Orville was 65 then, but he was active and alert, although he professed that he didn't want to talk too much about the technical aspects of the new plane. "I don't follow these things too closely," he confessed.

He also declined an invitation to fly in the ship with other dignitaries on a guest trip over the city. But his greyish eyes twinkled as he inspected the shiny DC-3 on the ground.

"The body is big enough to carry a sizeable payload and that is important," he said to this writer. "There is plenty of room and the seats are comfortable. They tell me, too, that it is so sound-proof that the passengers can talk to each other without shouting. This is a wonderful improvement. Noise is something that we always knew would have to be eliminated in order to get people to fly . . . Somehow it is associated with fear."

Impressed with the performance figures which the TWA Captain explained to him as they sat in the cockpit, Orville, remarked – "Two hundred miles an hour is fast enough. There is no other form of transport which can compete with that speed and still be safe. They should concentrate on safety and not speed. I don't know why everybody is in such a hurry, anyway . . ."

Later, after the ceremonies were over he had some other significant commentary: "It was always our hope and prayer that the flying machine would be used to carry passengers and mail and not as an instrument of destruction like the bomber," he philosophized. "The airplane should be used to bring all the peoples of the world closer together. Development of an airliner such as this is a big step in the right direction.

"The big thing that will bring this about is safety. I think they've built everything possible into this machine (the DC-3) to make it a safe and stable vehicle of the air."

Such words of praise for the new airliner were not new to Don Douglas' ears. When he delivered his Wright Memorial Lecture before the Royal Aeronautical Society in London back in 1935, Orville Wright had sent a cable to Lt. Col. J. T. C. Moore-Brabazon, President of the Society which said – "Development of the DC-2 airliner has been an outstanding feature in American Aviation. Mister Douglas' part in this has been second to none. We are proud of him."

Size, speed, safety – in referring to these three factors – the "Father of Aviation" had put his finger on the strongest characteristics that the DC-3 brought to the air world. It was big enough to carry half again the payload of any other airliner then flying, including the DC-2s. The speed was fast enough to cut travel time coast-to-coast to about 15 hours (eastbound) 17 hours (westbound) a strong enticement to the transcontinental traveler. Moreover, it had the capability of getting up high enough to safely cross the jagged mountains. And it was equipped with every known device to provide for the comfort and safety of its passengers and crew. Its safety record, after a rather rough beginning, was to speak for itself. In time it would become recognized as the safest airplane ever built. There are those even today in the era of the jets who still insist on "taking the three."

For the student of airline economics the DC-3 also painted a bright picture. Its all-metal construction (except for the fabric-covered control surfaces, rudder, ailerons and elevators) was easy to keep clean and in good repair. Flap covers in wing and fuselage (inspection holes) made it possible to get at control cables and other internal workings without a major disassembly operation. Mechanics could change an engine in two hours, thanks to the new engine mount in which the fuel lines and electrical connections were plugged into permanent fittings like an electrical plug into a wall socket. Wing panels could be taken off and a new one bolted into place with a minimum of effort. The result was maintenance costs dropped when the planes were on the ground in the shops. More important, the planes could be kept in the air without long maintenance delays.

Operational figures themselves told the story. The DC-3 cost about 71.6 cents per mile to run as against 67.4 cents for the DC-2s. But because of its additional seats – the seat-mile cost was 3.4 cents as against 4.8 cents. According to one report the planes cut operating costs (in terms of cost per passenger mile) from 7 cents to 4 cents, and from that moment on the airlines began to show signs of prosperity.

It was small wonder that the airline operators beat a path to Douglas' door and were standing in line to get their names on the order book. By July, 1939, according to Civil Aeronautics Authority records, American Airlines was operating 54 Douglas planes; Braniff Airways, six; Eastern Air Lines, 23; Northwest Airlines, six; TWA, 33; Western Air Express, three; Canadian Colonial Airways, four; Pan-American World Airways, ten; Pan American-Grace Airways, Inc., eight. Within 18 months after the first DC-3 had flown virtually all other types began to slowly disappear from the airways.

The same year, it was officially estimated, that 90 per cent of the world's air commerce was being carried in the DC-3s.

VI

Looking at the statistics of air transport covering the years 1935 to 1940 there is evidence that a whole new force exploded within the framework of the airline industry. The DC-3 is generally credited with igniting the fuse.

The year the first DC-3 spread its wings (December, 1935), according to figures released by the Department of Commerce in its *Air Commerce Bulletin*, there were 23 airline operators in the U.S. The cost of airline travel to the passenger was 5.7 cents per mile. The airlines were flying a wide variety of equipment, Boeing 247s, DC-2s, Ford Trimotors, Stinson Trimotors and Lockheed 14s, Curtiss *Condors* and even some of the old Fokker trimotors. Altogether there were some 460 aircraft in passenger service.

By 1940, however, the picture had changed entirely. There were, according to the Civil Aeronautics Authority (created in 1938) the new governing body for all civil aviation, only 358 scheduled airliners in operation, mostly DC-3s as we have pointed out above. Yet, these fewer planes carried 2,959,480 passengers, flew 108,800,436 plane miles. The average fare was down to .0506 cents per mile.

Grover Loening, one of the country's pioneer airmen and famed plane designer, in his book *Our Wings Grow Stronger*,

American Airlines "Flagship Oklahoma City" (Smith named planes after cities along American's route) was plane number 200 in the DC-3 series. Note American took delivery of first DC-3 (not sleeperplane) August 18, 1936. (Douglas Aircraft Co. Photo)

American Airlines began DC-3 Flagship Service on June 25, 1936 flying from Chicago to New York. First plane, a DST, carried thirteen passengers and crew of three. The loading ramp was a far cry from present day Astrojet techniques. (American Airlines, Inc. Photo)

took a look at the progress made in air transport and predicted – "The railroads are as obsolete today as the Erie Canal was in 1830 . . . The handwriting is on the wall for the steamship lines also . . ."

Even the insurance companies began to take a different look at the safety aspects of flying, their views greatly influenced by the advent of the bigger, sturdy DC-3s. Significantly, in December 1937 the newly organized Air Transport Association of America (ATA) announced that for the first time air travelers could buy a $5,000 trip insurance policy for 25 cents – the same rate as applied to travel by bus, rail, or ship. *Time* Magazine reported – "That insurance companies can now bet $5,000 to two bits against a passenger being killed on a flight of some 800 miles is one of the best pieces of publicity which U.S. airlines ever had."

Biggest impact of the DC-3s, however, is best illustrated by American Airlines' "CR" Smith who was in Washington petitioning the Interstate Commerce Commission for a boost in mail pay before the advent of the DC-3. American Airlines, Inc., he declared was losing $758,000 a year. "There is only one alternative," Smith said, "either raise the mail pay rate or the line will have to go out of business."

When American put its new DC-3s and DSTs to work the picture changed quickly – and for the better. The first full year of operations with the new planes, American raced to the forefront as the nation's No. 1

American Airlines inaugurated nonstop DC-3 flights between Chicago and the west coast on July 4, 1936. American's President **C. R. Smith** *(left) congratulates Capt. M. G. (Dan) Beard at the end of the nonstop flight from Glendale, California to Chicago which took 10 hours and 10 minutes. American Airlines' First Officer Bart Cox is at Beard's right, while three representatives of Fox's Studios in Hollywood are on the far right.*
(American Airlines, Inc. Photo)

airline; 25,000,000 passenger miles up on its closest rival (United) and 56,000,000 passenger miles ahead of TWA. *Fortune* Magazine in an article about Smith (February 1939), showed the airline was operating "in the black" and that American's earnings for 1938 would show a profit in excess of $100,000!

Smith, himself, declared: "The DC-3 freed the airlines from complete dependency on government mail pay. It was the first airplane that could make money just by hauling passengers. With the previous planes, if you multiplied the number of seats by the fares being charged, you couldn't break even, not even with a 100 per cent load. Economically, the DC-3 let us expand and develop new routes where there was no mail pay."

Admittedly, "CR" didn't know it when he made that statement, but the DC-3 would become one of the great champions of freedom everywhere. There was a whole new role cut out for it to play in the years ahead.

Movie stars, and starlets, were prominent among first DC-3 passengers. Here Shirley Temple, everybody's favorite in the mid-thirties, helps load film in DC-3's rear baggage compartment. (American Airlines, Inc. Photo)

Chapter 9

The Day Of The Skyliner

. . . or a day in the life of the American Airlines Flagship *Arizona*, Newark to Glendale in eighteen hours and forty minutes.

This chapter is an excerpt from an article "Airline in the Black" which first appeared in Fortune Magazine in February 1939. It was one of the best contemporary pieces written to describe airline procedures at the time of the Douglas Sleeper transport. Reprinted here by special permission of Fortune Magazine ©1939 Time Inc.

An hour after she had arrived from Los Angeles they washed the dust of a continent from the ship, and when they had her shining as brightly as a platinum ornament in a jeweler's tray a rubber-tired baby tractor hooked onto her tail and dragged her into American Airlines' hangar at Newark Airport. There two crews of mechanics – a dozen men in all – at once started giving her an inspection, for there was a chance that she might be scheduled to fly back to the Coast on Trip 7 – the Southerner – that night. They put tall ladders up by her nose and stripped the aluminum cowling from her 1,100-horsepower Cyclones preparatory to the engine check. They peered at her hydraulic landing-gear apparatus and examined her tires. They went into her cockpit and tested her controls, inspecting the hundred odd knobs and dials and buttons and switches and levers and gauges surrounding the pilots' seats, from the simple chronometers and altimeters to devices with cabalistic titles like Artificial Horizon, Turn and Bank, and Gyropilot. They wiggled her rudder and flapped her wing and stabilizer ailerons. They turned on her landing, navigation, cabin, and cockpit lights and replaced a couple of dimming bulbs. They pumped air in and out of the rubber de-icer boots on the leading edges of her wings, and checked the supply of wood alcohol and glycerin mixture that would prevent icing of her propellers. They went over every square foot of her glistening aluminum "skin," and every square inch of her three-bladed alloy propellers. They gave her two newly

On the ground at Newark Airport, serving New York City, an American Airlines DST is readied to start her long westward journey. She is listed in the timetable as Trip 3, the "American Mercury." (American Airlines, Inc. Photo)

The "Arizona" is powered with two Wright "Cyclone" engines each developing 850-horsepower. Photo at right shows engine wrapped in NACA cowling for streamlining. Photo (left) shows cowling removed so mechanics can check sinews of power. (Douglas Aircraft Co. Photo)

charged storage batteries for the ones she had flown from Los Angeles.

Presently they were joined by men from the commissary department, who entered the ship's cabin and took up the carpet for cleaning, stripped the berths and remade them with fresh linen, ran a vacuum over the seats, and washed the windows, walls, and ceiling. They checked the reading lights and the ventilators, installed fresh anti-macassars on every seat, and in every seat pocket made sure there were American Airlines timetables, packages of post cards stating that the seat was occupied, and printed messages from Mr. C. R. Smith, the President of the company, beginning with "How Did You Like Your Trip?" and ending with a request for suggestions on improving the service. Under every seat they placed a large cardboard carton for the accommodation of passengers who might become airsick. They tried the twelve-volt electric shaver in the tiny men's room at the rear of the cabin. They tallied the linen, the silver, and the plates and cups in the stewardess's serving pantry. They put copies of the latest issues of the *New Yorker, Time, Life,* and the *Sportsman Pilot* into binders and stowed them under the serving table along with the other magazines.

II

By evening the inspection had been completed. By evening, too, the ship – a Douglas DST fourteen-passenger sleeper with "Flagship *Arizona*" painted on her nose – had been scheduled not on Trip 7, but on next afternoon's *American Mercury, Trip 3.* By evening the New York reservations office had sold three of her berths clear through from Newark to Los Angeles, and one from Newark to Tucson. Nashville, her first scheduled stop, sold another to Los Angeles, and Dallas a fifth. New York reservations informed the publicity department in the same offices at 25 Vanderbilt Avenue that one of the passengers was to be Miss Gloria Goldilocks, coming in on the *Queen Mary* at 3:00 P.M. and going out on the Mercury at 5:10 P.M., en route between a six-month contract with Gaumont-British and a three-year contract with Metro-Goldwyn-Mayer. It went without saying that Miss Goldilocks would be assigned the plane's "Skyroom." The Skyroom was aft of the cockpit in the noisiest and shakiest part of the ship, but it was semiprivate and it was generally reserved for eminent travelers.

By morning New York reservations had sold three more spaces to Los Angeles and one tentatively to Nashville. The weather reports coming in almost continuously from the governmental meteorological service, from the airport ground observatories, and from dozens of pilots in the air suggested that by sundown Nashville's 1,000-foot

When the "Arizona" is not made up as a sleeper, passengers enjoy wide comfortable Pullman car seating in daytime version. (Douglas Aircraft Co. Photo)

ceiling might be closed in below the 400-foot minimum permitted by American Airlines and Civil Aeronautics Authority for let-downs. Reservations pointed this out to the Nashville passenger, but told him that if the Mercury had to take Atlanta or Memphis as an alternate airport he would be given train transportation to his destination. Nashville meanwhile made a similar proposition to its Los Angeles passenger and persuaded him to go out on the Southerner from Memphis if the Mercury was unable to get into Nashville.

III

Toward midafternoon the *Arizona* was towed out of the hangar and parked near the terminal. A little cart containing a storage battery was rolled up under her nose. Wires from the cart were plugged into the ship's electrical circuit in order to spare her own batteries the heavy starting load; the chief mechanic climbed into the cockpit and turned up her motors. At four o'clock the co-pilot assigned to the flight – "first officer" in the naval terminology of American Airlines – came out of the hangar and joined the mechanic. At five after four the flight pilot, or "captain," arrived from the Newark hotel in which the company maintains a suite of rooms for the use of its male personnel, and at four-ten the stewardess arrived from another Newark hotel designated by the company for its female personnel. The pilot, whose name might have been King, was an ex-army flier who had covered a million miles during his nine years with American Airlines. He was tall enough and handsome enough and rugged enough to have stepped into the hero's role in any movie epic of the airways without plastic surgery, dentistry, or an ounce of padding in his dark blue uniform. He was a union man, holding a card from the Air Line Pilots' Association, an A.F. of L. affiliate, but a very de luxe union man with very de luxe wages. Last year he had earned $3,000 base pay for merely belonging to American Airlines. In addition he had been paid on a sliding hourly scale for flying the maximum of eighty-five hours per month per pilot allowed by the Civil Aeronautics Authority – from a low of $4.20 per daytime hour with slower equipment to a high of $7.50 per night hour with Douglas Sleepers doing 195 miles per hour or better. With certain bonuses for the months in which he had flown more than 10,000 miles this had given him a total annual income of over $8,500; this night's flight alone – he would take the ship only as far as Nashville where a new crew would board her and fly her to Dallas – would net him $62.80.

The stewardess – Miss Jones, for convenience – was a registered nurse, an inch shorter than the five-feet-five maximum prescribed by American Airlines and five pounds under the 120-pound weight ceiling. She had been hired when she was twenty-six, the last year in which stewardesses are ever hired, and she was now twenty-seven, earning $125 per month. In three more years she would be forced to retire on account of her age, but the chances were that long before then she would quit the service and get married – probably to a passenger rather than to Captain King or any of the other 233 pilots and co-pilots in the company. Miss Jones was neither beautiful nor glamorous. Plenty of girls with better features and more figure had applied for her job and been rejected, it being against company policy to take on conspicuously attractive young women. But if she was somewhat usual in appearance, Miss Jones was undeniably a "clean-cut, clear-thinking young woman, adept in dealing with people, not too retiring nor too forward," as the stewardess's manual bade her to be. Furthermore, Miss Jones knew a great deal. She knew, for example, the right moment at which to present aromatic

Ladies' Powder Room (Douglas Aircraft Co. Photo)

Men's Lounge (Douglas Aircraft Co. Photo)

spirits of ammonia to a queasy passenger gagging in rough air. To curious travelers who were forever asking "What keeps an airplane up?" she could patiently explain that it was a combination of planing surface and speed, and that the vacuum created by air rushing over the top surface of a wing exerted twice the lifting force of air pressure on the lower surface. She knew how to describe the intricacies of instrument flying and the simplicities of contact flying. She knew the genuine art of escaping the attentions of occasionally amorous passengers while leaving them with the delightful impression that she was reluctant to escape. She knew that she should never use the word "trouble" in conversation with a passenger. An American Airlines ship might land "to make an adjustment" but not on account of "trouble."

The 'Arizona' has two lavatories in the tail section of fuselage. Each is equipped with wash basin and chemical toilet. (Douglas Aircraft Co. Photo)

These basic things and a great many others like them Miss Jones had learned during her training course at the school for stewardesses in Chicago. They were all down in her manual, and in case she should ever grow confused about any situation she had only to consult her copy of "The *Best* Way," a little mimeographed book that applies a Dale Carnegie brand of psychology to her dealings with passengers. Altogether Miss Jones was an engaging young woman, and in spite of a certain sexlessness resulting from thick stockings and an overtight girdle beneath her severely cut uniform, she would have little difficulty acquiring a husband. The prospect of so doing had been her chief reason for becoming a stewardess in the first place, and the same was probably true of most of the 117 girls in the service. Their success in this pursuit largely accounts for the 33 per cent annual turnover in American Airlines stewardesses and occasionally worries Mr. Newton Wilson, the Supervisor of Passenger Service, who has charge of them. Someone in the company is supposed to have suggested that if American Airlines hired girls that were just a wee bit less attractive than the incumbents both the marriage rate and the turnover would drop and over $10,000 a year might be saved in the operation of the training school, where it costs about $425 to prepare each candidate in a six-week course before she can be assigned to a run. But Mr. C. R. Smith would certainly veto any attempt to lower the quality of stewardesses. No one in the company has ever tried to calculate their goodwill value, but it is conceded that they are the most effective salesmen in the organization, and that as far as the predominantly masculine traffic is concerned they represent by themselves a good reason for traveling in airplanes.

IV

Captain King and Miss Jones went at once to the flight-control office in a small annex to the hangar. In this close and smoky place, full of the mingled noises of telephones and radiotelephones, radiotelegraphs, typewriters, and teletypewriters, King studied the Flight Release for Trip 3, containing a digest of the day's weather reports. In the Newark area conditions were "Genrly CAVU," meaning ceiling and visibility unlimited, with light west-southwesterly winds, the dew point at 34 and temperature at 39° Fahrenheit, and the barometric pressure 30.11 inches. Washington reported rain and some icing

For years American Airlines has been the favorite coast-to-coast airline for film stars. Here are some movie favorites on an American flight from Hollywood in the thirties. Included in the group are Mary Pickford, Douglas Fairbanks, Sr., Sir Alexander Korda, Murray Silverstone (then president of United Artists), Charles Chaplin, Dr. A. H. Giannini and Sam Goldwyn. (American Airlines, Inc. Photo)

at 4,000 feet, and southwest of Washington there were fity-mile head winds and a heavy overcast. Nashville still remained open but might close up at any time, and King would receive definite landing instructions by radio during the flight. Attached to the release was a pink slip titled "Pilot's Warning," which informed him that "KM (Camden): SRN BORDER SOFT. STAY ON RUNWAYS. 100 FT. PILE DRIVER ESE OF FLD MARKER. WA (Washington): CONSTR. E OF INTER OF BOTH RNWYS. NEW RNGE IN OPERATION WITH QUADRANTS REVERSED FROM OLD RNGE. NA (Nashville): CNSTR ON FLD MARKED." After studying the weather data and the other entries on the release, and noting that the ship was departing with 200 quarts of oil and 800 gallons of gasoline – enough to take her to Nashville, from Nashville to Memphis, her alternate airport, and to fly her for at least three-quarters of an hour beyond Memphis – King made out his Flight Plan, giving his magnetic courses, his wind-drift corrections, the horsepower he expected to use, the altitudes he expected to fly, and the times at which he expected to pass over the radio check points along the route.

V

Miss Jones meanwhile went over the passenger manifest. There was only one other woman passenger besides Miss Goldilocks, but she was a mother with a nonrevenue infant – under the age of two – and Miss Jones made a note to have a lower berth made up so that the child could be retired immediately, and to take aboard enough New York Milk and New York water to last to the Coast. Of the men, the reservations office had noted that two were first fliers who would require special attention and probably some reassurance when the ship hit the rough air beyond Washington. Another was a coast-to-coast commuter with whom Miss Jones was acquainted – he had confided several times that he was a "big Hollywood producer." Another was an Admiral of the Flagship Fleet – a sales-department title conferred on notables and on particular friends of American Airlines – with a card in his pocket and a thirty-five-cent piece of imitation parchment hanging on his office wall to prove it. The next two were neither Admirals nor first fliers nor commuters but ordinary businessmen traveling on scrip tickets at a 15 per cent discount from the regular $149.95 one-way fare. The last was an American Airlines publicity man taking a winter vacation and using some of the free air mileage that everyone in the company receives as a perquisite. If his space were sold anywhere the ship landed he would be deplaned and made to wait over. For that matter, even company executives traveling on business almost never take advantage of their privilege when there is a chance of selling an extra seat to a cash customer. C. R. Smith himself often rides the *Century* from Chicago to New York rather than discourage a passenger who might be going up for the first time.

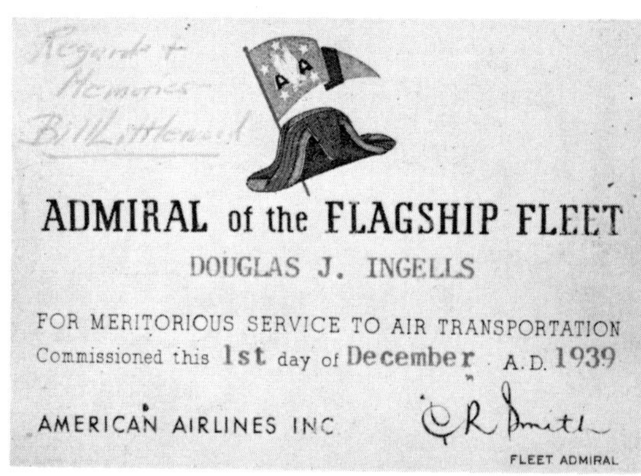
ADMIRAL of the FLAGSHIP FLEET
DOUGLAS J. INGELLS
FOR MERITORIOUS SERVICE TO AIR TRANSPORTATION
Commissioned this 1st day of December A.D. 1939
AMERICAN AIRLINES INC
FLEET ADMIRAL

Author is early Admiral's Club member. Commissioned in 1939.

Toward half past four all the preliminaries to Trip 3 began to converge on the actual take-off. Having run up her motors and tested her communications system by talking to American Airlines flight control and to WREE the Newark Airport traffic-control tower, the co-pilot accepted the ship from the chief mechanic. A few minutes later Captain King himself tried her controls, and, finding them satisfactory, signed the Flight Release, which stated: "I hereby acknowledge receipt of the foregoing clearance, including weather report, and consider all conditions including my own physical condition suitable for the scheduled flight." Had he not found weather conditions suitable he would have refused to sign and thus effectively canceled the trip, for it is against company policy to permit another pilot to volunteer to fly after one has turned down his assignment.

VI

At four forty the ship was pulled up in front of the terminal building. Miss Jones went aboard, slipped her metal name plate into a slot on the door leading to the cockpit, and made a rapid check of the cabin equipment. At four forty-five a delivery truck rolled up and unloaded big Thermos jugs and aluminum cases containing food that had been prepared by a caterer in Newark earlier in the afternoon. At four fifty-five an American Airlines air-conditioning truck came alongside and pumped warm air into the cabin to take off the chill until the motors and the steam heater were started. At four fifty-seven the bus from New York – a black Cadillac limousine seating ten persons – drew up at the terminal and the passengers got out and handed dollar bills to the driver, one or two of them muttering that it was a "damned outrage" that the fare wasn't included in the price of the ticket. Inside the terminal they queued up at a counter and had their names checked off on the passenger manifest. One man, somewhat tipsy, gazed at a photograph of Vice President Ralph Damon on the opposite wall and remarked to no one in particular that they were fine-looking fellows, fine-looking fellows. Another man bought a ham sandwich at the Union News lunch counter. Others purchased cigarettes, newspapers, and chocolate bars at the newsstand. The two first fliers lined up in the broad window in the waiting room and stared dubiously at ships landing and taking off on the field. The woman with the nonrevenue infant sat down in a corner and bundled the little one in the folds of her mink coat. The tipsy gentleman passed in front of her and tripped over her feet, apologizing with a sweeping bow that nearly knocked him down. A ticket clerk watched him narrowly, trying to decide whether he was drunk enough to deserve having his passage canceled.

At five o'clock some 330 pounds of mail and air express were loaded aboard the ship. It appeared that Miss Goldilocks and a Mr. Edward Belcher had not yet arrived at the terminal, for over the public-address system a plaintive voice kept repeating: "Miss Gloria Goldilocks and Mr. Edward Belcher, passengers on Trip 3, kindly step

The "Arizona" takes on mail and express. (American Airlines, Inc. Photo)

Rear baggage compartment is loaded. (American Airlines, Inc. Photo)

"Arizona" passengers enjoy full-course dinners aloft. With advent of DST, distance was measured by meals, not miles. (American Airlines, Inc. Photo)

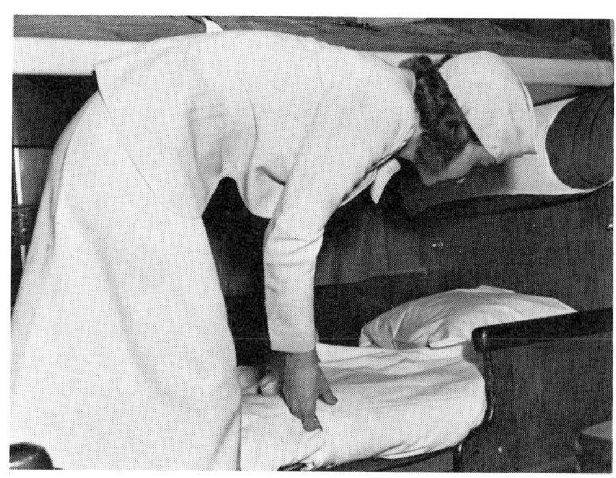

"Arizona" Stewardess makes up berth. (American Airlines, Inc. Photo)

to the ticket counter." Still no Miss Goldilocks, and at five-seven the voice boomed: "American Airlines Trip 3 for Nashville, Dallas, Tucson, and Los Angeles, now loading at Gate 5. Passengers will please go aboard. Please give your name to the stewardess, Miss Jones, as you board the plane." The men promptly threw on their overcoats and marched out in a sort of platoon to the ship, where they were greeted by Miss Jones, standing "in the men's dressing room with the binder resting on the wash basin," as regulations instructed.

At five-nine a Rolls-Royce escorted by two lesser vehicles raced up to the terminal and disgorged the luscious Miss Goldilocks in the midst of an incredible number of press agents, photographers, reporters, friends, and porters. Miss Goldilocks had seven suitcases and a Siamese cat on a leash. The suitcases weighed 200 pounds, and the press agents fought for the privilege of paying $108.75 for the excess over the fifty-five pounds allowed to transoceanic passengers; ordinary passengers are allowed only forty pounds. The clerk announced that the cat would have to travel in the baggage compartment, and Miss Goldilocks looked as though she might make a scene, but there wasn't time. At five-ten and one-half she ran through Gate 5 so fast that an orchid dropped out of her corsage. The ticket counter had given up Mr. Belcher, and as soon as Miss Goldilocks disappeared into the *Arizona* the cabin door was slammed and locked from the outside, and blocks were yanked out from the front of the wheels. Captain King touched a button on the dashboard of the cockpit and started the motors. The copilot talked to the Newark traffic-control tower through his radio-telephone and asked if it was all right for Trip 3 to take off. At five-eleven the ship turned and taxied toward the runway. Just before reaching it she stopped, and with his brakes on Captain King gunned each motor so hard that the plane strained and quivered along her whole length. Then she started rolling again and halfway along the runway left the ground so smoothly that none of the first fliers in the cabin realized what had happened until they saw the whole field rushing away behind them and the factory lights winking through the Jersey murk ahead. Up in the cockpit the Co-pilot stretched an arm out of the window and took down the little blue pennant that always flies above the cockpits of flagships on the ground because passengers never heard of a flagship that didn't have a flag. Then he switched his radio over from the frequency of the Newark Airport traffic-control tower to American Airlines flight control and announced that the Mercury was in the air.

With the thin whine of the on-course signal coming through his headphones Captain King flew the ship out on the southwest leg of the Newark range and passed over New Brunswick at five-twenty-three. The co-pilot reported the position to flight control, and on his Flight Log entered the time, the altitude, wind, temperature, horsepower, air speed, and magnetic course. He would make similar notations

On the ground at Nashville, the "Arizona" takes on more fuel and undergoes routine check. It is dark by time passengers board the plane again and some are ready to retire and sleep their way across the continent. Berths are all made up. (American Airlines, Inc. Photo)

at every check point on the route, so that the position would never be in doubt, and in case of a radio failure the ship could be flown back to her point of origin merely by following the data in reverse order. Over Camden at five forty-five he picked up American Airlines' flight control at the Washington airport and was told that two army planes en route between Mitchel Field and the Edgewood Arsenal in Maryland were almost directly above him at 10,000 feet and that a northbound Eastern Air Lines ship at 5,000 would be off Washington airport at six-five; the Mercury was then flying at 8,000, and the co-pilot transmitted back his weather observations, remarking that visibility was good except for smoke over urban areas. He made a note of this on one of a sheaf of forms in the cockpit, for in addition to keeping the Flight Log he was expected to compare actual weather conditions aloft with the ground station predictions and grade the meteorologist accordingly.

By the time the Mercury passed over Roanoke most of the passengers had finished their dinners of soup, lamb chops, vegetables, salad, ice cream, and coffee, served with the compliments of American Airlines at a cost of ninety cents per compliment. Over Bristol, Virginia, at eight-five, flight control announced that the landing at Nashville was now definite, but that the approach and letdown would have to be made entirely on instruments. Captain King proceeded to Knoxville where the co-pilot made contact with Nashville flight control. Another contact was made at Smithville, Tennessee, and then Captain King rode straight down the Nashville beam, occasionally getting a dash-dot in his headphones as the drift of strong lateral winds pushed the ship into the N twilight of the range. The signal volume steadily increased as the Mercury drew closer to the beacon; then it suddenly faded out altogether for a few seconds as they passed

While the "Arizona" roars on through the night sky, most passengers are asleep in berths. (Douglas Aircraft Co. Photo)

over the cone of silence directly above the ground radio transmitter. They were on top of the overcast at 3,000 feet, and as the copilot reported the position to flight control and prepared to switch over to the frequency of the Nashville traffic tower Captain King dropped the landing gear, adjusted his propeller pitch, and throttled down to an air speed of 120 miles per hour. He flew out the northwest beam for three minutes, made a procedure turn, and came back over the cone at 1,200 feet, losing altitude at the rate of 400 feet per minute. There were holes in the overcast now, and he could see the fuzzy, candy-pink glow of neon signs along a street; in a few more seconds he picked up the characteristic pattern of flashing beacons and boundary lights ahead and dropped down on Nashville as smoothly as he had taken off from Newark.

VII

At Nashville it took fifteen minutes to give the ship a quick visual inspection on the field; to refuel, change crews, discharge mail and a passenger and take aboard more mail and a new passenger, and to install in the stewardess's pantry Thermos bottles of coffee, Ovaltine, and hot water for tea. By ten o'clock Central time the Mercury was in the air again, heading southwest down the Memphis beam on the way to Dallas. It took a little over four hours to fly this leg of the trip, and a few miles east of the Dallas airport the westbound Mercury at 2,000 feet passed the eastbound Mercury at 3,000. West of Dallas visibility was limited only by the far horizons of the curving earth, and the pilot flew on contact with the miles of beacon lights that stretched in a great beeline across the plains. Beyond El Paso the sun came up behind the ship, and at Tucson a little before seven there were shadows. There was a wall of sharp-edged mountains ahead, and the ship flew across and between them for most of the next two hours. At ten minutes of nine Pacific time the Mercury landed at Glendale Airport on schedule, and after the passengers had been deplaned the ground crew washed the ship and then turned her over to the mechanics for inspection.

The "Arizona" is at the ramp and unloading her passengers at 8:50 A.M. (Pacific Standard Time — there is three hours difference). She has spanned the continent in 18 hours, 40 minutes, including all ground stops and bucking headwinds. Western terminus is the Grand Central Air Terminal at Glendale.
(American Airlines, Inc., Photo)

Chapter 10

Crash Fever

The proud Dutch airliner "Uiver," shown here back in regular scheduled service after the London-to-Melbourne race, was first DC-2 involved in a fatal crash. (KLM Photo)

On December 21, 1934, the proud Dutch airliner, *Uiver*, took off from Amsterdam Airport on a special Christmas Flight to Java. Aboard were three passengers, a crew of four and 54,000 pieces of mail. A sizeable crowd had gathered to watch the take-off. This DC-2 was the most famous airliner in the world, second-place winner in the London-to-Melbourne Race only two months before. Now, back in regular service again, she was the pride of KLM's fleet whose wings encircled half the globe. There were cheers as the big plane left the runway, climbed gracefully to altitude and disappeared southward beyond the horizon.

Less than 24 hours later there was mourning. The *Uiver* was missing somewhere between Cairo and Bagdad. Then, came the terrible news that everybody had feared. British Royal Air Force pilots found the plane, a tangled mass of charred metal, flipped over on its back and burned to a crisp on the rain-soaked sands of the Syrian Desert.

In Amsterdam, radio stations were silenced, flags flew at half-mast, Holland regarded the crash as a national catastrophe. Thousands of miles away in Santa Monica, California Don Douglas and the men who had built the *Uiver* were shocked at the news. It was the first of 40 DC-2s built to be involved in a serious accident. Douglas investigators were rushed to the scene. Was there something wrong with the DC-2 structurally, design-wise? They had to find the answer.

Days later, KLM *(Koninklijke Luchtvaart Maatschappijvoor Nederland enKolonien)* released its own report on what happened. The plane itself was absolved from all blame.

According to KLM, the *Uiver* hit the ground flying full speed, switches on, throttles wide open, stabilizer set for cruising, the landing gear full retracted. On the strength of these findings, the official report of the accident stated – "The experts have come to the conclusion that the machine was struck by a heavy flash of lightning which killed its occupants instantaneously. It continued flying until it struck the ground, where it crashed, somersaulted and the petrol burst into flames."

II

It was May 6, 1935, almost a year to the day since the first DC-2 made its initial test flight and was delivered to TWA. Captain Harvey Bolton, veteran TWAer, was at the controls of the *Sky Chief,* a DC-2 eastbound, Los Angeles-Albuquerque-Kansas City. Through his earphones Bolton was listening to the dispatcher at Kansas City, getting final instructions for a landing. There was trouble ahead.

The Kansas City tower advised that the field was "closed" because of bad weather. Bolton was told to make his landing at an emergency field about 130 miles west and north, near Kirksville, Missouri. It was 2:00 A.M. and Bolton aroused his passengers, among them Senator Bronson Cutting (New Mexico) and told them he was proceeding to the alternate field.

Over the emergency field, the TWA Captain found the whole area wrapped in a solid cloud bank. The air was rough. Circling blind until he had only a few minutes fuel left, Bolton finally found a "hole" in the murky atmosphere and began to feel his way down. The next instant, the ground came up and hit him. Pulling out trying to level off, he picked his way between a farmhouse and a barn, struck a fence, slammed heavily into a road embankment. The plane was a total wreck.

Bolton, co-pilot Kenneth Greeson, Senator Cutting and the 20-year-old sister of the TWA dispatcher at Kansas City who had been directing the flight, were crushed to death in the impact. The others (there were 11 passengers and hostess) got out alive.

It was the first fatal crash of a DC-2 in the U. S.

With one of their colleagues killed in the crash, Congressmen in Washington took special interest in the accident. The investigation dragged on for months. Not since Rockne was killed was there so much public furor. There were charges and counter-charges of what happened. Inspectors reported that the plane was improperly dispatched from Albuquerque; the reserve tanks didn't contain the required minimum for forty-five minutes flying time. Jack Frye, TWA president put the blame squarely on the government weather forecasters. Bolton was told the ceiling was 7,000 feet, directed to fly out of his way using reserve fuel, only to find himself in zero-zero conditions, Frye maintained. Some 900 pages of testimony later the Bureau of Air Commerce issued its own conclusion – *The Sky Chief crashed because of bad weather and bad weather reporting! The investigation and testimony revealed nothing wrong mechanically or structurally with the aircraft.*

III

The night of February 9, 1937, is also a memorable date in Douglas company records. What happened in the semi-darkness of the night sky over the Golden Gate Bridge in San Francisco gave Douglas engineers something to think about and a case of the shudders. This time there wasn't any bad weather. Everything was perfectly normal. Yet, something went radically wrong with the brand new silvery-winged United Air Lines' DC-3 at the end of its short, two-hour hop from Los Angeles to San Francisco. Until that moment, the new DC-3s had had a perfect record.

Captain Alexander Raymond ("Tommy") Thompson, a million-miler for United, was at the controls of the plane. The co-pilot was Joe Decesaro; hostess, Ruth Kimmel. There were eight passengers back in the cabin. The plane took off from Los Angeles at 7:00 P.M. right on schedule. At 8:44 P.M. Thompson was over San Francisco. He could see the lights of the city below. The night was clear and calm. He contacted the radio dispatcher at Mills Field. The plane would land on the east-west runway.

People on the ground saw the airliner approaching. It roared over the field at about 700 feet and out over the bay where it began banking to line up with the runway. Observers saw it coming in, head-on, wheels down, right in line with the concrete landing strip. Then, suddenly, it went into a 45-degree dive, vanished with a loud WHAM! behind a large dike between the field and the bay.

Next morning a derrick raised the wreckage. The plane was on its back, fuselage ripped open like somebody had wielded a

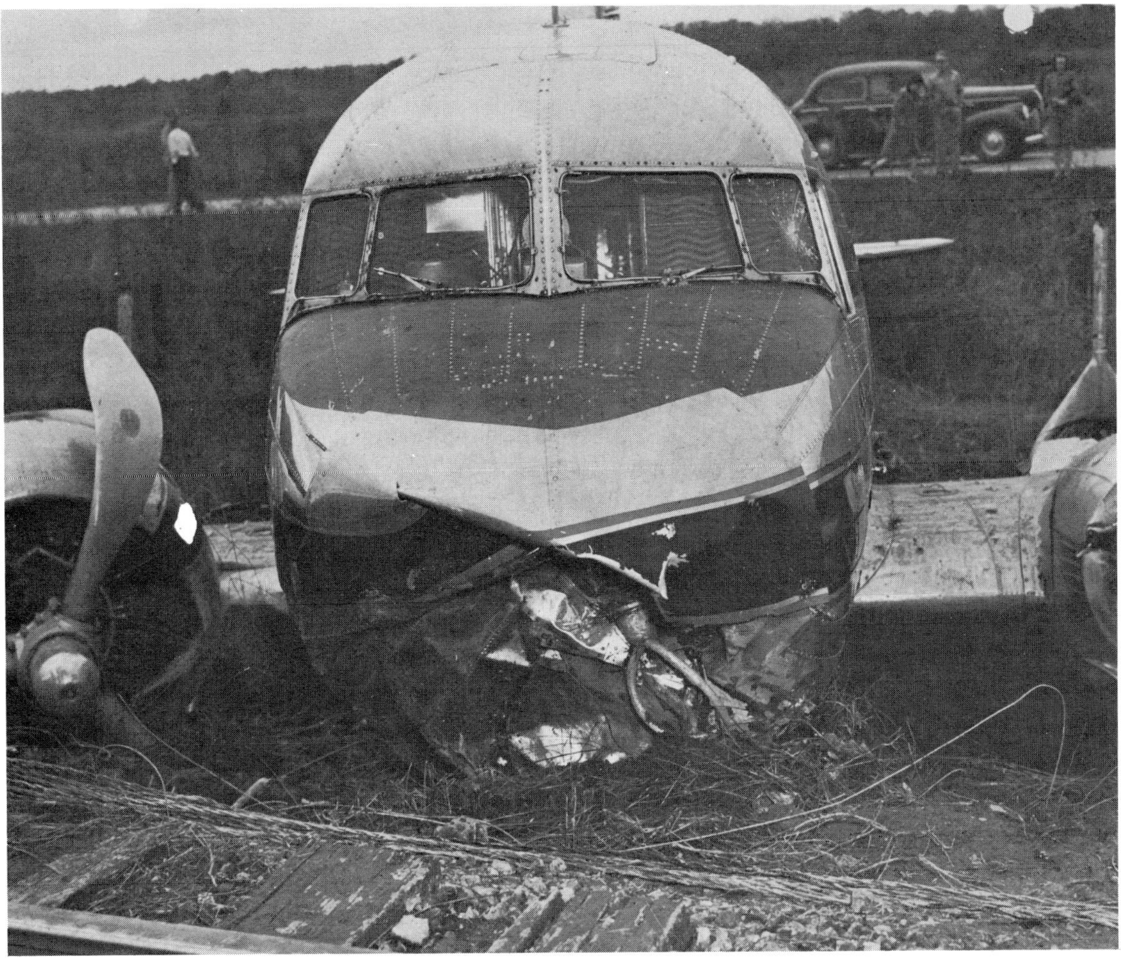

It has been said that the DC-3's were the first passenger planes so structurally strong that you could walk away from a crash landing. Here is one that "mushed in" and although there was considerable damage, occupants were not seriously injured. The plane was put back into service again. (Civil Aeronautics Board Photo)

giant can opener, the tail shredded. Inside, were the bodies of the crew and passengers, their seat belts still fastened. Apparently they had drowned!

Nobody knew what happened. Crash investigators were completely baffled. There wasn't the slightest clue. They were ready to chalk this one up to "pilot error" when, quite by accident, the cause came to light.

One day in March, about five weeks after the crash, an American Airlines' pilot was about to take off from Newark in his DC-3 Flagship. Gunning the engines and testing the rudder, elevators and ailerons, just before heading down the runway for take-off, he found the controls were jammed! He couldn't budge the big control column no matter how hard he yanked back on it. Checking to see what was wrong he found the trouble – *the radio mike had fallen off its hook and was jammed in a V-shaped well between the moveable control column and the cockpit wall.* He pried the mike loose. The controls worked perfectly. The plane took off, completed its flight.

The alert Captain reported the freak incident and a warning went out to all airlines. When aviation reporter C. B. Allen of the *New York Herald Tribune* heard about it, he put two and two together and started asking questions. When he finally got all the answers the story was out. This is what happened to "Tommy" Thompson. This is what caused the tragedy in San Francisco Bay.

United investigators took another look in the cockpit of the wrecked airliner. There was the mike jammed down in the control well. It was bent and crushed. Thompson had fought with all his might to pull the wheel back and stop the plane from its fatal plunge. He lost. But others gained by his unfortunate experience. A good pilot had not died in vain.

Nobody blamed anybody because, certainly, the mike accidentally fell off its hook. Anything could have caused it to fall. But Douglas engineers promptly designed a leather-booting that covered the control column well. It could never happen again.

IV

During "Dangerous April" 1937, there was another strange accident. TWA Captain Frederick Lawrence Bohnet with 10 passengers aboard his DC-2 was mushing down through the overcast making his final approach into Pittsburgh. Another TWA Airliner, Captain A. M. Wilkins in command, was approaching from the west ready to follow Bohnet down. Wilkins, however, noticed Bohnet was having trouble. The ship was wobbling, one wing would drop, then the other, and the pilot didn't seem to be able to control it. The next instant, the plane rolled over on its back and dived straight into the ground.

The crash occurred near the little town of Clifton, Pa. All aboard were killed instantly. But the whole thing had been witnessed by an expert and rescuers reached the scene in time to find evidence of what had caused the accident. Ice had formed on the wings around the hinged joints where the ailerons were; it didn't jam the controls but it built up to where it changed the airfoil contour and disturbed the smooth flow of air. The aileron control was useless.

Back at the factory in Santa Monica they went to work on the problem. It might not happen again in a thousand years, but it could happen and did under just the right weather conditions. Douglas wanted built-in safety to make such a thing impossible.

Consequently, a few days after the fatal accident, a Douglas test pilot with test observers aboard was up in a DC-2 flying over the Tehachapi Mountains. The weather was stinking. Ice conditions! They had purposely waited for just such an atmosphere condition. And they purposely flew right into it. But nothing happened. They had made a subtle change in the DC-2.

This is the way Arthur Raymond described it – "We added a few inches to the underside of the wing where the ailerons hinge on. This reduced the flow of air through the slot. It also reduced the possibility of ice forming at the crucial point."

There never again has been any report of similar trouble.

V

There were other crashes. The airlines were going through a period in which, seemingly, they had caught a severe case of "Crash Fever." In little over one month – December 1936 through January 1937 – there were five major airline disasters. The fever seemed to get worse, not better. There were charges that planes were not structurally sound. In one case, this was proved to be true, although it was not a DC-ship involved in the accident. Pilots pulled some stupid blunders that were proven in crash investigations. Some lived and even admitted it. The weather kicked up some of the worst storms in history, and took its claim and share of the blame. There was, indeed, just cause for alarm and concern.

A Western Airlines' plane crashed in the mountains somewhere between Salt Lake City and Los Angeles. Less than a month later another WAL ship, a Boeing 247, crashed near Saugus, Utah, killing famed explorer Martin Johnson. A Northwest airliner fell eighty miles west of Elk River, Idaho. Braniff lost an airliner on take-off during a test run at Dallas, Texas. Four days later a United ship with 12-passengers aboard plowed into the mountains only ten miles from the Burbank, California terminal.

American Airlines with a record of 86,000,000 passenger miles and not a single fatality lost its Flagship *"The Southerner,"* a DC-2, in flat country around Little Rock, Arkansas. The crash was headlined as America's "Worst air disaster." There was a rumor that a madman shot the pilot!

TWA's Flight No. 1, the *Sun Racer,* out of Newark bound for Pittsburgh crashed on the crest of Cheat Mountain on Chestnut Ridge, the westernmost of the Allegheny "hogbacks." Hostess Nellie Granger, bruised and bleeding, crawled down the mountain and led rescuers to the scene.

Two passengers were still alive and lived to fly again.

An Eastern Airlines DC-2 taking off from the field at Daytona, Florida in the early morning hours of August 10, 1937, ran into high tension wires; the crew and two passengers killed instantly. It was Eastern's first fatality in 180,000,000 passenger miles of flying.

Northwest Airlines' Captain Nick Namer with more than 10,000 hours of flying behind him, a pioneer over the tough, rugged Northern air route that stretches from St. Paul to Seattle, was killed in a crash on Bridges Peak just north of Bozeman, Montana. Nine others were found in the wreckage of the new 225-mile-an-hour Lockheed 14 airliner. Crash investigation showed the ship had developed "tail flutter." The Bureau of Air Commerce promptly grounded all the planes.

What was wrong?

There were all kinds of excuses. Accusing fingers pointed in every direction. Some said that it was the newness of the equipment. Others blamed one disaster after another on "Pilot error" and airline operations procedures. There were some cases of engine failure, but usually there were other factors, too, that built up to the disaster. There were also accusations that the planes themselves were unstable and unsafe.

It was after a series of crashes involving the DC ships that a nasty and vicious rumor began its rounds. When Don Douglas heard it he was furious. The rumor had it that the DC-3 had bad stalling characteristics. To spike the rumor Douglas sent one of the DC-3s to Langley Field, Virginia, home of the National Advisory Committee for Aeronautics (NACA) laboratories, invited the government agency to put it through any test they desired with respect to the ship having any critical stalling characteristics. The DC-3 came out with flying colors. NACA said it was one of the most stable airplanes ever built, under any and all known flight conditions!

There is always danger of mid-air collision with foreign objects. Vultures of India still carry on their undeclared war against aircraft. This is what happened in a collision at 7,000 feet between a C-47A and one of the big feathered birds. DC-3's in airline service have survived many similar collisions. One even made it back safely after a bomb exploded in the baggage compartment. (USAF Photo)

There was an encouraging ray of hope in the same crashes, despite the rash of accidents and the terrible loss of life and property. The bigger planes were proving they could take it. More important, some of the crash victims were walking way from the wrecks. It had seldom happened like that before. Prior to the time when the DC ships went into service, word of an airliner crash usually meant everybody was killed. Newspapers even had their headlines set up in type – AIRLINER CRASHES – ALL ABOARD KILLED.

The facts were plain. The newer, bigger planes were rugged, built to take a lot of punishment in the air and even during crash landings. Take the case of what happened to Trans-Atlantic pilot Henry Tindall ("Dick") Merrill. The famous flyer who had twice flown the Atlantic was flying for Eddie Rickenbacker as a Captain on one of the DC-2s that made up Eastern Airlines' "Great Silver Fleet." Merrill brought his ship down on a ridge near Port Jervis, New York without a single loss of life.

Led astray by bad weather reporting (it could have been radio static. And Merrill, himself, admitted it might have been overconfidence.) Merrill thought he was coming down out of the overcast and "really rough air" to find Newark; instead, there was the ground and a raw hillside dead ahead.

According to W. T. Critichfield, one of the eight passengers who survived the crash, Merrill's expertness at the controls saved the ship and the lives of its passengers. The pilot brought the ship down, saw the ground rushing up and pulled up quickly, slicing the tops off some trees. Then, somehow, he managed to belly it in. When they found the wreck it was minus its wings and the fuselage was battered and warped, but the machine had survived and so did its occupants. Not-so-modest Dick Merrill credited the plane's ruggedness, not his own pilotage, for being alive!

VI

Despite the rash of crashes air transport was growing steadily. Each year from 1935 to 1939 air traffic jumped about 19 per cent over the previous year. In 1939, when virtually all of the carriers were using DC-equipment, the traffic increase was a whopping 42.2 per cent! Correspondingly, the safety factor was also increasing *because the bigger planes were flying more passengers more miles.* The National Safety Council which uses the passenger miles yardstick to measure its safety statistics put air travel on a par with the automobile and bus travel so far as risk was concerned. Actual figures showed that the average death rate (1938-1940) per 100,000,000 passenger miles flown or carried was 2.8 for the Scheduled Air Transport Planes; 3.7 for passenger automobiles and buses. Transport pilots told their wives that it was safer flying their regular runs than it was driving to and from the airport!

The student of air transportation, perusing the records can easily understand what happened. The speed and comfort of the modern airliner was a strong enticement to the man in a hurry. It is no secret that the businessman going places filled up the seats in the pre-World War II airliners. The businessman, however, also demanded reliability and the DC-ships scored high in this category. They permitted the airlines to set unprecedented records in maintaining time-table operations. In short, they were in the air more than they were on the ground which wasn't always true of the planes before them.

There were other signs pointing towards *safety* in the air, the only effective weapon against fear, aviation's biggest bugaboo. As a direct result of the "crash fever" the government once again stepped in to take steps toward "safety-izing the air." There were stiffer Federal regulations for pilots and planes. The airlines themselves banded together in the Air Transport Association of America (ATA) to build jointly toward better operational techniques, the development of the new safety devices and their application. Pilots, themselves, also decided to do something about the situation and the Airline Pilots Association was formed in affiliation with the union of Railroad Brotherhoods. And in each of these areas, it is evident, the DC-transports were influential in setting the pattern.

Unquestionably, the biggest single step forward came with the passage of the Civil Aeronautics Act of 1938 which has been called the "Magna Charta of Civil Avia-

Many changes through the years have been made in the CAA. Today it is known as the FAA (Federal Aviation Agency). The Air Safety Board has become the Civil Aeronautics Board. The responsibility, however, has not changed; FAA and CAB still rule the industry. Today's CAB is comprised of these members: Left to right, John G. Adams, Whitney Gillilland, Charles S. Murphy (Chairman), Robert T. Murphy (Vice Chairman) and G. Joseph Minetti. (Civil Aeronautics Board Photo)

tion," one of the most far-sighted pieces of legislation ever enacted by our Congress. The act was unusual in two respects: (1) The airlines, themselves, fought for it even though it meant harnessing their whole structure, planes, plans, operations, pilots, routes, fares and safety standards with the known red-tape of government regulation. (2) For the first time it put all civil aviation under a single government agency (The Civil Aeronautics Authority) and it made the Federal Government recognize air transportation in its proper right, spend money for improvement of airways facilities, enforce and monitor operations and flying techniques and, in short, give purpose and mission to the whole air transport industry.

For purposes here, let's look at how the DC-ships helped bring about this important act of Congress. To begin with, they are universally credited with getting more people to use air transport. Statistics prove this. In turn, the air traveler began to demand more air service, safer regulations. Air travel became a way of life. The public demand put the pressure on Congress and the President to do something that would bring law and order

President Franklin D. Roosevelt signed the Act – (it is officially known as the McCarran-Lea Bill) sponsored by Senator Patrick A. McCarran of Nevada and Representative Clarence Lea of California on June 23, 1938 and, as someone said – "civil aviation was given its new constitution." The new law automatically took aviation away from the Post Office Department, the Interstate Commission and the Bureau of Air Commerce, put it in the hands of the Civil Aeronautics Authority, with the agency reporting directly to the President. The Authority consisted of an Administrator (Clinton M. Hester, an enterprising attorney in the Treasury Department and close friend of FDR's) and a board of five members. They were to be the judges and referees in all matters pertaining to Civil Aviation. In addition, there was also created a three-man Air Safety Board appointed by the President. Its job – to investigate all accidents and publish reports on the cause and prevention of airplane crashes.

One of the first acts of the new agency was to rewrite the laws governing regulations and requirements pertaining to air transport equipment, personnel and operations. When it came to setting standards for transport equipment Don Douglas and his designers and engineers were called to Washington to help write the specifications and requirements. "We made the trip so many times," Arthur Raymond recalls, "that we considered setting aside one of our DC-3s and using it as a shuttle between Santa Monica and the Capital."

Such things as single engine performance for the twin-engined transports; all-metal construction for passenger-carrying planes; flying aids and navigational aids in the cockpit; anti-icing devices, structural limitations, stalling speeds, the use of wing flaps, and many other features which the DC-ships had pioneered were taken as standard requirements for safe air transport plane. "The DC-2," Clinton Hester declared, "because of its known performance characteristics was the instrument we turned to in drafting many of the new standards pertaining to air transport plane construction, maintenance, and operations. I am convinced that without it we could not have had a very vital tool with which to begin to carve the shape of commercial aviation's future."

VII

Hester took over the reins and the CAA began to cut its teeth on things August 22, 1938. The Air Safety Board also began to wield a big stick. One thing pleasing to Don Douglas was that a published survey of the airliner accidents through January 1939 stated that in no incident where a DC-2 or DC-3 was involved did investigations disclose any evidence of structural failure in the aircraft itself. With courage and conviction, however, the Air Safety Board put the blame on bad weather reporting, lack of adequate airways facilities, cut-throat practices of the competitive airlines to fly in defiance of severe weather conditions, other airline operational practices. The CAA immediately took action to remedy the situation in these areas.

It all but came out flatly and ordered a standardization of equipment and operational procedures within the air transport industry. That put the DC-3 definitely in the spotlight of favoritism. Congress appropriated more money than ever before in its history for modernizing the federal airways, increasing radio facilities, improving airports. The CAA also took steps to revitalize the industry, revamping certain route structures, encouraging mergers to bring about stronger financial stability, setting more sound practices in the distribution of mail pay and generally spreading the wings of air commerce to include communities that never before had enjoyed air transportation. Air safety inspectors were "thicker than flies" around airports. They were also riding the airliners night and day, here, there and everywhere, to see that new recommended procedures and operations techniques were being put into effect.

The result soon began to bear fruit. On March 26, 1939, a Braniff Airlines DC-3 crashed near Oklahoma City killing eight passengers. But from then on, until a Pennsylvania-Central Airlines' DC-3 crashed on August 31, 1940, near Lovettsville, Virginia, the airlines enjoyed a period of peace and quiet seldom equaled by any form of transport. The record was unmarred by even a minor accident!

This achievement did not go by without recognition. In December 1940, the *Collier Trophy* was awarded to – *"the airlines of the U.S. for their outstanding record for safety in air travel during 1939."*

The citation, read by FDR when he presented the trophy at the White House also said – "With especial recognition of Doctors W. M. Boothby and W. Randolph Lovelace II of the Mayo Foundation for Medical Research and Captain Harry G. Armstrong, U.S. Army Medical Corps, for contribution to this safety record by their work in the field of aviation medicine generally and pilot fatigue in particular."

If the DC ships hadn't already enjoyed their own *Collier Trophy* (Chapter Six) they, unquestionably, would have shared in the 1939 award. The truth is, they were planes that "lifted the air traveler up to altitudes" where it was necessary for man to do something about oxygen masks and pressurized cabins, the contributions to aviation for which Boothby, Lovelace and Armstrong were honored.

Significant during this period of the perfect safety record is the fact that for the first time in their history the airlines of the U.S. began to show definite signs and intent that they could pull together in their effort to further the new dimension in transportation. The shining example of this solid front occurred during the week of September 20, 1938, less than one month after the Civil Aeronautics Authority took command.

Colonel Edgar S. Gorrell was first head of the Air Transport Association (ATA) and more than anyone else can be credited with keeping the airlines from being completely militarized during the war. (Air Transport Association Photo)

Roaring up from the Carribbean, one of the worst hurricanes in history hit the New England Coast. Roads were inundated and motor car transport was at a standstill. Rail lines were knocked out, radio stations silenced. The whole eastern seaboard was an isolated, devastated area, completely cut off with the outside world. There were thousands homeless, pestilence threatened, damage ran into the millions.

Naturally, during the blow the airliners were grounded. But the next day they were in the air again, the only line of communication. Normally, it was a route (New York-Boston-Hartford-Maine) that belonged exclusively to C. R. Smith's American Airlines. The *Flagships,* shuttling back and forth, under normal operations carried about 200 passengers a day. The morning after the hurricane, however, more than 1,000 persons wanted seats. There was desperate need for nurses and doctors and medical supplies; for rescuers and technicians and workers to help dig through the debris and start over again.

American Airlines couldn't possibly handle the task alone. It called for help. First to come to the aid was Edgar S. Gorrell, head of the young Air Transport Association. The dynamic "Little Colonel" got on the telephone talking with TWA, United and Eastern airline presidents, all members of his association. He didn't *ask* them, he *told* them, if ATA was to mean anything, they should divert their planes to help American during the emergency. Then, he called Hester and got the CAA to permit the other carriers to fly over American's franchise route. Literally, only minutes, after Gorrell hung up the phone, after "clearing the decks for action," the planes of the different airlines were taking off on missions of mercy heading for the stricken area.

Stuart G. Tipton, today's President of the Air Transport Association. (Air Transport Association Photo)

For a solid week the airlines, working together, ferried in more than 1,000 rescue and reconstruction workers and brought out more than 1,500 stranded persons. In addition, they carried 60,000 pounds of needed supplies and 57,000 pounds of mail. It was air transport's busiest week in the history of airline operation. The airlines were credited with a major role in helping to minimize a national disaster. The ships that performed the mission were all DC-2s and DC-3s.

Historians also were to recognize that in this moment of glory the DC-ships proved for the first time the true value of *airlift* in time of emergency. The time would come in the not-too-distant future when the same planes would have to put it to practice on a much larger scale. Then, it would be a decisive factor in the turning of the tide of a World War.

A squadron of 33 Douglas B-18 bombers flies over Diamond Head, Oahu, in the peaceful Pacific skies before Pearl Harbor when the DC-bomber was our "frontline" protector and guardian. In foreground is the famous Royal Hawaiian Hotel. Picture was taken in April of 1940. (Official Army Air Corps Photo)

Chapter 11

The DC-Bombers

One day in August, 1934 Don Douglas went to his office and found another letter there which would have far-reaching impact on the future of the Douglas Aircraft Company. It was almost the same story of the Jack Frye letter all over again. The Frye letter, it must be remembered, put the company in the big transport field. Now, almost two years to the day later, the new letter would ultimately put the company in the middle of a hot bomber competition. The result would be a record-breaking order for a new bombardment airplane from the U.S. Army Air Corps. Paradoxically, the DC-1 and the DC-2 would influence the design of the bomber – designated officially, the XB-18 – and prior to the outbreak of World War II these medium bombardment aircraft were America's operational frontline striking weapons.

The letter Douglas opened was really a circular sent out by the Materiel Division, Wright Field, Dayton, Ohio in which the Air Corps procurement people outlined the specifications for a new production bomber. In text it said that the Air Corps was desirous of a machine that would carry a bomb load of 2,000 pounds, 1,020 miles and return. The plane *must* have a speed of 200-mph, with a *desired* speed of 250-mph. The *desired* range was 2,200 miles. It could carry a crew of four or six and must be armed to defend itself. The circular also said that interested companies must submit bids for construction of up to two hundred and twenty airplanes!

There was also a time element involved. The Air Corps circular said, to be eligible for the competition, a *flying airplane* had to be submitted to Wright Field by August, 1935!

This was the thing he read that "bugged" Douglas. The truth was, he had been thinking about making a bombardment type airplane designed around the DC-1 configuration for quite some time. It was only natural, perhaps, that he should have such thoughts. The DC-1 in its record-breaking spree, had carried greater payloads, flown faster, higher and for greater distances than any bomber currently in service with the Army Air Corps. With such a performance record behind her, why wouldn't she make a good bomber? There didn't seem to be any insurmountable engineering or production problems to change the fuselage design to carry bombs instead of passengers. And it shouldn't be too difficult to cut a few holes here and there for installation of gun turrets.

What was troubling Douglas wasn't making a bomber out of the DC-1 or the DC-2 basic designs. He was pretty sure this was possible. But to get a bomber design flying in a year's time. The fabrication process. Flight testing. That was cutting things pretty close. Every time he walked through the factory he shuddered at the thought – *where in hell could they put another assembly line to build the bomber, if they came up with a design and it won the competition?*

The summer of 1934, the whole plant was filled with DC-2 fuselages and wings moving along the assembly line. Things were really getting into "high-gear" for the DC-2 production. The orders were piling up for the new transport. Business was booming. Douglas certainly didn't want to disrupt the smooth flow of the DC-2 production. Still, with typical farsightedness, he was looking ahead. The commercial air transport market, he felt certain, would hit a saturation point sooner than most people might believe. Maybe, say 200 of the DC-2's. Then what?

The challenge of the new bomber competition seemed to be a logical answer. If they could get this contract then the future would be brighter.

Besides, there was a personal reason why the challenge was appealing to Douglas. Ever since he had helped design that early twin-engined bombardment airplane, the

Martin MB-2 twin-engined bomber which Douglas helped design when he was with Glenn Martin Company in early 20's. (Douglas Aircraft Co. Photo)

Martin MB-2, Douglas had had ideas about the kind of new bomber, incorporating the latest aeronautical advancements, which he wanted to try out.

For a while, Douglas couldn't make up his mind about announcing that they would enter the bomber competition. He called in Carl Cover to talk about the Air Corps circular. The latter, who had flown the DC-1 on its maiden flight and was Chief Test Pilot for the Douglas plant at the time, also wore another hat with the organization. He was the Douglas "liaison man" between Santa Monica and the Materiel Division, Air Corps procurement people at Wright Field, from which came all the Air Corps design proposals and bids, the test center for the Army's wings. If anybody would know what the situation was back in Dayton, Carl Cover should know – and Douglas wanted to know what Cover felt the chances were for winning the competition.

Born in Roxbury, Pa., where he spent his early years, Cover in 1917 entered the Officers Training School at Berkeley, University of California and went from there to Texas, where he received flight training at Brooks and Kelly Fields. He was commissioned an officer in the Air Corps in June of 1918. In 1926, he came to Santa Monica as Air Corps resident representative. At the time the Douglas Company was engaged in filling its first orders for military planes. Three years later he transferred to the Air Corps Reserve in order to go to Honolulu to assist in the formation and operation of the Inter-Island Airways as operations manager.

He returned to California a year later and joined the Douglas organization, as Chief Test Pilot and manager of the military sales program. For the next thirteen years, but with one single exception (the XB-19), he was first to fly every new model turned out by Douglas. From 1938 to 1943 he held the rank of Vice President with the company.

When Douglas called him into the office that day in 1934 to talk about the bomber thing, Cover had just recently returned from a trip to Dayton.

"Carl," Douglas greeted him, "what do you think of this? He tossed the Air Corps circular across the desk.

Cover, of course was aware of the circular. He didn't hesitate with his answer.

"I think," he told his boss, "that we should take a crack at it. There are two other companies that will probably submit entries. Martin, I understand, has a souped-up version of the B-10. . The word is out that Boeing has a new design, a four-engine plane, they call the Model 299 . . ."

Douglas interrupted. "Four engines . . .?"

Then, he rememberd, the Circular had said *multi-engine*. There was nothing that said the new bomber couldn't be a trimotor or a four-motor. Perhaps, he remembered, too, that the Frye letter mentioned only a trimotor. But the DC-1 had finally emerged as a twin-engined aircraft.

He put the thought out of his mind about the four-engined concept. He had no idea of going in that direction.

The two men had talked before about a bomber version out of the DC-1 or the DC-2. In fact, he had asked Cover to "sound out the Wright Field people" on such a project *before* he had ever received the Air Corps circular. It was one reason Cover had made his last trip to Dayton.

Now, he reported, that "the bomber project boys at Wright Field were quite enthusiastic."

"If we come up with a design," Douglas asked, "what are our chances of winning the competition?"

"Well, the Martin is plenty fast," Cover told him. "The B-10 has flown faster than some of the pursuits. . . The B-12 is supposed to be better than that . . . I don't know much about the Boeing project . . . Nobody does."

He concluded: "I think if we can come up with a vehicle in time, that's the problem as I see it. Then, I think we can win the contract."

Obviously, Douglas had already made up his mind.

"We'll get the plane in time," he declared. "You can tell them back in Dayton, we'll be in the race."

II

There followed another round of long sessions with Raymond, Kindelberger, Oswald, Herman, Stineman, Shogran and the others who had designed the DC-1 and the DC-2. This time Cover sat in on some of the meetings to fill them in on ideas he had gleaned from the military people. There was no substitute in this business for "personal contacts". Carl Cover was Air Corps. The engineering gang took his suggestions seriously. As before, with the DC-1 project, the preliminary design study meetings dragged on; lights burned late as they thrashed out the problems one by one. Strangely, the "talk" had a familiar ring.

"I think we can go with the basic DC-1 wing," Arthur Raymond suggested. "We stretched it for the DC-2, I don't see why we can't stretch it again. A little more wing should do the job. Besides, it will save a helluva lot of retooling and a lot of time . . ."

Douglas agreed, but he pointed out a big problem. Where the wing joined the fuselage, this would have to be a different kind of joint. The DC-2 fairing and stub-wing technique simply wouldn't work. The low-wing configuration was OUT. It posed a structural bugaboo because of the bomb bay and the bomb bay doors, which desirably should be located as close as possible to the center of gravity for a stable platform.

The bomber, it was finally decided, would be a mid-wing aircraft. The fuselage underbelly would extend *below* the wing slightly. There was no reason, however, why the DC-2 tail – rudder and vertical stabilizer, the horizontal stabilizer and elevators – shouldn't work for the bomber.

"With minor modifications," Bailey Oswald admonished, "the DC-2 empennage should suffice. It's the front end of the fuselage I'm worried about. The bomber configuration out of an airliner won't be easy without upsetting things."

He was concerned, and rightly so, about where to put the bombardier's compartment. Where to locate the gunners and the gun turrets. The bomber had to have defensive armament. How to cut all of these holes in the fuselage, put in all the extra stuff and not change the aerodynamics of the aircraft, without throwing the weight-and-balance characteristics all out of proportion. These were factors that would take some doing. Yet, it had to be done.

There were other problems. Beefing up the structure itself, the airframe, where the cut-a-ways were affected to provide the gun ports and the bomb bay. Beefing up the under-carriage to take the additional weight and probably a faster landing speed. Redesign of the engine nacelles because of the mid-wing configuration.

So it went until finally they believed they had a design that would meet the requirements of the Army Air Corps specifications.

Kindelberger summed it up – "The damn thing is going to look like a DC-2 only a little bit pregnant!"

They called their bomber design, the DB-1 – *Douglas Bomber Number One.*

The Air Corps gave it another designation:

XB-18

About the time they were ready to turn the engineering plans over to the shop people and start work on the DB-1 Carl Cover returned from another trip to Dayton. He reported: "The whole place is buzzing with rumors about the Boeing 299. They're saying it's THE bomber of the future, a virtual *Flying Fortress.*"

The competition was going to be tough. Douglas was going to have to hustle. The DB-1 had better be *damned good!*

By late spring of 1935, the Douglas entry was rolled out of the plant at Santa Monica. There was great secrecy. But those who did get a glimpse of the DB-1 were impressed. She bristled with armament. Where the bombardier sat in the nose, below the pilots' compartment and forward, she had the look of a rugged, pugnosed fighter. She looked tough enough. But she also looked very much like the DC-2! They put her through a rigid flight test program, and they were glad she resembled the DC-2, performance-wise. The DB-1 was blessed with the proven flight characteristics of the airliner, already accepted as one of the best designed and best-built planes in the world.

The Douglas entry was ready, and they flew the DB-1 to Wright Field. It was early July, 1935. They had beat the deadline.!

When they landed at Wright Field, one of the competitor's aircraft was already on the flight line, the Martin B-12. It, too, was a mid-wing aircraft with a span of 70 feet, six inches, a wing area of 678 square feet. The fuselage was 45' feet, three inches from nose to tail, capable of carrying a crew of four, pilot, co-pilot, bombardier and rear gunner. A distinguishing feature was the bird-cage-like nose turret and bombardier's compartment. The fuselage was long and narrow and crew seats were in tandem, pilot, and navigator in a forward position under a canopy, and gunner just behind the trailing edge of the wing under another canopy of bullet-proof glass. She carried three .30 caliber machine guns, one in the nose turret, two in the rear gun-

XB-18 bomber, popularly called the BOLO. (Douglas Aircraft Co. Photo)

ner's position. The maximum bombload was 2,260 pounds. The B-12 was powered with two Pratt & Whitney engines each developing 775-horsepower. She reportedly had a top speed of 218 miles per hour. Her gross weight was 12,884 pounds. She had a range in excess of 2000 miles.

The Martin B10 series (the B-12 was merely a modified version) already had a reputation. The Air Corps the previous year had ordered 103 of the B-10's, some of them already were in active service. The design had also won for Glenn Martin the Collier Trophy for 1932. And at the very moment a flight of the Martin B-10's led by Lieutenant Colonel Henry H. Arnold was making history on a 7,360-mile round trip between Washington, D.C. and Fairbanks, Alaska.

By comparison, however, the DB-1 or the XB-18, whichever one chose to call her, as she stood there on the flight line at Wright Field along side the B-12, was a giant. The Douglas entry had a wing span of 89 feet, six inches – almost five feet more wing than the DC-2. She had a fuselage 56 feet, 8 inches from nose to tail (eleven feet longer than the Martin) but five feet *shorter* than the DC-2. She had a gross weight of 25,000 pounds, almost double the gross weight of the Martin, three tons more than the DC-2. The DB-1 had a six man crew: Pilot; co-pilot in side-by-side seating the same as the DC-2 in a roomy cockpit; bombardier in the nose, lying down on a prone position platform; a nose-turret gunner; a navigator; and also a rear-turret gunner located in a top turret just forward of the vertical stabilizer. The plane was powered by two Wright *Cyclone* engines each developing 930-horsepower. Its top speed was reported to be 217 miles per hour with a bombload of 4,400 pounds, a 2400 mile range. She had a service ceiling of 24,000 feet. Certainly, here was a real contender.

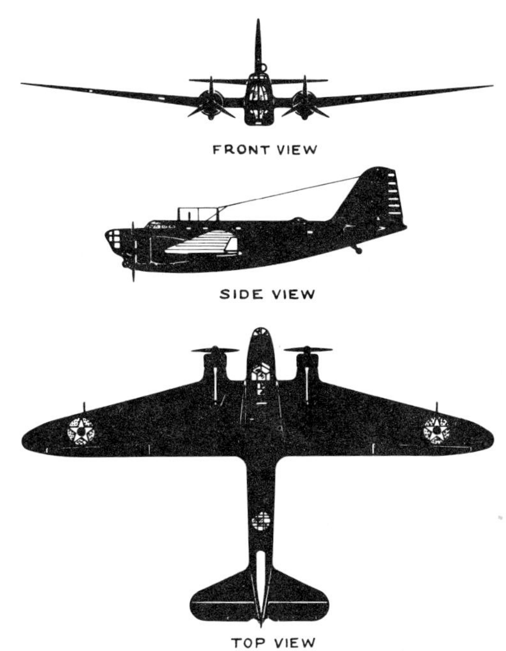

Planview of B-18A Bomber. (Army Air Corps Photo)

Martin B-12 bomber, one of the contenders in the 1935 bomber competition at Wright Field. (Army Air Corps Photo)

The famous B-17 series "Flying Fortress" was first of four-engined monoplane bombers. Prototype was Model 299 entered in competition with the twin-engined B-18. The Model 299 crashed and burned during trials at Wright Field. (Army Air Corps Photo)

It was mid-August before the Boeing entry arrived in dramatic fashion. The so-called "Flying Fortress" came roaring out of the west – nine hours, non-stop from Seattle, Washington to Dayton. And she was a giant! Wing span – 103 feet, 9 inches and 1,420 square feet in area! Gross weight – 34,873 pounds! Four Pratt & Whitney *Hornet* engines, a total of 3000 horsepower. Top speed – 250 mph. Maximum range in excess of 3,000 miles. Service ceiling – above 30,000 feet. Bristling with gun turrets, in the nose, belly, atop the fuselage, on the sides. A six-man crew. Bomb load – near five tons!

There never had been anything like this before. She was the *sky dreadnaught* that General "Billy" Mitchell had been preaching about for so long.

There wasn't any question. The Boeing entry had the inside track. There were those, however, who said she was "too far ahead of her time." And this, probably would be her greatest hurdle. Like battleships, sky dreadnaughts cost a lot of money. The 299 – "Flying Fortress" concept – was going to be hard to sell to the Air Corps appropriations people in Washington.

The twin-engined Douglas and the twin-engined Martin still had a chance. Provided they could meet the stiff Army Air Corps requirements as set forth in the year old circular.

The competition evaluation began. For weeks there were various tests for the three entries. Speed trials. Endurance trials. Time to climb. Service ceiling. Weight carrying trials. Armament firing tests. And on the ground the planes had to pass other requirements in structure and design, equipment installation, maintenance.

In the middle of the competition, tragedy struck. The Boeing entry on take-off ran into trouble. Later it was discovered somebody had forgotten to unlock the elevator locks. The 299 crashed and burned!

The crash prolonged the evaluation proceedings. There were many controversial arguments, pro and con, to give the big contract to Boeing anyway, on the basis of the ship's performance before the crash. The decision dragged on. It was Christmas time before the Air Corps announced the winner of the bomber competition. Both Douglas and Boeing won.

The big contract for 103 of the XB-18 bombers went to Douglas. But Boeing also got a service contract to build thirteen YB-17's. For the time-being, however, the new B-18 production models, with slight modifications, would as rapidly as possible join the Air Corps bombardment squadrons as

Douglas B-18 "Bolo" in flight. Plane won competition. Note resemblance to DC-2 in rudder and empennage and wings. XB-18 was definitely descendant of the Douglas Commercial Transport family. (Army Air Corps Photo)

the front-line bomber. Modified as the B-18A and the B-18B before the assembly line would shut down on these models, the Douglas Company would build more than 500. The last was delivered in 1939 about the time that Hitler started World War II in Europe.

Before the war was over Douglas, at its new Long Beach plant, would be building Boeing B-17's – three thousand in all – a shining example of the American free-enterprise system at work under democratic process in time of emergency. To carry this a bit further: The B-17's, designed by Boeing, built by Douglas, were powered with engines designed by Wright Aeronautical Corporation and Pratt & Whitney, built by Studebaker and Buick; equipped with turbo-superchargers designed by General Electric, built by Allis Chalmers!

III

They gave the B-18 a popular name – *Bolo*. Probably because she was considered to be the Air Corps' sharp-edge offensive weapon with striking power and range enough to protect our shores 1,000 miles seaward. She had the range to bomb an approaching potential enemy flotilla a thousand miles from our shores. But experience with the new bomber demanded changes. In the original design the bombar-

Douglas B-18A was modified version of B-18. Note shark-styled nose change and different nacelle configuration. Planes were used later for anti-submarine warfare. (Army Air Corps Photo)

dier's compartment was cramped, interferring with accurate sighting. In a new configuration, they gave her a shark-like nose. The bombardier position was reversed, above the nose turret instead of below it. This became the B-18A. The change was made on the 134th *Bolo* to come off the assembly line. They also put in more powerful engines, increasing the horsepower. The B-18A *Bolo* also was designed with water-tight outer wing panels and had hydraulically retractable landing gear and flaps. And they had increased her fuel capacity to give her more range.

With these modifications, the *Bolo* was sent to Air Corps units in the Canal Zone, in Hawaii, the Philippines. She became the first modern offensive weapon in the Pacific theater of operations. The first indication of an airpower build-up in the Pacific where seapower was regarded as our mightiest arm of defense.

At Pearl Harbor, when the Japs struck, she won two distinctions. The first wave of Jap planes caught a lot of *Bolos* on the ground; they were among our first aircraft victims of the infamous attack. She was also one of the first planes to take to the air and search out the Japanese Carrier force.

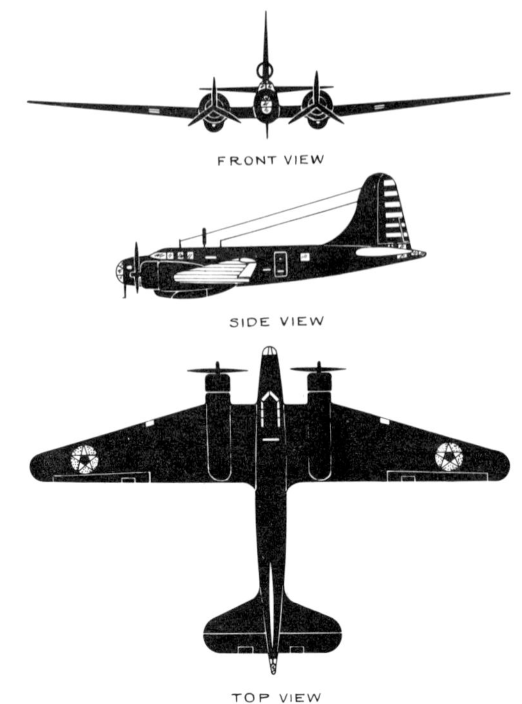

Planview of Douglas B-23 bomber. (Army Air Corps Photo)

Back home there was another job for her. They changed the nose again. The shark-like bombardier nose was replaced

Douglas B-23 "Dragon" takes off on test flight. B-23 had DC-3 wing, but incorporated B-19 rudder configuration. Note the tail turret gun position and "greenhouse" for bombardier in nose. (Douglas Aircraft Co. Photo)

with a bulbous plastic radome. With delicate and sensitive micro-wave gear in the nose, she became a new kind of weapon. Submarine detector. Operating from bases in England she helped spot the Nazi subs that were virtually annihilating the first convoys, Britain's lifeline. In this role she put the Air Corps ahead of the Navy – she was really doing a Navy job.

She was doing the same task, very effectively, off our own shores. It can be said *Bolo* saved millions of tons of shipping.

But the B-18's saw very little actual combat. There were only isolated cases of her being used as a bomber – in the early island campaigns when the Japs were on the offensive and they were the only bombers we had in the Pacific arena. Patrol duty over the Panama Canal and anti-submarine warfare. She did, however, fill the need until the bigger B-17's and the B-24's came along to become the real muscle of bombardment aviation.

Meanwhile, things had been happening back in Santa Monica. The DST and the DC-3 were flying and setting remarkable records in the skies as commercial transports and aerial freighters. If they made a bomber out of the DC-2, Douglas believed they could make a better bomber out of the DC-3. The end product became the B-23. The first B-23 was flying even *before* Pearl Harbor.

She showed a family likeness to the DC-3 (virtually the same wing) and a resemblance to the B-18. But gone was the shark-nose and the paunchy belly. She was long and slim, and sleek and trim. Capable of speeds above 280-mph! So fast they eliminated the nose turret entirely – it wasn't likely an enemy could get in front of her. The nose turret gone, she had a spacious bombardier's compartment providing one of the most stable airborne bombing platforms ever designed.

They called her the *Dragon*. She had a range of almost 3,000 miles with a bombload of 4,000 pounds. A service ceiling of 31,000 feet. Improved Wright *Cyclone* engines gave her a combined horsepower of 3200 horses. She carried a six man crew. And she was one of the first bombers to try out the .50 caliber machine gun. The heavier caliber gun was mounted in a tail turret, the first to appear on any bomber. A similar installation – in the years ahead – would appear on the B-29's.

Yet, inspite of these improvements there were only 38 of the B-23's ever built. She simply hadn't kept up with the latest aerodynamic advances – and the priority was on the big heavy bombers like the B-17 and the B-24. Before she was really off the drawing board, the B-23 was an obsolete aircraft.

They relegated her to the role of a trainer and for off-shore patrol work. Later twelve of the Army B-23's were converted into UC-67 transports.

She had gone the complete circle. Originally she was basically the DC-3. They made a bomber out of her – the B-23. Then, they refurbished her as a utility transport.

The DC-bombers vanished from the scene.

Reportedly there are still some B-18's flying in Central America, converted into flying freighters although this is difficult to confirm or imagine, because they were never cheap to operate. Some B-23's, however, are still flying and have joined the elite group of executive aircraft.

The DC-bomber story would not be complete without a brief review of what happened in the years just prior to Pearl Harbor and during World War II. "Douglas accomplishment between September 1938 and the end of the war fills a truly prodigious catalogue of combat and transport aircraft, designed, fabricated and delivered to our own Armed Forces and our allies by sheer force of will, skill and manpower," writes Crosby Maynard, Assistant to Vice President Public Relations, Douglas Aircraft Co., Santa Monica, "At wartime peak in 1944 net sales reached $1,061,407,485 as against $130,840 in 1922 (when Douglas began operations.) Instead of 68 employes in a small California seaside city, the company had 160,000 employes, spread over six plants and much of the world."

"The loft operation on the second floor of a planing mill had zoomed to become the fourth largest business in the United States.

"In 1944, engineering personnel touched a peak of 5,301. Completely new plants had been established at Long Beach, California; Tulsa and Oklahoma City, Oklahoma; and Chicago, Illinios."

Certainly, it can be said that design and production of the B-18's and the B-23's started the Douglas company into the design and development of a whole series of specialized bombardment aircraft for the Army, Navy and our Allies.

Perhaps the most famous of these bombardment aircraft was the twin-engined Douglas A-20 (attack bomber) which the British called the *Havoc*. Produced in several versions and configurations, including the BD-1, BD-2, the P-70 *night fighter* and the photographic reconnaissance models F-3 and F-3A, a total of 7,478 was built. The actual construction was spread among Douglas plants at Santa Monica, Long Beach and El Segundo, plus 240 built by the Boeing Airplane Company. In March 1944, production reached a rate of 32 per month. The innovation of a moving assembly line for wing sections and fuselage sections contributed very heavily to the high rate of production.

In round figures this was better than a plane-a-day production rate! For Donald W. Douglas it was another crowning achievement. He remembered, perhaps, listening to the radio and hearing Franklin D. Roosevelt tell the nation – and the world – in 1939 that the American aircraft industry would be expected to rise to a production rate of 50,000 units a year. Friends who were with him during that broadcast said that Douglas assumed a very pensive look and then remarked for all to hear – "We can do it." And before the end of the war – between 1942 and 1945 – Douglas provided, in all, 432,000,000 pounds of aircraft, equal to 16 per cent of the entire output of aircraft in the United States during the war period!

Including the A-20's, the SBD's (Navy carrier-based bombers) and the C-47's, this represented a total figure of 29,385 aircraft.

Near the end of the war, the A-20 had grown into an improved version the A-26 (later re-named the B-26) which would remain one of the prime attack weapons in the USAF, performing notable feats in the Korean conflict which lay ahead.

Not only did Douglas produce bombers

Douglas A-20 attack bomber. Originally it was DB-7 design which French bought early in the war. A-20 was modification and became the "Havoc" which saw action with British at Dieppe. (Douglas Aircraft Co. Photo)

by the numbers but in 1939 he built the biggest plane of its day — the first of the truly BIG intercontinental bombers. They called it the XB-19. She had a wing span almost the length of a football field; a winged goliath weighing 164,000 pounds. The B-19 first flew on June 27, 1941 from the same field and under the same conditions that had seen the initial takeoffs of the *World Cruisers* and the DC-1. At high noon, the factory whistle at Santa Monica blew three long blasts and from every department Douglas workers poured on to the field to see the takeoff.

Perhaps more than any other airplane the XB-19 was a true "flying laboratory." She pioneered so many things. The first big plane with a tri-cycle landing gear. The first plane to use hydraulic "booster" controls. First to have remote controlled gun gurrets; a 20-mm cannon in the tail. First military plane to have berths for the crew, a galley and many other innovations designed to make possible long-range sustained flight. Capable of flying from U.S. territory to any potential enemy and return. And part of her long fuselage was designed to be pressurized (although they never did try it) — a pioneer step toward high-altitude bombing operations. First to use the new high-horsepower (in excess of 2,000 hp. each) both radial and in-line engines.

She taught us many things. But she died an infamous death. They scrapped her at Davis Monthan Air Force Base in Arizona — made pots and pans out of her. But she had taught us things about big airplane construction which unquestionably made possible the huge planes now programmed. Her only fault, perhaps, was that for her day she was too big and underpowered. The thrustpower of the Jet Age was not available when Douglas started construction of the B-19 in the spring of 1937!

As soon as the jet engines became available, however, Douglas was there with a bomber design. The experimental XB-43, a twin-engined jet with the engines in the tail, was the first U.S.-built jet-propelled bomber design to take wing in 1944. Sig-

Douglas A-26 attack bomber. Later designation was changed to B-26 (not to be confused with Martin B-26 Marauder). The B-26 was called the Invader. They saw plenty of action in Korea. (Douglas Aircraft Co. Photo)

Biggest bomber built before World War II was the Douglas XB-19. Wings were so thick that mechanics could crawl out to engine nacelles and make repairs in flight. Only one was ever built. Plane was used for flying test-bed, but perhaps her greatest contribution was the "know-how" in building large structures within aerodynamic limitations. First Douglas DC-4E, which would become the Skymaster (C-54) followed the XB-19 fuselage configuration. (Douglas Aircraft Co. Photo)

nificantly, it was the last "bomber design" to be built by Douglas.

The DC-bombers had really started something. Or should one say the DC-1, DC-2 and DC-3 really *started it all* and gave us new military wings as well as wings for commercial transport?

One thing is certain: The DC-2's and the DC-3's in their own configuration as transport planes would play a leading role in wartime operations.

Chapter 12

The "C" Stands For Cargo

There wasn't much talk of war in the winter of 1932-33 when the DC-1 was taking shape in the jigs at the Douglas plant in Santa Monica. Nobody paid much attention to the announcement that the Nazi Party leader, Adolph Hitler was made German Chancellor; that Spain by Parliamentary edict dis-established the Church; that Germany withdrew from the League of Nations and the disarmament conference; that President Roosevelt recognized the Soviet Union as the government of Russia. All of this was far away. Nobody really cared. Here at home, the U.S. was fighting on an economic front to pull itself up by its bootstraps from the depths of the worst depression in the nation's history.

"It wasn't easy to generate much interest in air travel when we went to Douglas to build our airliner of the future," Jack Frye once declared. "Bankers, whose banks were closed, were looking at the breadlines not the airlines. Only a handful of far-sighted investors would listen."

But Douglas had listened. He was willing to gamble. So was TWA. The DC-1 project was, indeed, a kind of a symbol of a new day dawning. Certainly, it lifted the spirits of the workers in the Douglas organization.

Something else happened that winter lifting the spirits of a forgotten people; it would change the concept of the airplane and its use for all time. It was almost as though Destiny itself had written the future for the DC-ships *before* the DC-1 ever even rolled out of the factory.

It was a terrible winter, that January and February. Blustering snowstorms roared down from the north, blanketing most of the country. The weather was particularly bad in New Mexico, southwest Colorado, south Utah and northern Arizona. Hundreds of Indians on reservations in these sections faced starvation.

Orders flashed from the War Department in Washington to the Commanding Officer of the Air Corps station at March Field, Riverside, California – less than 75 miles from the Santa Monica factory where the DC-1 was being hatched. In command at March Field was a young Lieutenant Colonel named Henry Harley "Hap" Arnold, veteran airman of World War I, who had worked with Don Douglas in 1917-18 when the latter was a staff member, a civilian engineer, for the Aeronautics and Aviation Committee on the Council of National Defense. Arnold and Douglas saw eye to eye on most things. The two would work closely together in shaping the nation's airpower. Both would be called on to do the impossible in World War II not too far in the future.

Gen. Henry Harley "Hap" Arnold. (Douglas Aircraft Co. Photo)

After they had accomplished the fact, "Hap" Arnold who became a five-star general, Supreme Commander of the United States Air Forces in that war would write about the terrible winter of 1932-33 in his book *Global Mission*.

"The isolated Indians in the villages faced starvation," Arnold wrote. "I was asked if we could help from the air. We had never been confronted by such a problem, but I said *Yes*.

"Our first question, as we took on this job was not how to cope with the weather over that mountainous territory with its high winds, but how to pack the sugar, flour, potatoes, etc., so that the bundles we dropped wouldn't break on the frozen ground and spill their contents. Captain Charlie Howard, with his famous 11th bombardment Squadron of *Condors*, made one test after another at March Field. Finally, we were able to pack the different commodities so well that, as one of my sergeants said – *We could drop a dozen eggs without breaking a damned one*. Our bombers operated from various airports along the TWA line from Kingman, Arizona, east to Amarillo, Texas, and for several weeks, at the direction of the Indian Agents, we located the scattered villages and hogans buried in the deep snow and bombed them with food."

The trouble was the old twin-engined, fabric-covered, Army biplanes were bombers, not cargo planes. It took a lot of improvision and ingenuity to utilize them for the mission. This fact fired "Hap" Arnold's imagination.

Shortly after the DC-1 made its initial flight in July of 1933, Arnold was standing on the flight line at Clover Field adjacent to the Douglas plant, watching the DC-1 silver airliner and talking with his friend Don Douglas. He was, perhaps, recalling the episode of the "Big Drop" during the winter past which had saved the Indians.

Anyway, Douglas remembers, Arnold turned to him and remarked something like this – "Doug, what we need is a cargo ship along the lines of the DC-1. The day is almost upon us when the ground forces will be dependent upon an aerial supply line. The hell of it is, if the Air Corps were to buy some of these planes, the appropriations people would think the top brass wanted plush jobs to fly around in. It would be hard to convince them we were buying an aerial mule. Maybe, that's what we need – an aerial mule."

Douglas didn't say anything. But he had told George Strompl one day when they were walking down the assembly line where the DC-2's were moving along, that ultimately they would reach the saturation

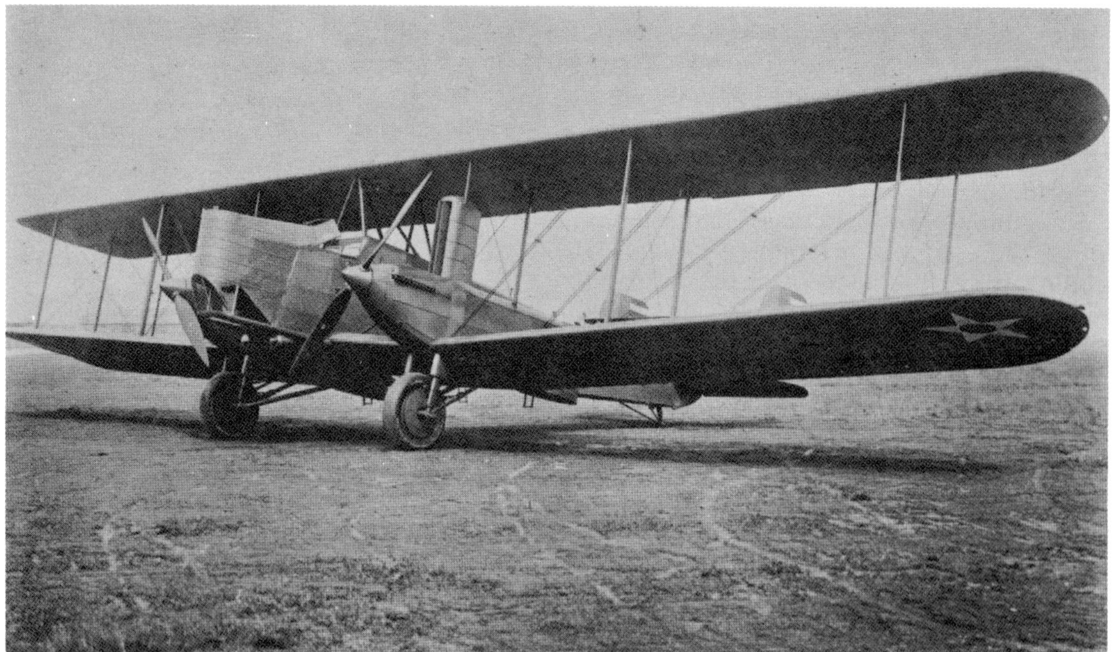

This Curtiss B-2 "Condor" was largest of our bombers in 1933. It was not easily adaptable as a cargo plane. (U.S. Army Air Corps Photo)

point with the airlines, where the carriers would have more DC-2's than the traffic called for. It would be smart, he thought, to look at the possibility of military orders for this type of plane. He also knew that Jack Frye already had approached him about an idea for making the DC-2's into aerial freighters.

The idea undoubtedly occurred to Douglas to make a *cargo version* of the *commercial airliner.* He knew also that his sales people were working on a presentation for the Air Corps procurement people of the Materiel Division at Wright Field. The word was out that the Air Corps was looking for a new transport plane.

Paradoxically, the time would come sooner than either Don Douglas or "Hap" Arnold ever dreamed of, when they would be haggling over the specifications for a military cargo plane that would bear the designation C-47.

There would be more Model C-47's – the standardized military version of the DC-3 – built by the numbers, than any other single aircraft type, in the world including the mass fleets of bombers and fighters.

"Hap" Arnold's *aerial mule* would become a reality and perform Herculean tasks.

II

Building cargo planes for the Army Air Corps was no new assignment for the Douglas Aircraft Company. In his booklet *"U.S. ARMY AIRCRAFT, Heavier-than-air 1908-1946",* Editor James C. Fahey, lists the Douglas C-1 as the first plane designated officially by the Army Air Corps as a cargo transport. The C-1 was a biplane similar in configuration to the famous Douglas "Round-the-world" *Air Cruisers.* It had a wing span of 56 feet, 7-inches, measured 35 feet, 4-inches from rudder to propeller hub tip, was powered with a Liberty V-1650-1 Motor (singled engined) with a horsepower rating of 420 and its gross weight was 6,483 pounds. The Army bought nine of the C-1's in 1925. There followed the C-1A (only one was ever built)

Officially the Army Air Corps designated this the first Cargo plane. It is a Douglas C-1 transport. Pilots sat in open cockpit forward and above passenger cabin. Note round windows which later would become feature of first DC-4 transport. (Army Air Corps Photo)

and the C-1B and the C-1C, all improved versions. The latter, the C-1C had a gross weight of 7,440 pounds. They had added four feet to the wing span and another 12-inches to the fuselage length. It had a top speed of about 120-mph. The Army bought 17 of these ships. They were attached to squadrons, here and there, and flown on freight-carrying missions wherever there was an emergency need. There was no parent organization, but it was evident the military minds were thinking about an aerial transport system and the need for cargo plane development. This was *before* Lindbergh's flight to Paris, and the resultant impetus and public interest this epoch flight brought about in aviation and the utility of air transportation.

The five-year period, between 1928 (one year after Lindbergh's non-stop, New York-to-Paris flight) and 1933 when the DC-1 appeared, saw amazing strides in commercial air transport. During the same period, it was evident that our military aviation was lagging behind civilian development. A closer look showed the U.S. a fifth-ranking airpower. This inadequacy was clearly demonstrated in early 1934 when FDR cancelled the civilian mail contracts and turned flying the mail over to Army fliers. There occurred a " terrible week in the sky" with army planes involved in a series of fatal crashes, the complete cancellation of all airmail, and public clamor for a sweeping investigation of what was wrong. Almost a month before the Army fliers turned the mail back to civilian operators – about the time that TWA introduced its first DC-2's into service – a War Department Board, headed by former Secretary of War Newton D. Baker, began a study of the operations of the Air Corps and its proper relation to civil aviation.

One result of the Board's study was the recommendation that the Air Corps focus more attention on the revolutionary cargo and transport planes which the airlines were flying. The Board said, in effect, that if a war should ever come, the military would need planes to carry personnel, troops and supplies, and that, maybe, some of the commercial transports could do the job. It virtually directed the Chief of the Air Corps, Maj. General Benjamin D. Foulois to give the matter "serious consideration."

"Benny" Foulois, the first military aviator (he learned to fly in the Wright Brothers' first military airplane in 1909-10) agreed with the Board's recommendation. But during the hearings, Foulois pointed out that there was a need for the development of a specialized military air transport or cargo plane. He said that the conventional passenger-carrying airliners of the era, in his opinion, were not capable of hauling heavy military material, by virtue of their design and structural details. He also revealed that the Army Air Corps had already been studying the matter for some time, and that his people had pushed the development of a project with the Fairchild Corporation to design and develop a special military cargo airplane.

The plane in question, the Fairchild XC-8, was a single-engined monoplane powered with the new Pratt & Whitney R-1340, 450-horsepower, air-cooled engine, which gave it a top speed of about 130-mph. It was, however, smaller than the Douglas C-1C, and even the improved versions, the Fairchild C-8 and the C-8A developed a lot of "bugs" which ultimately resulted in cancellation of any further orders and even the "grounding" of some of the planes. Fortunately, the idea of a specialized military cargo plane did not die.

Despite their disappointment over the Fairchild project, Foulois and his staff came up with specifications for a new type of cargo plane whose prime mission would be *"the movement of supplies and personnel to front line airdromes, and for the evacuation of sick and wounded."* The specs called for a plane with a payload of 3,000 pounds, top speed of 150-mph, cruising speed of 125-mph, a range of 500 miles. Bids for such a transport were sent out to the aircraft industry.

When Don Douglas saw the specifications, it was quite natural that he should think about a military version of the famous DC-2. Already proved in airline operation with the DC-1 and the DC-2's that were flying all over the world, Douglas saw in the DC-2 a plane that could be adapted to meet all the military requirements and exceed most of them in performance figures. He submitted a formal proposal to build twenty planes (modified DC-2's) for the Air Corps at a cost of $61,775 each, plus $20,500 for the engines.

Writing in their book *"GRAND OLD LADY – story of the DC-3,"* Colonels Carroll V. Glines and Wendell F. Moseley, described what happened, a classic word picture of government "red tape" entanglement.

"After all the bids were in," according to Glines and Moseley, "flight tests were held with the models in existence. (The Fokker Trimotor, the Ford 'Tin Goose,' a Bellanca and the latest Fairchild entry.) The Douglas DC-2, modified to meet the demands of the Air Corps, placed first with the 'aggregate figure of merit' of 786 points, while Fairchild placed second with 599.7 points. When the results of the tests were sent to Washington, the contracting officer recommended that the award of the contract be given to Douglas even though he (the contracting officer) noted that the approved 'Requirements Program for 1936' called for *the procurement of thirty-six cargo aircraft of the single-engine type.*"

"General Foulois did not agree," the authors of the GRAND OLD LADY continue. "He claimed that thirty-six, twin-engine craft could not be legally ordered. But after an opinion from the Judge Advocate General was tendered, the General (Foulois) approved an order for eighteen Douglas aircraft, to be designated the C-33."

Performance-wise, the new C-33 – a militarized version of the DC-2 – could carry a useful load of more than 6,000 pounds, fly at speeds in excess of 165 miles per hour, and for non-stop distances of over 900 miles. She was also modified to meet the Army's needs for carrying bulky cargo, and she introduced many innovations.

"Two methods of loading were provided," according to Glines and Moseley. "In one, a hoist was attached to a tripod on the top of the fuselage and the cargo was lifted into the cabin by a winch permanently attached to the forward bulkhead. In the other, tracks were used and the material was drawn into the cabin by a system of pulleys and cables.

"In addition to the cargo facilities, modifications were made which would allow the C-33 to carry nine standard Air Corps litters or twelve commercial-type passenger chairs. Thus, the original specifications for a cargo craft which could haul bulky cargo into the front line area and haul wounded men out was satisfied."

III

It was 1936 when the first C-33's were delivered to the Air Corps. The first order was for 18 planes. The major change from the commercial DC-2 was that the C-33 had a larger empennage and a special cargo door.

There were far more sweeping changes in the structure of the Army Air Corps itself than in the conversion process from the

Gen. Benjamin Foulois. (Army Air Corps Photo)

DC-2 airliner into the Army C-33. On March 1, 1935, for example, the General Headquarters Air Force was created to give the U.S. a new striking air arm. Some nine months later, on December 24, 1935, "Benny" Foulois was relieved as Chief of the Air Corps, replaced by Brig. Gen. Oscar E. Westover. Three days later Don Douglas' friend, "Hap" Arnold, promoted to Brigadier General, became the new Assistant Chief of the Army Air Corps.

There was nothing strange about the fact that Arnold, shortly after his appointment

The Douglas C-33 Military transport. It was a DC-2 with a larger rudder and tail and a cargo door. (Army Air Corps Photo)

The Douglas C-39 transport had a DC-2 fuselage, a DC-3 tail and more powerful engines than the C-33. This plane was one of those assigned to the Tenth Transport Group, Fairfield Air Depot, near Dayton, Ohio. Planes did not take on camouflage until after Pearl Harbor. (Army Air Corps Photo)

to the new job in Washington should place a phone call to Don Douglas in Santa Monica. Arnold had been reading reports in the paper about the new Douglas transport, the DST, which had made its first flight on December 17, just before he got his new assignment. He wanted to get "first hand," Douglas' own version about the DST and the DC-3 models which, the Douglas Company had announced, were coming along. Moreover, "Hap," stubborn as an army mule about his ideas for the *aerial mule,* made it one of his first official acts as Assistant Chief of the Air Corps to "stir up a lot of interest in bigger, faster transport planes."

Satisfied with the reports he got from Douglas, Arnold urged his people to study the prospect of converting the DC-3 into a military cargo plane. Douglas accepted the challenge after the Air Corps decided to go ahead with the idea, and the C-39 transport was born. Busy with a flood of orders from airlines all over the world for the DC-3's, and snarled up by change after change after change in the military specifications and requirements, the first C-39 was not delivered to the Army until 1938. But the Air Corps ordered a total of 35 of the ships which, along with the C-33's, became the nucleus for the Army's first systemitized air transport operation. They called it the Tenth Air Transport Group, organized in 1939 at Patterson Field, near Dayton, Ohio. Paradoxically, it was on this same site in 1910 (then, it was called Wilbur Wright Field) that General Arnold learned to fly. And here, more than a quarter of a century later his "dream" of a military air transport operation was born.

Patterson Field, at the time was home base for the Fairfield Air Depot, one of a whole nationwide system of Supply Depots under the Air Corps Materiel Division based a few miles down the highway at Wright Field, test center and procurement center for all Air Corps operations. The Tenth Transport Group started their own airline, linking the Fairfield Air Depot with others located in Middletown, Pa., Sacramento, California; Oregon and Utah. The "silvery aerial freighters" of the newly organized transport squadrons flew daily schedules between the depots. The C-39's got a chance to prove themselves.

Typical was what happened one day when Major Murray C. Woodbury, commanding the Tenth Transport Squadron at Patterson Field got a wire from the War Department. The message said:

"RUSH ARMY TRANSPORT PLANE WITH MEDICAL AID TO BATTLE CREEK AND PICK UP INJURED CONGRESSMAN SCHAEFFER FOR REMOVAL TO HOSPITAL IN WASHINGTON. URGENT. PROCEED AT ONCE."

By mid-morning that day, one of the Douglas C-39's equipped with a stretcher cot, carrying two orderlies and an army surgeon was enroute Dayton, Ohio to Battle Creek, Michigan. That same evening doctors at Walter Reed Hospital told reporters that the Congressman had passed through his crisis. They praised the transport squadron's "emergency airlift."

Day and night the planes flew, carrying aircraft engines, vital spare parts and key personnel, here and there to the expanding Air Corps squadrons, part of the build-up of the U.S. Air Power, geared to the imminent danger of war in Europe. The need for air transport was vital.

Then, when war did come in Europe, with Hitler's invasion of Poland, September 1, 1939, there was new emphasis placed on more and more orders for the military air transport planes. There followed a hodgepodge of requests from the War Department. The Air Corps people kept the wires hot between Washington, Dayton and the Douglas plant in Santa Monica. The Air Corps wanted a "special plane" for a hundred different "special purposes." Over-night, the *rubber airplane* was stretched and stretched again in a hundred different directions. There were so many different designations – C-41, C-42, C-48, C-47, C-49, C-50, C-53, and so many modifications, C-41A, C-47A,B.C.D., C-49A-B-C-D-E-F-J-K – that it was almost impossible to keep up with the numerical and alphabetical model designations, (see accompanying table). Yet, all were basically derived from the DC-2 and the DC-3 commercial airliners. In all, there were more than fifty different versions of the DC-twin-engined ships built for the Army Air Corps.

"It got so, as the war progressed, we found ourselves swimming in thicker alphabetical soup than during the early day's of the New Deal's WPA, NRA, PWA," remarked one Douglas official. "Even the guys who built the planes didn't know which model they were working on, but to us they were all DC-3's."

General Arnold, himself, once remarked to the author when we were sitting in the General's own "personal aircraft" a modified DC-3, in these words: "This thing is getting out of hand. We've got to settle on a standardized military transport plane."

MODEL	YEAR ORD	YEAR DEL	NUMBER BUILT	CUSTOMER	ENGINE/REMARKS
COMMERCIAL & EXPORT					
DC-1	32	33	1	TWA	2 X WRIGHT ENGINE
DC-2	33	34	130	VARIOUS	2 X WRIGHT ENGINE
DST	34	36	803 (DST and DC-3)	VARIOUS	2 X P & W OR WRIGHT ENGINE
DC-3	34	36		VARIOUS	2 X P & W OR WRIGHT ENGINE
USAF, CARGO					
XC-32	36	36	1		2 X 750 WRIGHT ENGINE; COMM. DC-2 REDESIGNATED C-32, 14 PASS.
C-32A	42	42	24		2 X 740 WRIGHT ENGINE
C-33	36	36	18		2 X 750 WRIGHT ENGINE; DC-2 LARGER TAIL & CARGO DOOR
C-34	36	37	2		2 X 750 WRIGHT ENGINE; SAME AS XC-32; REVISED INTERIOR, 14 PASS.
C-38	CV	37	(1)		2 X 930 WRIGHT ENGINE; C-33 WITH DC-3 TAIL (DC-2½)
C-39	38	39	35		2 X 975 WRIGHT ENGINE; DC-2 FUSELAGE, DC-3 TAIL, CARGO
C-41	38	39	1		2 X 1200 P & W ENGINE; SAME AS C-39 WITH ENG. CHANGE, PERSONNEL CARRIER
C-41A	40	40	1		2 X 1200 P & W ENGINE; DC-3 MOD CABIN
C-42	38	39	1		2 X 1200 WRIGHT ENGINE; SAME AS C-39 WITH ENG. CHANGE, REVISED INTERIOR
C-47-DL	41	41	953	SKYTRAIN	2 X 1200 P & W ENGINE; DC-3 WITH CARGO DOOR & FLOOR
C-47A-DL	42	42	2832	"	2 X 1200 P & W ENGINE; 24 VOLT SYSTEM
C-47A-DK	42	42	2099	"	2 X 1200 P & W ENGINE
C-47B-DL	43	43	300	"	2 X 1200 P & W ENGINE; SUPERCHARGER FOR CHINA OPERATIONS
C-47B-DK	43	43	2808	"	2 X 1200 P & W ENGINE
TC-47B-DK	43	44	133	"	2 X 1200 P & W ENGINE; TRAINERS R4D-7
XC-47C-DL	CV	43	(1)	"	2 X 1200 P & W ENGINE; TWIN FLOAT AMPHIBIAN
C-47D	CV	46		"	2 X 1200 P & W ENGINE; C-47B WITH BLOWER DELETED; SOME TO AC-47D, RC-47D, VC-
C-47E	CV		(6)	"	2 X R-2000 ENGINE; MODERNIZED C-47 FOR AIRWAY CHECK
YC-47F-DO	CV	51	(1)	"	2 X R-1820 ENGINE; REDESIGNATED FROM YC-129, TURNED OVER TO NAVY AS R4D-8
C-48	41	41	1		2 X 1200 P & W ENGINE; 21 PASS., COMM. DC-3 FROM UAL
C-48A	41	41	3		COMM. DC-3, STAFF TRANSPORT
C-48B	42	42	16		2 X 1200 P & W ENGINE; 21 PASS., COMM. DST
C-48C	42	42	16		2 X 1200 P & W ENGINE; COMM. DC-3
C-49	41	41	6		2 X 1200 WRIGHT ENGINE; COMM. DC-3, BUILT FOR TWA
C-49A	41	41	1		2 X 1200 WRIGHT ENGINE; COMM. DC-3, DOOR ON LEFT SIDE, BUILT FOR DELTA A.L.
C-49B	41	41	3		2 X 1200 WRIGHT ENGINE; COMM. DC-3, DOOR ON RIGHT SIDE, BUILT FOR E.A.L.
C-49C	41	41	2		2 X 1200 WRIGHT ENGINE; DC-3, SIDE SEATS, BUILT FOR DELTA AIR LINES
C-49D	41	41	11		2 X 1200 WRIGHT ENGINE; SAME AS C-49C, BUILT FOR EASTERN AIR LINES
C-49E	42	42	22		2 X 1100 WRIGHT ENGINE; COMM. DC-3
C-49F	42	42	9		2 X 1200 WRIGHT ENGINE; COMM. DST
C-49G	42	42	8		2 X 1200 WRIGHT ENGINE; COMM. DC-3
C-49H	42	42	19		2 X 1200 WRIGHT ENGINE; COMM. DC-3
C-49J	43	43	34		2 X 1200 WRIGHT ENGINE; COMM. DC-3

MODEL	YEAR ORD	YEAR DEL	NUMBER BUILT	NAME	ENGINE/REMARKS
C-49K	43	43	23		2 X 1200 WRIGHT ENGINE; COMM. DC-3, TROOPER INTERIOR
C-50	41	41	4		2 X 1100 WRIGHT ENGINE; COMM. DC-3, DOOR ON LEFT, BUILT FOR AMERICAN AIR LINES
C-50A	41	41	2		2 X 1100 WRIGHT ENGINE; COMM. DC-3, TROOPER INTERIOR BUILT FOR AMERICAN A.L.
C-50B	41	41	3		2 X 1100 WRIGHT ENGINE; COMM. DC-3, TROOPER INTERIOR, BUILT FOR BRANIFF AIR LINES
C-50C	41	41	1		2 X 1100 WRIGHT ENGINE; COMM. DC-3, AIR LINE INTERIOR, BUILT FOR PENN-CENTRAL A.L.
C-50D	41	41	4		2 X 1100 WRIGHT ENGINE; COMM. DC-3, TROOPER INTERIOR, BUILT FOR PENN-CENTRAL A.L.
C-51	41	41	1		2 X 1100 WRIGHT ENGINE; COMM. DC-3, TROOPER INTERIOR, BUILT FOR CANADIAN-COLONIAL A.L.
C-52	41	41	1		2 X 1200 P & W ENGINE; COMM. DC-3, TROOPER INTERIOR, BUILT FOR UNITED AIR LINES
C-52A	41	41	1		2 X 1200 P & W ENGINE; COMM. DC-3, TROOPER INTERIOR, BUILT FOR WESTERN AIR LINES
C-52B	41	41	2		2 X 1200 P & W ENGINE; COMM. DC-3, TROOPER INTERIOR, BUILT FOR UNITED AIR LINES
C-52C	41	41	1		2 X 1200 P & W ENGINE; COMM. DC-3, TROOPER INTERIOR, BUILT FOR EASTERN AIR LINES
C-53	41	41	193	SKYTROOPER	2 X 1200 P & W ENGINE
XC-53A	CV	42	(1)	"	2 X 1200 P & W ENGINE; FULL SPAN FLAPS
C-53B	42	42	8	"	2 X 1200 P & W ENGINE
C-53C	43	43	17	"	2 X 1200 P & W ENGINE
C-53D	43	43	159	"	2 X 1200 P & W ENGINE
C-68	42	42	2		2 X 1200 WRIGHT ENGINE; DC-3
XCG-17	CV	44	(1)		GLIDER; CV FROM C-47
C-117A-DK	45	45	17		2 X 1200 P & W ENGINE
C-117B-DK					2 X 1200 P & W ENGINE
C-117C	CV	53	(11)		2 X 1200 P & W ENGINE; REVISED C-47
U. S. NAVY, TRANSPORT					
R4D-1	40	42	CV	SKYTRAIN	2 X 1050 P & W ENGINE; SAME AS AIR FORCE C-47 NUMBERS BUILT INCLUDED IN C-47 SERIES TOTALS
R4D-2	41	41	CV		2 X 1050 WRIGHT ENGINE; SAME AS AIR FORCE C-49
R4D-2Z			CV		
R4D-3	41	42	CV	SKYTROOPER	SAME AS AIR FORCE C-53
R4D-4	42	42	CV	"	SAME AS AIR FORCE C-53C
4Q			CV	SKYTRAIN	
R4D-5	42	43	CV	"	SAME AS AIR FORCE C-47A
5E			CV	"	
5Q			CV	"	
5R			CV	"	
5S			CV	"	
5T			CV	"	
R4D-6	42	44	CV	"	SAME AS AIR FORCE C-47B
6E			CV	"	
6Q			CV	"	
6R			CV	"	
6S			CV	"	
6T			CV	"	
6Z			CV	"	
R4D-7	43	45	CV	"	SAME AS AIR FORCE TC-47B
R4D-8	50	51	(98)		DC-3S, CONVERTED FROM R4D

IV

The Official "PILOT TRAINING MANUAL FOR THE C-47" describes the airplane in this manner – *"The C-47, and its modified versions C-47A and C-47B etc., is a 2-engine, all metal, low-wing monoplane, used for transport of supplies, paratroop operations, glider towing, and the evacuation of wounded.*

"The airplane has two 1200-Hp Pratt & Whitney, 14-cylinder, R-1830-92, Twin Wasp engines, with Hamilton Standard hydromatic, full-feathering three-bladed propellers. The C-47B is designed for high-altitude flying. It has R-1830-9C engines, each with a 2-speed internal blower.

"The hydraulic landing gear is of the conventional type. There is a large cargo door at the left of the main cabin and a smaller cargo door on the left side of the airplane behind the pilots' compartment. The plane has two main sections.

"In the forward section is the pilots' compartment, radio operator's and navigator's compartment, and a space for cargo behind the co-pilot's seat. Radio equipment is in the forward section.

"The rear section consists of main cabin, lavatory, and spare parts compartment. The main cabin is marked off in stations for cargo loading; it has two rows of seats for troop carrying and a static line for operation with paratroops. For long-range operation it carries from two to eight auxiliary fuel tanks in the forward part of the main cabin. There are litter attachments in the main cabin for use when the airplane is employed in the evacuation of the wounded."

The airliner and the Army cargo plane were so identical in profile that you could put a C-47 without its olive drab wartime colors, along side a DC-3 and to the casual observer he'd swear they were the same airplane. Perhaps, the only big outward difference in their appearance would be the big cargo door on the side of the C-47's fuselage. And it was this "barn door-like" aperture that posed one of the big problems to Douglas engineers during the transformation from DC-3 to C-47.

"It was easy to draw the lines on the blueprints and cut a big hole in the side of the fuselage of the DC-3," Arthur Raymond recalls. "But when we discussed it with the scructures people and the aerodynamicists, they shook their heads. I remember one guy saying – *'if you cut a hole that big in that spot, get the damn thing in a little rough air and the whole tail end will fall off!'* So, we cut the hole, anyway, because that was the way the Army wanted it. The structures gang beefed up the longerons and formers and bulkheads until tests proved they could take it."

The structures people had another problem. The reason for the big door was so they could drive a jeep or two up a ramp into the cabin. Maybe, even a small field piece. If they did that, the standard floor of the DC-3 would simply collapse under the weight. There was only one answer: *beef up the floor structure.* They did that, too. Then, they put the fuselage on the scales and weighed it.

"Crazy, man, crazy!" joked one of the workman. "How can they do this to an aircraft? They took out all the soundproofing, all the plush interior, left us with a raw interior, a damn truck bed, but the thing weighs more than it did in the first place!"

It was no joke to "Doc" Oswald and his aerodynamicists and the weight-and-balance experts. "We got some pretty crazy results in the early wind tunnel tests," Oswald remembers. "But by adding here, taking off there, like sculptors playing with clay, changing a fairing shape, maybe a little difference in the rudder and the stabilizer, we finally got the stability we wanted. And, of course, it helped because we had DC-3's flying as testbeds so that we could jerry-make the changes gradually until we got the desired safety performance."

That's the way it was, one problem after another. But one by one the Douglas "gang" for the most part comprised of the men who had designed the DC-1, DC-2, and DC-3 skyships and built them, came up with the solutions. Tear out the seats and put in bucket seats along the walls. Make the Sky Pullman into a moving van interior. Find a way to make it a "locomotive" for pulling gliders. Make the engines so they could breathe at high altitudes and fly over the Himalayan mountains, "The Hump," because the Japs had closed the Burma Road. Then, undo all this and "plush-up" some of the interiors again for the Generals, as VIP transports. In some cases, the military demanded more *plush-plush* than did the airlines. But then, that was part of the contract, the C-47 had to be a Jack-of-all-Trades. Nothing like this had ever happened before.

Truly, she became the "workhorse with wings."

The first C-47 took-off on its initial flight from Clover Field in mid-1942 about five years and six months after CR Smith's first DST spread its wings over the same site. There were thousands that would follow. Most important, perhaps, was the fact that the old "workhorse or warhorse or whatever they chose to call her" was *in the works* and moving along the assembly lines, when the Japs pulled their sneak attack at Pearl Harbor.

She was ready to train the first paratroopers and organize the "Jump Squadrons" at Fort Benning, Ga., the guys who would drop behind Hitler's Fortress Europe on D-Day. She was ready to haul men and machinery and the supplies of war to bases around the world, wherever Americans were sent to make their stand for the right to be free. She blazed new sky trails across a thousand skies. If her sisterships – the DC-2's and the DC-3's changed the world geographically and ideologically – the C-47 *SECURED* it. GRAND OLD LADY, indeed! She might better be called *"America's Joan d' Arc, angel with wings."*

Let it be said for historians to record and remember: She was there to do the job because a free-enterprise system and a competitive air transport and airframe and engine industry, with its own money and its own know-how had produced an airliner, the DC-3, which stood ready to be drafted and serve her country on a moment's notice. In this one case – oh, there may be others – it was *not true* that the war gave impetus to progress. Progress was already there. The DC-ships were its shining symbol.

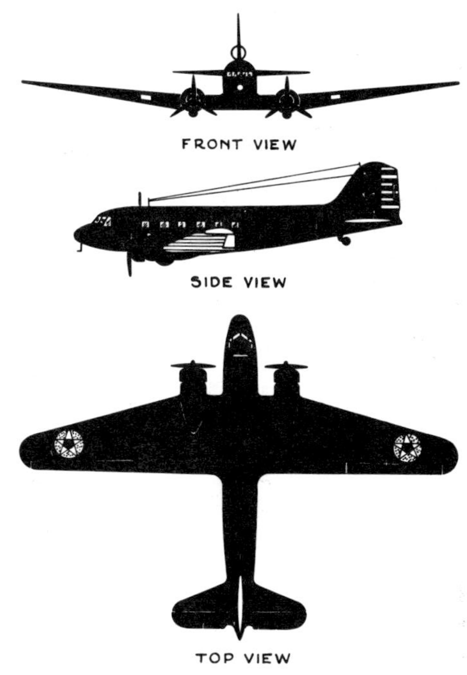

Planview C-38, C-39, C-41, C-41A, C-42. (Army Air Corps Photo)

V

The impact on the Douglas Aircraft Company was phenomenal. Douglas Santa Monica was bursting at the walls producing the first mass order of C-39 transports. Quite naturally, when the Army decided on the standardized C-47, there wasn't enough room. One plant couldn't do the job. The C-47 gave birth to a new factory addition at the Douglas Long Beach plant

The C-47 "Skytrain." It was a DC-3 with large cargo door and beefed-up floor. Distinguishing feature is navigator's dome on top of fuselage. (Army Air Corps Photo)

Altogether in one configuration or another there were more than ten thousand military versions of the DC-3 built. This was scene at Douglas plant in Oklahoma City during peak production period. (Douglas Aircraft Co. Photo)

and a whole new factory at Oklahoma City.

BUSINESS WEEK magazine in its April 3, 1943 issue would report – *"Barely a year after the project was O.K'd by the Army and only five months after tooling up began, completely assembled C-47 ("Skytrains") cargo planes are rolling out of the Douglas Aircraft Company's big new plant near Oklahoma City. . . . Size of the building can only be indicated by the fact that there are nearly two miles of double brick wall, especially insulated for air conditioning. White cement floors in working areas help miles of fluorescent lights to keep illumination above a 55-foot candle level."*

"Faced with a dearth of experienced mechanics in the Oklahoma area, which until a few months ago had no industrial plant employing more than 2,000 workers," BUSINESS WEEK continues, "Douglas sought nonconfusing simplicity for its green crew – Not only in plant lay out, but also in functioning. Every machine and assembly operation is simplified. Parts bear easily understandable names rather than numbers. Work is delivered to the worker either by mechanical conveyors or by stock girls."

A Douglas Company press release datelined LONG BEACH, CALIFORNIA, June 19, 1940 told the other side of the story. *"With dedication of a $12,000,000 defense plant and the simultaneous groundbreaking ceremony for a $12,619,000 addition,"* said the release, *"this city today celebrated acquisition of an aircraft factory soon to be acknowledged the greatest in this or any other country. . . .*

"Already in production for several months on parts and assemblies, the Douglas company's Long Beach plant now employs 7,000 men and women with personnel rapidly increasing toward the scheduled peak, when 30,000 will be producing attack-bombers, military transports (C-47's and C-54's) and four-engine bombers at a record rate."

Describing a high-point of the celebration, the Douglas release added – *"Overhead and adding its thunderous crescendo to the tumult of cheering below roared the world's mightiest warplane, the Douglas B-19 bomber which appropriately had timed a routine acceptance test flight by the Army Air Corps to coincide with this precisely climatic moment."*

With the mass orders for the C-47, Douglas suddenly found himself producing more planes for the military than he had ever dreamed of. For more than a decade the Douglas Aircraft Company would be the leading manufacturer of both commercial airliners, military transports and bombers.

In the process, it can be said that the DC-ships, particularly the C-47, led to new production techniques, assembly-line operations, that would change the whole complexion of the aircraft industry. It marked the beginning of an economic change. The day would come when the projected growth of the Aerospace Industry would employ more people than any other work force.

It was really, however, the mass orders for the C-47 that started this industrial revolution.

Her record in history on that point alone, would be sufficient to fill volumes.

But the DC-ships were destined to play many other roles. In tribute to their versatility and ruggedness, one high-ranking Air Force General, after returning safely to his base in a C-47 which had been badly shot up turned to his aide with a "glad-to-be-alive" look on his face.

It happened in England and the General remarked – "This, by God, is an *airplane.* All the rest of the damn things are just machines."

United Air Lines started the first scheduled all-cargo plane service in the nation late in 1940. Before Pearl Harbor, planes were called on for big airlift missions. UAL learned a lot about air cargo operations that was helpful in wartime operations. (United Air Lines Photo)

Chapter 13

The Four Far Corners

The Douglas DC-2's and DC-3's, wearing the insignia of the nation's airlines went on war emergency status long before their military counterparts, the C-47's, were even out of the factory jigs. The moment Hitler marched into Poland in September, 1939, America's wings for commerce became wings for defense.

Almost immediately, the airlines themselves imposed a defense priority system. Who is there among veteran air travelers, for instance, that does not remember being "bumped" by some star-shouldered general, production trouble-shooter, scientist or serviceman? Those were the days when rows of seats up front in the old DC-3s were "blocked off," and SECRET cargos rode under the canvas-covered tie-downs. The "Arsenal of Democracy" was dependent upon its aerial lifeline.

A United Air Lines' converted cargoliner made headlines early in 1941 when it carried a bulky, half-ton Diesel engine crankshaft from Chicago to San Francisco. It was bound for Pearl Harbor. For the first time, such a huge piece of machinery had moved by air.

On another cargo flight, a DC-3 flew a complete telephone exchange from Chicago to a big magnesium plant near Las Vegas, Nevada. It was to be the nucleus for a vital communications center for Los Alamos, White Sands and the "Manhattan Project."

At Fort St. John, a vital outpost in Alaska, they needed a saw mill to build barracks for men working on the Alcan Highway, part of America's defense logistic's plans. A commercial cargo DC-3 plane flew in the whole unit. When fire destroyed the infirmary at Nome, Alaska – two DC-3 airliners flew in a 26-bed hospital complete with X-ray equipment, hypodermic needles and rubber gloves. The shipment arrived 48 hours after the request came over the teletype.

In a move designed to strengthen our air defense along the Pacific, after Jap subs had been sighted too close in American waters, the Air Corps needed pursuit planes

Pan American World Airways' loading dock for the Pacific Clipper ships was a busy place in 1939-40. This was typical scene at Treasure Island, near San Francisco, hopping-off spot for the Orient. Pacific (China) Clippers were vital link with our bases in Honolulu and the Philippines. (Pan American World Airways Photo)

In 1939 the Pan American World Airways "Atlantic Clipper" was also a vital link with England and all of Europe not yet torn apart by Hitler wolves. Clippers carried top priority cargoes. Crews were major asset in training pilots on four-engined equipment and in flying long over-water routes. They had pioneered most of routes around the world, by far the most experienced in over-water flying. (Pan American World Airways Photo)

in a hurry. Curtiss P-40s, the only line fighter planes we had at that time, were flown over the Rockies in United Air Lines' cargo-liners. The tiny pursuit fuselages rode inside the DC-3's bellies while the wings were slung in special brackets underneath. Planes carrying planes; nobody ever heard of it before!

When General Claire Chennault's American Volunteer Group (AVGs), the "Flying Tigers," needed tires, American Airlines' *Flagships* flew 20,000 pounds of rubber from New York to Los Angeles. There, the shipment was transferred to Pan American's Boeing flying boats, – the "Clipper Ships" – and flown across the Pacific to the China bases.

There was no official declaration of war, but we were in it. Commercial air transport was pioneering a whole new pattern in logistics. The airlines were ready when the nation was thrust into the conflict on that day of infamy, December 7, 1941. That meant the DC-3s were ready, for at the time the DC-skyships were virtually standard equipment on all U. S. air carrier operations. The Douglas C-32's, C-33s, and C-39s, first of the Army Air Corps modified DC-2's and DC-3's were also ready – the back-bone of the fledgling Army air transport system. Moreover, the moblization plan, carefully worked out in advance by the airlines and the military, had been largely based on the performance capabilities of the Douglas commercial skyliners.

Overnight, more than half of the commercial airlines' fleet of 350 DC-2s and DC-3s became the nucleus of the Army Air Transport Command (ATC) and the Navy Air Transport Service (NATS) whose routes were to stretch around the world. The Military Airlift Command (MAC) – an outgrowth of ATC and NATS – would become the largest and longest airline in the world. It was born with the DC-3 which exchanged its silver wings for the olive drab colors; out of mufti into uniform.

It was a big question mark in the minds of some military authorities as to whether the DC-3 could handle the global job which had to be done. These were landplanes, the skeptics said, and their payloads were

American DC-3's shortly after Pearl Harbor engaged in mass troop movement to South America, where Nazi take-over threat seemed imminent. (American Airlines Photo)

limited by CAA peacetime regulations to 5,000 pounds on long hops, (600-700 miles) whereas under existing beliefs, the length of our war supply lines called for giant flying boats. The overwhelming size of the task demanded super transports.

The DC-3s were given the job in the beginning because they were the only transports that were being manufactured in large quantities. They immediately proved themselves startlingly competent. In the hands of Air Transport Command and commercial airline pilots, they demonstrated that they could carry more than twice the load permitted them by Civil Air Regulations, so great was the margin of safety built into them.

II

The first major action with the DC-3 occurred on Sunday, December 14, 1941. Records of the Air Transport Association of America, the trade group representing the scheduled airlines, reveal that morning, the War Department called the ATA for assistance in the air movement of certain special troops. There was threat of enemy action in South America.

Colonel Edgar S. Gorrell, ATA President and the man, who is credited with having drawn up the airlines' mobilization plans, got his orders direct from the War Department. Immediately, he teletyped instructions to the airlines to put ATA's plan into effect. A lot depended on what happened. Gorrell had managed to convince General Arnold, Chief of the Air Forces and President Roosevelt, that ATA's member airlines could operate better under private management; that they could best serve their country without being completely taken over by military control. It was an unprecedented blow struck for the free-enterprise system. FDR reportedly had drawn up an executive order giving the airlines to the military to run the whole

Pan American World Airways DC-3's flying in Latin America and South America were credited with holding together the economic structure of our southern neighbors. Air Transport was certainly the vital tool for trade and commerce. (Pan American World Airways Photo)

air transport operation. Gorrell had talked him out of it. Now, this was the supreme test. If the carriers couldn't come through, Roosevelt would draft them into the service lock, stock and management.

According to the ATA, minutes after the War Department request was received, pilots in the air were ordered to land their planes, discharge their passengers, refuel, and fly to secret assembly points. The airliners were on the ground at specified Army posts to pick up the troops – in some cases – *before* the troops themselves were ready to disembark.

The mass troop movement by air involved some twenty DC-3's most of them from C. R. Smith's big fleet of American Airlines' *Flagships*. The planes flew southward over the Carribean to hot spots in Brazil. True, the force was small, but the DC-3 helped put a keen, sharp edge on the Monroe Doctrine. We meant business; that no foreign country should get a foothold in the Western Hemisphere. The effect was a discouragement – the truth, a "cleaning up" – of the pro-Nazi activities in the South American countries.

The records also show that long previous to our entry into the war Pan American World Airways employed DC-3s, to break the hold that Axis airlines held on the economic life of the South American continent, thus helping the State Department to ally these nations with the U. S. Subsequently, these same planes flew a total of more than 8,000,000 plane miles in Latin America, and between these countries and the United States, supplementing normally inadequate rail facilities and replacing war-halted surface transport insofar as vital commodities were concerned. The effect was to strengthen the economic structure of our southern neighbors.

Many claim that the lightning-swift demonstration of troop mobility made possible by air transport saved the day in South America. The airlines, for the most part, were able to hang onto the reins of the U. S. Scheduled Air Transport System, a factor that was to put America far ahead in air transport operations in the post-war era. The military-airline team proved its own logic.

III

Within a month after the Brazil troop movement, another carrier, Northeast Airlines, was to make history with a C-39 aircraft. With Northeast's Vice President Operations, Milton H. Anderson, and Frank C. Barker, Superintendent of Communications aboard, the plane, piloted by airline Captains Hanzen Bean and Donald H. Stuart blazed the trail north from Presque Isle, Maine to Gander, Newfoundland. "Purpose of the flight," Anderson said, "was to determine the feasibility of a scheduled airline route to Labrador and

Newfoundland – the first leg of the North Atlantic aerial lifeline to Great Britain."

The first survey flight was made on January 11, 1942. By Valentine's Day, the line was operating over the route in regular scheduled operations. Flying in blinding snow storms, with temperatures far below zero, over uncharted wilderness, the planes carried generators, quonset huts, radio and navigational aids and supplies to establish the northern bases. Such strange places as Mocton, New Brunswick, Stephenville, Goose Bay, Gander began to appear on the airline map. The latter was to become one of the biggest and busiest air gateways in the world.

While DC-ships shuttled back and forth with men and equipment to activate the initial way stops, others stretched the line farther north and eastward. In one of the new C-53's, Anderson and Captain Alva V. R. Marsh, Northeast's Operations Manager, Radio Operator Stewart and Flight Mechanic Gabry, on April 24, 1942 made the first flight to Narssassuak (Bluie West 1) on the east coast of Greenland. This flight, made with the airplane overloaded – 4,000 pounds beyond its original design specifications – proved the DC-3 type was capable of flying long overwater hops. Moreover, navigational and operational procedures that were pioneered during these stages became the "Bible" of all farther north operations. It is noteworthy, too, that the plane was almost shot down by ground fire from American gunners because our *own* troops in the area had not been notified of a "commercial airliner" operating in the lower Arctic regions.

Later, in May, Northeast pilots flew their DC-3 to Iceland, landing at Kalkadadarnes and Reykjavik, adding another 750-mile segment to the Atlantic crossing. Then, on the Fourth of July, 1942, they flew on to Stornoway and Prestwick, Scotland. In the belly of the ship was a complete radio range station. Set up under trying conditions and adverse weather it made Stornoway a vital air link in the trans-ocean chain.

The whole operation was the beginning of the Air Transport Command's North Atlantic Division whose planes at the peak of the war, were shuttling back and forth over the northern route, one every four minutes. It is significant, too, that the man who headed up this ATC operation was General Lawrence G. Fritz, one-time TWA Operations Chief, and one of the first line pilots to check out in the DC-1. Man and machine were proving up to the supreme test.

After the war, Larry Fritz summed up the record of the DC-ships with these words of praise – "It was a magnificent job, setting up and operating bases in Newfoundland, Labrador, Greenland and Iceland with the twin-engined aircraft. . . . It taught us invaluable lessons in winterization of planes and engines. . . . At the same time, it put us far ahead in the development of navigation aids and weather services. . . . Finally, we reached a point where the airways' aids across the North Atlantic were better than those over the U. S."

IV

"Who holds Alaska, holds the world!" These prophetic words of General "Billy" Mitchell must have been ringing in the ears of General Robert Olds, Commanding General of the Air Ferrying Command, when he directed Northwest Orient Airlines, under contract to the military, to establish a new air route to Alaska.

Maj. Gen. Lawrence C. Fritz. (USAF Photo)

Typical of the flight crews of United Air Lines; who chalked up more than five million miles of flying in Alaska for the Air Transport Command in World War II, is this group (left to right) Flight Radio Operator J. B. Smithers, First Officer M. A. Christensen and Captain Hugh Coleman. (United Air Lines Photo)

UAL pilots made friends wherever they flew. Ask Capt. Robert Ashley, one of United's Alaskan pioneers, shown here with a "friendly native." Huskies, once the prime mover via dogsled in the far north were joined by the DC-3 which put wings on things. Note the Air Transport Command (ATC) insignia in background. ATC simply took over part of airline fleet in beginning of crisis. (United Air Lines Photo)

About the same time that Anderson, Bean and Stuart in their C-39 aircraft were winging out from Presque Isle to Newfoundland, another special, winterized DC-3 Northwest airliner, was roaring northward from Minneapolis - St. Paul heading for Fairbanks, Alaska. By March 29, 1942 they were flying daily operations Stateside to America's far north territorial possession.

Names like Grand Prairie, Fort St. John, Fort Nelson, Watson Lake and White Horse in Canada, Northway, Big Delta in Alaska, suddenly became important way stations on the new Alcan Airway. Before the summer was out, United Air Lines' crews, flying DC-3s had pioneered another route from Patterson Field, near Dayton, Ohio to Anchorage, Alaska. Meanwhile, Western Airlines' and Pan American DC-3's had opened a coastal airway from Seattle to Fairbanks, Anchorage and Juneau.

With the Japs increasing their activities in Aleutian Island waters, the Douglas planes extended the routes to bases on Kiska, Attu, Adak, Agattu. The once-frozen land of the north serviced only by small planes and the "Bush Pilot" operators, became a busy aerial supply route. Navy versions of the DC-3, the first of the R4D's operating with newly born Naval Air Transport (NATS) squadrons, used the Douglas transports to service fleet units building up in the area.

It was D. W. "Tommy" Tomlinson, he who helped father the DC-1 into the sky, in Navy blues as a Commander, who helped in the formation of the NATS organization and directed many of its activities. "If there hadn't been any DC-2's and DC-3's," Tommy declared, "there wouldn't have been a NATS in the early days of the war when fleet supply by air was so vital to survival. It was like being able to go to the ship's store and buy 'air transport' right off the shelf – ready-made and a capable performer. No individual could be more proud than I was of having been a part of the early development of the DC-1 which made it possible to have such a utility weapon in stock when it was needed most."

Of the Alaskan-Aleutian flying operations, Tomlinson recalls – "It was a challenge that put the planes to supreme tests. The cold and the salt-water atmosphere played strange tricks with engines, tires, metal skin and frame, hydraulic lines, brakes and other mechanical features. Oil became thick as molasses. Rubber fittings

Eastern Airlines' crews in planes of THE GREAT SILVER FLEET (mostly DC-3's) blazed the trail across the Caribbean to complete first leg of Air Transport Command's south Atlantic operation. (Douglas Aircraft Co. Photo)

crystallized. Grease froze in wheel bearings. Windshields iced up and frosted over. We learned the hard way, by guess and by God, how to winterize the machines for adaptation to the sometimes 40 and 50-degree below zero temperatures. The DC-ships came through with flying colors. There never was a more rugged airplane built and they proved it themselves."

When the Japs bombed Dutch Harbor, it was the DC-2 and DC-3, many of them yanked off the regular domestic airline schedules and still in gleaming silver paint, that flew troops, ammunition, weapons and serums to bolster the defenses of the islands whose occupation by the Japanese might have changed the whole course of the war.

The Navy, in an official "well-done" statement after the Japs gave up in the Aleutians said – "Retaking of the Aleutians would have been postponed for months if Air Transport had not been able to fly in men and cargo quickly and in great quantities."

V

The same thing happened in Africa. The miracle was that the same planes, those that were called upon to fly in the Arctic cold were able to fly on a moment's notice in the fiery furnace of the desert. Dust, and storms, tropical fungi tried to ground them, but the planes flew on. It was a tribute to engineering, design, construction of the DC-ships written indelibly in the annals of man's conquest of the sky.

While Northeast's DC-3's were pioneering the "Ice Berg" route (Newfoundland, Labrador, Greenland, Iceland, Scotland) their sister ships of Eastern Airlines' *Great Silver Fleet* were heading south out of Miami across the Caribbean to Trinidad via Borinquen Field, Puerto Rico and Port-au-Prince, Haiti, the first leg of the Air Transport Command's South Atlantic Route. On May 1, 1942, regular Transport service between Miami and Trinidad was inaugurated with the converted-to-cargo airliners. The new airline proved Uncle Sam's answer to the threat of the Axis submarines, thicker than porpoises in the Caribbean waters.

Within a month, the ships opened up a new gateway to South America, extending the run from Trinidad over the jungles and crocodile-infested rivers to Georgetown, British Guiana, thence southward down the coastline to Belem, Brazil and on to Natal, the hopping off point to Africa. In the cargo-laden fuselages of the twin-engined Douglas "luxury liners" was a new kind of payload – rugged, heavy machinery and equipment necessary for cutting runways out of the dense jungles in setting up vital communications stations. Sometimes, the ships flew 16-18 hours a day — stopping only for fuel and change of crews — over the 4,000-mile finger from Miami to Natal.

This was just the beginning.

Some 2700 miles eastward was the small Gold Coast town of Accra, Africa. Already it was being girded as a vital supply point for the planned African campaign. With the South Atlantic infested with Hitler "Wolf Pack" subs daily taking a heavy toll of shipping, the air route was a priority measure. Short-range bombers and fighters had to fly across. But the distance was too great unless. . . .

There was no answer. About half-way across, some 1400 miles from Natal was a barren piece of land, 34 square miles in total area — Ascension Island, discovered by Portuguese, Joao de Nova in 1501 on Ascension Day. And rising up in the center of the rock was Green Mountain, whose flat-top could be made into an airstrip, an anchored air base smack in the middle of the South Atlantic.

Toward this tiny dot, eight hours out from Natal, in the summer of 1943 headed Eastern Airlines' survey crews in specially-fitted DC-cargo ships. The materials and machinery they needed to make the base liveable and operable they brought along with them. Before the year was out hundreds of fighters and bombers were hopping across the Atlantic in a steady stream. The "Rock" became as important to the over-all war effort as the Rock of Gilbralter was in another era. The DC-ships stopped there only long enough to put the place on the map, roaring off the Ascension runway toward the Dark Continent and Accra to complete the 8,000 mile Miami-to-Africa airline.

There to meet the planes as they landed on African soil was George Strompl, who was manager of "Douglas Town" a maintenance base established at Gura. Strompl had volunteered for the job which was so secret that even he referred to it only as "Project 19," a joint Douglas/military operation. By the end of 1942 the base was employing several thousand natives, our own military personnel and hundreds of Douglas workers, who as civilians, had volunteered for the overseas positions. It became the major overhaul base for fighters and bombers.

"It was here that we began to see the true character of the fabulous DC-1 which ten years before was merely a few lines on paper and metal image in the minds of Jack Frye and the boss," Strompl recalls. "When we saw the first of her decendants, the DC-3s come in, after winging their way across the vast stretches of open Atlantic, it made our hearts swell with pride. The 'rubber airplane' was stretching itself performance-wise far beyond its original design specifications. We actually did things with the ships that we never put into the reports because the gang back in Santa Monica would think we were just plain nuts."

The work done at "Douglas Town" was credited by Field Marshall Montgomery as one of the most vital assets contributing to the turning of the tide that kicked Rommel out of Africa.

"The chain of fields from Miami to Natal," the General said, "contributed directly to the winning of the North African Campaign."

Equally important, it was this route that let the DC-3s, C-47s and Navy R4Ds gird the earth to turn up in China, Burma, Australia, and the Philippines in the early days of the war. They also made possible Pan American's stupendous feat of straddling the African continent with a chain of airfields leading to the Mediterranean and the Orient. With the completion of the new aerial highway, the planes flew daily routine hops from North America to Egypt, Persia and India.

VI

The greatest achievement of the DC-ships, however, was lifting the Burma Road high into the sky and maintaining an "Open Door" policy with Free China in the days when the Japs had cut off all ground communications.

In this moment of glory, the wing joined the wheel and the sail as a dominant force in changing history and geography. Even the great towering peaks of the Himalayas, perhaps, the most treacherous chain of mountains in the world, could not shackle these man-made wings. Before the war

When the DC-ships started turning up in China-Burma area they found CNAC planes were already operating in this region. This DC-2 belonging to Chinese National Aviation Corporation shows how Chinese coolies worked to refuel planes. Sometimes the DC-planes flew in their own aviation gasoline to become "flying tankers."
(Pan American World Airways Photo)

ended, cargo by air was to traverse over the high road in a greater volume by far than ever before had moved over the historic Burma Road by surface transport.

"Flying the Hump" was spectacular in its accomplishment, but even more so in its effectiveness in changing military strategy and speeding the course of victory.

Actually the route was pioneered before Pearl Harbor by the China National Aviation Corporation (a Pan American World Airways-Chinese Government operation) DC-2's and DC-3's which flew from Hong Kong to Chungking, China's provisional capital, then south to Rangoon and Calcutta. The mainline airway over the backbone of the Himalayas, however, was from Assam in northeast India to Chungking. There is little argument that this is the most dangerous stretch of flying weather and terrain found anywhere in the world.

Towering, jagged slabs of rock each like fingers of death up to heights of 25,000 feet. Below, steaming, impregnable jungles cover the valleys, thousands of square miles of uncharted and unexplored territory. Monsoons come in torrential downpours making ground operations almost as dangerous and impossible as air operations.

This CNAC aircraft, a DC-3, was one of first to pioneer "flying the hump." It flew regular scheduled service from Hong Kong to Chungking, China's provisional capital, then south to Rangoon and Calcutta. CNAC was flying over the humpback of the treacherous Himalayas long before outbreak of World War II—proof that the airlines had blazed the skytrails to the four corners and the then top of the world.
(Pan American World Airways Photo)

And the weather generally is variable, *usually from bad to worse.* Yet, into the face of these hazardous conditions, the DC-3's took off, climbed above the peaks, rode out the storms, maintained their schedules.

Later joined by their sister ships, the C-47's of the China-India-Burma section of the Air Transport command, the Curtiss-Wright C-46's and the much larger Douglas C-54 *Skymasters*, the operation grew to 5,000 flights a month; 44,000 tons of supplies.

This airlift, alone, is credited with supporting General Stilwell's campaign in Burma and the actions of Chennault's Fourteenth Air Force. More important, it carried the bulk of the initial materials and men which made possible the China bases for the big B-29 *Superfortresses* that struck the knock-out blow at Nippon's heart.

VII

The global war was still young, but already the DC-3 and her military family had proved to be the implements which man used to change all previous geography of the globe. The DC-ships shrunk great oceans to the size of mere lakes. They leaped over the highest mountain peaks, over the steaming jungles, across the polar wastes to bring transportation and contact to cities and towns that heretofore were isolated from the outside world. Though on war missions, they were blazing the commercial air routes that gave us a new concept in trade and changed the way men think, and act and learn to live together.

In the process, they put a new word in the dictionary that was to change military planners' minds about logistics for all time to come. That word is AIRLIFT. Its import is that of a whole new force as vital to the waging of modern war as the weapons themselves.

Flying the new world air routes which they pioneered, the DC-ships wrote a new chapter in transportation history in the movement of people and things.

Anything and everything moved by air. Dynamite, eggs, war dogs, gold bullion. Beetles from the Fiji Islands to fight other beetles which were destroying war crops of hemp in the Honduras. All went into the cargo holds of the aerial freighters.

Growth of the Air Transport Command saw bigger planes join the DC-3 in China. Here is one of first Curtiss C-46 "Commandos" which greatly increased airlift capacity during Burma Road crisis. (USAF Photo)

It didn't matter the size. When a newly established island air base needed big gasoline trucks, they cut the tank trucks up in sections, piled them into the planes' fuselages, flew them in, and then welded them together again at the destination. They did the same thing with heavy road-building machinery that was used to carve out airstrips in once impregnable jungles so the bigger four-engined planes could follow.

Talking to the joint Air Transport Users Conference meeting in Washington, in July, 1945, Colonel James W. Aston gave ample testimony to the amount and variety of cargo carried. "During the peak of operations," he said, "we were flying 6,000 tons of cargo a day. This is almost three tons per mile flown. This cargo has been limited to 'valuable freight,' certainly, but not to 'light freight,' nor has it been limited to type. The planes carried anything which, whole or in part, can be put through the big cargo doors, and there are few items short of the heaviest machinery frames that cannot thus be handled."

In his book "Air Transport At War," Reginald M. Cleveland draws a vivid word picture of the kinds of cargo that moved by air.

"The holds of the cargo ships became, indeed, an odd miscellany of items. . . . Panama hats, baby chicks, and 100,000 false teeth were flown by Pan American Grace Airways DC-2's converted into flying box cars over the 1,678-mile route from Balboa, Canal Zone to Lima, Peru. . . . Insecticide, penicillin, serums, vaccines, medicines, sunglasses, plastics, raw fish, dynamo parts, textiles, mining machinery and tools were also among the articles to take wing on this long trek.

"Another odd passenger was a cow transported by a crew to a remote base along the coast of the Indian Ocean to provide fresh milk for personnel stationed there. Among top priority passengers were two sheepherders, flown to an airbase in Scotland. They had been required to keep wandering sheep off the runways that had been built across sheep ranch feeding grounds."

It was General Harold L. George, war-

Lt. General Harold L. George. (USAF Photo)

time commanding general of the Global Air Transport Command, however, who translated all of this into meaning and impact.

"There is evidence," General George said, "that air transport so remarkably developed by this war, can become the medium of mutual understanding for all nations when peace comes. Distances between the world's capitals are measured now in hours. The leaders of nations can meet face to face and settle their differences by personal arbitration rather than by long-range negotiations."

It would be thus from this time forward, the meetings of Churchill and Roosevelt, Truman and Stalin, Eisenhower and Krushchev – Yalta, Potsdam, Washington – they would change the course of history.

Air transportation introduced a new kind of statesmanship. It has been said that DC stands for "*Diplomatic Convenience.*

In wartime, it stood for *Direct Contact* with the enemy and the DC-3 or its counterpart, the C-47, was in the skies over every front.

There was thunder aloft as the C-47's of the Troop Carrier Air Division, 12th Air Force, laden with tough and well-trained paratroopers started across the channel to hit the enemy behind the lines in France. The transports kept coming and coming in an endless stream. On D-Day in 1944, more than a thousand "Gooney Birds" were there. (Official USAF Photo)

Chapter 14

Cry Of The "Gooney Bird"

On June 6, 1944, Don Douglas along with millions of other Americans was listening to radio reports from war correspondents on the beaches at Normandy with the first wave of the Allied invasion armies. It was D-Day. The Allies were striking at Hitler's continental fortress.

"The sky is darkened with swarms of cargo planes, and the roar of their motors is like the thunder of the war gods," Douglas heard CBS reporter Charles Collingswood describe the action.

"The steady stream of transports keeps coming and coming and coming in an endless train," Collingswood continued. "The awe of the thing actually has stopped gunfire and fighting in some sectors. . . Men look skyward with unbelieving eyes.

"With their stripped-down interiors and special attachments on the fuselage and wings, some of the planes are carrying jeeps, small cannons, ammunition and spare parts for infantry tanks . . . Others, as tow-planes are pulling one, and sometimes, two troop-carrying gliders."

Altogether, more than 1,000 DC-3's and C-47's, flying at gross weights nobody ever dreamed of and performing unbelievable tasks, took part in this greatest airlift of all time. In the first 50 hours, when the fighting was the most fierce and the beach-head faced its do-or-die test, the planes carried more than 20,000 paratroopers and their weapons of war across the English channel.

William Randolph Hearst, Jr., who saw the first of the planes take off from their bases in England, wrote in an editorial — "I am certain this type of plane will go down in history as one of the greatest planes of the war!"

In her war role the DC-3 had many names. The British named her the *Dak* or *Dakota*. The Russians, who had concluded a licensing agreement to manufac-

The "Skytrains," C-47's, towing troop-carrying gliders come in low over the Normandy coast on D-Day. White stripes on wings and fuselage identified planes as part of invasion force. (Official USAF Photo)

ture the DC-3 in the Soviet, also had a name for it – the *Ilyushin IL-2*. Our own GI's called it the *Doug, Old Fatso*. Officially, she was designated the C-47 by the Air Force. The Navy called its version, the R4D. More popularly, she was known as the *Skytrain* or the *Skytrooper*.

But to the thousands of pilots who flew her, and to the hundreds of thousands of servicemen who rode in bench-like bucket seats for which the wartime models were famous, the plane was, and probably always will be affectionately called – *"The Gooney Bird."*

There are tall tales of how she got that name. Some say it originated in the South Pacific on the small atolls where the real-life Gooney Bird (a king-size seagull-like specie) makes its home. When the twin-engined Douglas' appeared overhead, they were the first metallic birds to be seen in the skies over some of these isolated islands. It was natural they should be given the nick-name.

Then, there is the explanation that comes from an Air Force Colonel, an intellectual type, who claims the plane's cognomen was derived from the word *goon* which Webster defines as a "stupid person." The Colonel defends himself, thusly – "We called them the *Gooney Birds* because these planes were just plain stupid. They didn't know they couldn't do the things they did!"

Where she got the name *"Gooney Bird"* will probably forever be argued about by the men who flew her. There are many con-

The C-47's carried an army to Europe, their interiors loaded with paratroopers and their equipment. This is one of the C-47 "Skytrooper" versions. She had bench-like, metal bucket seats along each side. Note "girlie" pictures on forward bulkhead. (U.S. Army Photo)

The Big Drop. On D-Day the sky blossomed with parachutes as an invading army descended to the countryside of southern France. This particular action took place somewhere between Nice and Marseilles, part of "Operation Uppercut." (Official USAF Photo)

Russians were given some C-47's under Lend-Lease agreement. They also got parts and tooling, but never acknowledged that planes were U.S.-built. Designated their version the IL-2, claimed it was built in Russia. Later IL-2 became commercial airliner in Russia and was for a long time backbone of Soviet air transport. Douglas never received any royalties. (USAF Photo)

flicting stories. Crosby Maynard of the Douglas PR staff for years tried to pin down the first instance where the C-47 was called a *"Gooney Bird,"* and one source he turned up certainly pre-dates the popular claim that the nickname came into being during the war years.

According to Crosby, he received a letter from Colonel Ted Graff, a veteran of the Tenth Transport Group organized at Patterson Field in 1939 (See Chapter Twelve) who claims they called the C-39 transports *"Gooney Birds"* and originated the name. The first C-47 hadn't even been built yet.

The author, who did one of the first stories for the Dayton Daily News about the Tenth Transport Group, working with Ted Graff (then a captain), can corroborate this: The "gang" at Dayton who flew the first C-39 transports, memory recalls, often referred to their charges as *"Goonies."* It seens unlikely anyone before them ever used the name. There were damn few C-39's in the spring of 1939.

Before the war was over, the Bunyanesque tales about the DC-3 and her sister ships began to pour in from the four far corners. Pilots, who are famous for exaggerated yarns, found themselves unable to top some of the stranger-than-fiction exploits.

Whenever possible, Douglas engineers and tech representatives who were everywhere, checked the stories, and the company's files are jammed with documentation of the accomplishments of the *Gooney Bird.* Some of the reports were so fantastic and unbelievable that even the men who had designed and built the ships shook their heads. Impossible! "No airplane could have done that, not even ours!" became an oft-repeated remark around the birthplace of the DC-3 in Santa Monica.

Yet, one story after another about the DC-ships came from all over the world as the war progressed.

II

On April 18, 1942 sixteen Mitchell bombers (B-25's) loaded with 500 pound bombs took off from the decks of the U.S. Aircraft carrier *Hornet* afloat some 688 miles eastward from Tokyo, Japan. Within a few hours the planes, led by famous Army flier James H. ("Jimmy") Doolittle, then a Lieutenant Colonel on special duty, roared over the Japanese capital city and gave the Japs a taste of Pearl Harbor "surprise" tactics.

The raid, designed primarily to boost American morale, was considered an epochal success despite the fact that all of the planes but one crash-landed somewhere in China. (The one, landed near Vladivostok, Russia; the crew escaped to Iran, but the plane was never returned.) Of

Captain Charles L. Sharp of Fort Worth was pilot of CNAC plane which flew Jimmy Doolittle out of China after famous Tokyo raid. (Pan American World Airways Photo)

the eighty pilots and crewmen who took part in the sortie, eight were captured off the China coast, three were shot, others were imprisoned. Many of the airmen, however, made their way back safely with the help of the Chinese underground.

One of those who got out was Doolittle. "I wouldn't have made it though, if it hadn't been for one of the DC-3's," the famous flier confided to Don Douglas at a later date.

It was true. Doolittle had made it past the Japs and out of China to an airfield in Burma. He managed to get aboard the last China National Airways Corporation (CNAC) DC-3 out of Burma before the Japs took over. "That was some trip," Doolittle relates, "There were 75 passengers on that airplane including one damn tired, silver-leafed Colonel named Doolittle.

"When I saw that many persons being loaded into the ship I wouldn't have given a plugged nickel that we would get off the ground. The fact is, I told Captain Sharp, the pilot, that if I had any sense I'd walk home."

According to Captain Charles L. Sharp, of Fort Worth, Texas, who at the time was CNAC's Operations Manager in the area, this is how they jammed that many bodies into the DC-3 normally designed to carry a maximum of 21 passengers – "The side arms of the seats were removed allowing three adults to sit in a double seat, a total of 28. Then, there were 22 kids who sat on the laps of the seated passengers. That made a total of *fifty!* Four native Indians rode in the waist cargo bin and six others in the forward mail compartment, leaving 14 standing in the aisle."

The story of pilots, like Sharp, and what they did is without parallel for courage and selflessness. Civilians all, they waged a battle for humanity as gallant as the struggle of General Joseph Stilwell's weary forces in the sweltering jungles below them.

"It was CNAC's six Douglas DC-3 transports," wrote Bill Clemmens, war correspondent, "flying high above the bloody battlefields of the Irrawaddy, and higher still over the great barrier peaks of Arakan Yoma, which offered the only means of

China National Airways Corporation (CNAC) pilots and planes were flying wartime air transport long before U.S. entered the war. Here is one of CNAC's planes, a DC-3 which helped pioneer flying the Hump. Note the old Curtiss "Condor" biplane in background. (Pan American World Airways Photo)

escape to thousands of British, American, Chinese and Indian civilians trapped by Japanese blood-maddened armies.

"Many came from as far away as Rangoon, escaping first to Mandalay, then to Lashio, just a step ahead of the advancing Japanese. Gathered into Lend-Lease trucks, they were convoyed over Burma's winding jungle roads by the shark-snouted fighters of General Claire L. Chennault's 'Flying Tigers,' the famous American volunteer group. At concentration points deep in the jungles, they hid during the daylight hours.

"Then, at dusk they were loaded aboard the twin-engined Douglas transports. As soon as the first pilot flashed back an 'all-clear' a second transport was loaded and departed, followed in turn by the other ships of the fleet. By the middle of the night, the first transport had returned; its cargo — six to eight thousand pounds of medical and combat supplies — was quickly transferred to waiting army trucks, and a second file of passengers went aboard to be spirited away into the darkness.

"Each night, until help came from the United States Ferrying Command and some Royal Air Force ships and pilots, these overworked DC-3's spirited 400, sometimes more, over the worst flying country in the world, a forbidding land of dense tropical jungles broken by narrow valleys and studded with 10,000-foot peaks."

It was against this background that "Charlie" Sharp and his fellow pilots performed a "transport miracle." Short of planes, and with no reserves, the brunt of the flying fell on seven CNAC veterans — Sharp, Captain H. L. Woods of Colorado Springs, P. W. Kessler of Chicago, Robert Angle of Santa Monica, Frank Higgs of Columbus, Ohio, Hugh Chen and Moon Chin, Pan-American-trained Chinese pilots.

With the odds a thousand to one against them, they managed to get several flights across the barrier and back again every night, flying mostly in bad weather, constantly on the alert for the heavily armed fighters of Nippon's air squadrons. If their luck held, and the weather was too bad for the Jap fighters to venture aloft, the CNAC pilots could each make four trips over the mountains and back into their Burma field before daylight.

Wheeled off the runways, their planes were covered over with netting of camouflage until the curtain of darkness, or heavy clouds in which they could hide, permitted them to fly again. If they were "cursed with good weather," or if they had to detour too many Japanese raiders, they hid away on the Indian side of the frontier until just before sunset when they streaked back into Burma for their cargoes. Altogether, these planes were credited with having rescued more than 8,000 persons from battle-torn Burma. Their last flights, reports indicate, were made when the Japs were actually within range of the evacuation field.

These men who flew the planes, remember, had other evacuation-under-fire records behind them, — Shanghai, Nanking, Hankow, Hong Kong. They had been flying war-time transport for more than 54 months, *before the United States ever got into the scrap!*

III

Germany attacked the Soviet Union on June 22, 1941. The terrible Panzer divisions and the screaming Stuka bombers in rapid succession took Minsk, Smolensk, Kiev, Kharkov, Orel, besieged Leningrad. During the days of evacuation of that city (Leningrad) the Douglas transports were in the thick of things. Back in Santa Monica, Douglas workers learned about it from the first-person accounts as related by members of the USSR Purchasing Commission on a tour of the plant.

"All available C-47's were used to bring food to and evacuate the citizens of Leningrad," Colonel V. I. Bakhtin of the Red Army Air Forces explained. "They flew in with food and supplies and took off with loads of aircraft workers, engineers, women, children, old people — all those important to the prosecution of the war and those in urgent need of evacuation.

"With German and Finnish troops surrounding the city, the flak was terrific but the giant transports came through. Our guerilla forces are also indebted to these ships for delivery of ammunition and supplies to almost inaccessible areas."

Under Lend-Lease arrangements the Russians were getting hundreds of C-47's.

The planes were flown to Alaska by American ferry pilots and then turned over to the Russian airmen. It was there on one occasion that a U.S. Air Force Colonel on an inspection trip of our far north bases, learned something about the psychological attitude of the Red pilots that he will never forget. Colonel T. B. Holliday, Chief of the Equipment Laboratory at Wright Field came back to report – "I saw them do things with an airplane that marked them as absolutely fearless, or just plain damn fools."

According to Holliday he saw one young Russian Lieutenant climb into the cockpit of a C-47, his first experience in the left-hand seat. "The plane started down the runway, engines roaring wide open, and the tail of the plane wasn't even up, when suddenly the pilot pulled up the gear," Holliday said, "The ship was airborne whether it liked it or not. She staggered and shook, but she made it!"

Later, Holliday through an interpreter, remarked to the Red pilot that he thought it was pretty rough treatment, asking an awful lot of the airplane.

"The kid looked at me," Holliday recalls, "and said – 'What's the matter, Colonel, are you afraid to die?' "

IV

Wherever they flew on their wartime errands, the DC-ships took punishment far and beyond man's wildest expectations. Regulations and restrictions were thrown to the winds. The planes, themselves, defied all the laws of aerodynamics.

Plane No. 4823, one of the C-53 personnel transports delivered to the Air Corps in November, 1941, is a good example. Somehow, the ship found its way to the Royal Australian Air Force. One day, during the New Guinea Campaign, manned by an Aussie crew it was flying from a forward airstrip across the Owen Stanley mountains

The "Goonies" could take it and they could dish it out. This one crash landed after a mid-air collision over the Owen Stanley Mountains tore off six feet of outer wing and nine feet of aileron. Nobody was hurt in crash landing, but plane was declared a total washout. (Official USAF Photo)

Here is another example of the "Gooney Bird" ruggedness. Jap suicide (Kamikaze) fighter pilot attacked this C-47 and when he failed to shoot it down with gunfire, he rammed it. Plane made it back to base in spite of the sudden draft. (Douglas Aircraft Co. Photo)

toward Australia when, at 12,000 feet, they hit a tropical thunderhead.

The impact flopped the plane over on its back. From this inverted position it went into a dive executing an inside loop-the-loop. The pilot fought, unsuccessfully, to control the ship as it plunged towards the jungle at terrific speed. Finally, however, the controls began to respond and the pilot managed to pull out at 4,000 feet. They had flopped over, looped, and dived 8,000 feet before recovery.

Aboard were 26 passengers and a cargo payload of about 6,000 pounds. The cargo consisted of the passengers' personal gear, loose freight and an old-fashioned pot-bellied, cast-iron stove, none of which was lashed down. When the airplane went over on its back the passengers were hurled violently against the ceiling. Their gear was tossed about, and the stove knocked a hole in the roof big enough for a small kangaroo to jump through. Passengers were cut and bruised, but nobody was seriously injured.

When the ship landed at the Australian base despite its damaged and shook-up condition, Wesley Lamar, a Douglas Company service man was there to check it over. "I found wrinkles in the wing running from the leading edge aft and outboard across the entire length of both wings," he wrote in his official report. "The stabilizer was wrinkled in the same fashion. Rivets had been torn away as far back as a foot from the leading edge. One rib was hanging by a single rivet!

"The pilot (we never did get his name) inquired if it was safe to fly the airplane some 600 miles over water to his original destination. Naturally, I advised against it. Disregarding the advice, he had the cargo removed and took off, anyway.

"What's more he made it safely . . ."

Then, there was the case of "Whistlin' Willie," a C-47 operating out of an airfield near Chungking.

"We were on the ground taking on a load of gas when a swarm of Jap Zeroes strafed the field," reported Captain Harold Sweet. "I think that plane must have taken a thousand bullets. It looked like a sieve.

"Miraculously, the engines would still run. The radio was still workable. We decided to patch it up and try to fly it. A gang of Chinese coolies covered the holes with pieces of canvas cut from the awning of a missionary's tent.

"This done, we flew the ship with 61 refugees aboard to a base in India. A near monsoon rain loosened the patches and – over the roar of the engines – we could hear the ship giving off an eerie whistle! One shrill tone was added to another until the plane became a howling banshee."

For two hours the plane screamed through the hostile skies. Finally, Sweet brought it down, still intact, but looking more like a piece of Swiss cheese than an airplane.

Consider, too, the harrowing experience of Captain Robert J. Haines while flying the Hump in a DC-2. "Trying to get around a typhoon I wound up in a strange mountain pass," Haines related. "At about 16,000 feet in the heavily loaded plane, I was caught in a sudden updraft that kicked us up to 28,000 feet. It was the fastest rate of climb I had ever experienced . . .

"There was nothing to do but try to keep the plane on an even keel. Then, just as suddenly, the ship started down. It was like being swept over Niagara Falls in a barrel. In little more than two minutes, we dropped from 28,000 to 6,000 feet – almost four miles, straight down, plummeting like a rock.

"When we stopped it was with such a jar that I just didn't think planes could be built to take that sort of punishment."

The record of "Old Miscellaneous" (her crew dubbed her that) the tenth C-47 built for Uncle Sam and the first to join General George C. Kenney's Far East Air Forces, is another example of the ruggedness and durability of these ships that never seemed to give out. The plane was built at Santa Monica and delivered to the Air Force in February of 1942. It was sent to Australia via surface freighter and assembled there. In May of the same year it went into active service, transporting troops and supplies to the battlefronts.

Before she returned to the U.S. – retired with honors to participate in a nationwide bond tour – the ship had flown more than 2,000 missions and close to 3,000 operational hours. She took off from crude jungle airstrips and from bomb-pocked runways. She flew over oceans, mountains and jungles. She wore out 12 engines, had new wing tips, elevators, rudders so frequently that pilots called her the "shop worn angel." It's all in her log book.

When she arrived back in the States there was this letter of recommendation placarded in her cockpit for all to see:

"This ship is the oldest, fastest C-47 in the Southwest Pacific, so into whomsoever's hands she falls, treat her kindly and she will always get you to your destination."

The ships could take it; and they could dish it out.

Captain Hal M. Sorugham of Frankfort, Kentucky with Lieutenant Elmer J. Jost of Berwyn, Illinois (both assigned to the much-decorated 64th Troop Carrier Group) as pilot and co-pilot, respectively, were flying their C-47 in the skies over Burma when suddenly two Jap Zeroes jumped them.

But let Schrugham tell it in his own words . . .

"When we saw the Jap fighters, I swung the C-47 into a dive and hugged the ground as the enemy fighters peeled off for what looked to them like a sure kill.

"The first Zero made a pass at us, but we were too close to the ground and the pilot zoomed up without scoring any hits.

"The second Zero came right down on us. As he got within inches of our plane I gave the throttle an extra tug and got just a little burst of speed to keep him from crashing us amidship. As it was, the Zero missed our fuselage and slashed into the tail. The impact cut off all but a foot and a half of our rudder. But the Zero plunged into the ground.

"We watched him crash and explode. Then, in spite of the fact that our own ship had practically no empennage, it could still be controlled and we flew her back to our base."

Since the mid-air collision had been witnessed by ground forces, who also saw the Jap plane die, the C-47 crew was credited officially with having downed an enemy fighter plane!"

Writing in *Collier's* magazine, James H. Winchester, pictured the DC-3 in a war role that saw the transport plane masquerading as a bomber.

"One night in India a bunch of transport jockeys were whooping it up in a hut," Winchester wrote. "For months they'd been flying their unarmed planes over the Hump, and, in the process, ducking hot metal thrown up by the Japs. This night, fortified by a few noggins of jungle juice, they decided to retaliate.

"Taking a few old carbine and gasoline drums, the boys fashioned several home-made blockbusters, loaded them into the cabin of the weary old C-47 and took off. A couple of hours later they swooped low over a surprised Jap airfield in Burma. While a few shoved the bombs out the cabin door, the others shot up the field with Tommy guns, carbines and hand grenades tossed from the cockpit and windows."

Such stories are legion. During the Sicilian invasion, a large caliber naval shell passed straight through one C-47 fuselage, but the plane continued on its mission of dropping supplies. Crew members said they "pushed guns and ammunition out the gaping hole made by the shell." The plane got safely back to base. Another C-47 flew safely home after one engine had been completely torn out. His plane so badly damaged by shell-fire, one pilot decided to ditch it in the Mediterrean; but the plane refused to give up and bounced off the waves and into the air again. So, he flew it on home. In Europe's skies, too, there is the story that paratroopers mounted a machine gun so it could fire out the door of their C-47.

V

Back from an inspection tour of the North Africa shortly after the invasion of the Dark Continent had begun in the fall of 1943, General "Hap" Arnold took time out to write Don Douglas a personal letter which Arnold requested Douglas read to all the men and women "whose loyalty and zeal on the production lines gave us a transformation from weakness to strength."

Just as the Germans used air transport to drop an invasion army on Crete from Greece, Douglas C-47's of the 51st Troop Carrier Wing retaliated with an air drop to recapture Greece. Here planes are lined up at base somewhere in Italy ready for take-off. They dropped British paratroopers into Greece and towed gliders loaded with British Infantry. Then they moved on to another field in Greece to pick up supplies and cart them to starving Athenians. (USAF Photo)

Arnold's letter said further:

"I want to repeat to you some things I said recently about your C-47. This airplane is proving its worth in combat. One of the most remarkable examples was the arrival in battle of parachute troops flown to Africa from bases in the United Kingdom.

"No parachute attack in history had been made over more than a fraction of this distance. . . . The Germans, for example, in the invasion of Crete from Greece had to hop only 85 miles. On November 29, forty-four C-47 transports took off from an English field carrying British paratroopers to be dropped at an airdome 35 miles southwest of Tunis . . . 1,500 miles, non-stop from the United Kingdom to North Africa.

"Not an engine or plane faltered and, still in tight formation the transports rendezvoused over the Mediterranean with strong fighter and bomber escorts. Proceeding *en-masse* to the battlefront, the formation first bombed and strafed an important airdome. Then, the parachute army descended to capture and hold this vital field. The entire flight was completed, the drops successfully made and all the planes returned safely."

Douglas also read with inward pride the letter's closing words – "The performance of the C-47 is a tribute to the skillful management and to the diligent workmanship of the men and women in your organization."

It was a similar story on Guadalcanal. Following the battle of Savo Island, fourteen especially-equipped Marine Corps C-47's were flown from San Diego to New Caledonia and, under the Southwest Pacific Combat Air Transport Command (SCAT), they maintained daily service into Guadalcanal.

These C-47's, and others that were added to SCAT command, flew a total of almost 1,000 trips, aggregating 1,000,000 miles into Guadalcanal; and on each trip out, they carried our wounded back to base hospitals.

One day Douglas looked up from his desk to see a Marine, Captain Grant W. McCombs, an original member of the famous SCAT organization (Southwest Pacific Combat Air Transport) standing before him. McCombs had asked personally to meet the "man who is responsible for the design of the C-47." On leave, he had come to visit the plant.

"Bug Killer"— that's what GI's called the C-47 spray planes that came to help fight the jungle insects which were considered worse enemies than the Japs. This picture was taken on Saipan; "Gooney Bird" sprayed the island almost every day. (USAF Photo)

"There isn't a Marine on Guadalcanal who doesn't credit the C-47's with saving the island for us more than once," McCombs told Douglas at lunch. "Take, for instance, that day when Jap dive bombers blew up a ship which had rushed in gasoline two days after the enemy had destroyed our fuel dumps. That meant there was no gas on the island and no way our fighter planes could get up. They called on the C-47's and we started flying gas in, 600 gallons at a clip. That kept up for a week before surface ships got in. That was the only reason our fighters and dive bombers were able to get aloft."

The C-47's were also the backbone of the New Guinea Campaign. "When the Japs pushed over the Owen Stanley Mountains and advanced to within 40 miles of Port Moresby," General Kenney reported, "it was these transports which rushed from Australia the force of 3,800 Allied troops which defeated and drove back the enemy.

"The same C-47's also flew in the force of 7,000 Yanks and Aussies which cleared the Japanese from North Papua, and later from Salamaua and Lae.

"Besides being the sole source of supply

for these troops, they executed the wholesale paratroop action in the Markham Valley, and supplemented it by landing hundreds of additional troops on a captured airfield. They also helped build airfields in the impenetrable New Guinea jungles, there being one instance, where they flew in 19 bulldozers, 32 jeeps, graders, scrapers, field camp equipment and arms, as well as a crew of engineers."

It was the same way in Europe.

On September 29, 1944, at the headquarters of the 9th Troop Carrier Command in England, they got an urgent call for help from Brig Gen. Harold L. Clark whose 82nd U. S. Airborne battalion was fighting to turn the tide of the German line at Cleve. Clark needed more men, ammo, weapons, gasoline, rations and he needed them in a hurry or the Germans stood a chance of wiping out his whole unit.

The situation was ticklish. The 82nd had moved in the day before and occupied a German fighter airstrip in the middle of Holland. It was small, little larger than the area of five football fields. Moreover, the Germans wanted it back.

Success of the operations, according to General Clark, would depend entirely on speed. The *Skytrains* would have to come in, land and take-off in a hurry. There probably would be heavy ground fire.

In answer to his request the Troop Carrier Command readied 200 of its C-47's for the job.

According to Lieutenant Joseph D. Guess, Correspondant for *Air Force* magazine, official journal of the USAF during the war, who went along in one of the transports – "The planes took off, one after the other, and they carried with them 132 jeeps, 73 quarter-ton jeep trailers, 31 motorcycles, 3,374 gallons of gasoline, 60,730 pounds of rations, 657,995 pounds of combat equipment, 882 fully-equipped men . . . The whole operation was accomplished in three hours. Not a single ship was lost."

The war moved to a close. Germany surrendered. The "knock-out" bombs were dropped on Hiroshima and Nagasaki. There were peace feelers from Japan. Nippon had had enough. Then, suddenly, it was all over.

In Europe, General of the Armies, Dwight D. Eisenhower, unreservedly, declared that the DC-3 was one of the four weapons that won the war. Writing in his book *Crusade In Europe,* Eisenhower, says – "Most senior officers regard as the most vital to our success in Africa and Europe were the bulldozer, the jeep, the two-and-a-half-ton truck and the C-47."

None of these, paradoxically, was designed for combat!

At MacArthur's headquarters, General Kenney, air boss of the Pacific, summoned in Colonel Gordon A. Blake, the commanding officer of the Seventh Army Airways Communications Squadron.

"How quick can you set up a control tower and an air traffic control unit at the airdrome near Tokyo?" Kenny wanted to know.

It was urgent. MacArthur wanted to fly the occupation troops and surrender teams into the area as quickly as possible.

"Give me 48 hours and twenty-five C-47's," Blake answered.

Before the day was over Blake had dispatched two special C-47 airplanes that had been modified as airborne communications stations. The planes had been fitted with a complete Signal Corps Radio Station. They were the first American planes to land on the Jap airfield. Within hours Blake had established radio contact.

Two days later other C-47's landed, bringing in the necessary materials to step-up the needed air traffic control facilities. Blake led them. With him it was a very personal matter. He had been one of those in the control tower at Hickam Field, Honolulu, the day the Japs hit Pearl Harbor 32 long months ago.

Now, on August 28, 1945, when the big Douglas C-54 plush-job carrying General MacArthur and his staff roared over Tokyo, it was Blake, who contacted MacArthur's pilot and said over the radio – "Clear to land. . . ."

Later, his GI's kidded him about it – "The only guy on earth who had the power to keep MacArthur from landing in Tokyo!"

VI

The DC-3 and its sister ships, no matter their official designation or nick-name, had been in on the beginning and they were in on the ending of the most terrible war mankind has ever known. There was wide ac-

The "Gooney Birds" were in on the beginning and they were in on the end of the greatest war in history. This picture taken in February 1945, shows C-47 air-dropping supplies to troops on Corregidor Island, where they had landed previous day to retake the famous fortress. C-47's also landed the first advance troops at Tokyo airdrome after Jap surrender. (USAF Photo)

claim and praise for the jobs they did on the homefront and all over the world.

"The greatest air bombardment of all," one General said, "was the material that came out of the sky from the cargo holds of these transport planes. Our bombers smashed the enemy into submission; but our cargo planes kept the bombers flying. Delivery of the weapons and materials to ground, sea and air units was the big factor in the turning of the course of victory."

One of the highest tributes of all came, however, from the late Secretary of the Air Force Harold L. Talbot, years after the war was over. The occasion was the presentation of the Exceptional Service Award to Donald W. Douglas, Sr., at an Air Power Symposium luncheon held in the Presidential Room of the Hotel Statler in Washington, D. C. August 21, 1953. The award is the highest civilian decoration awarded by the Air Force for non-combat service.

The citation reads: "Donald Wills Douglas distinguished himself by rendering exceptional service to the United States Air Force and his country through his contribution to the development of military and civilian aviation over the past 40 years.

"The soundness of his technical skill is best illustrated by the DC-3 (C-47) which unquestionably ranks as the *best single airplane ever built!*"

Perhaps, as Douglas accepted the award he was thinking that it was this same Harold Talbot, a lifelong friend who, twenty years before, had come to him and suggested – "Doug, you should go after that TWA bid. It won't hurt to get into the transport field, and I'll help you all I can."

Talbot was a member of TWA's Board of Directors. It was no secret Talbot, probably more than anybody else, had influenced Douglas to build the DC-1, and that decision, indeed, had influenced the course of history.

The sky would never be the same again since the all-metal "Gooney Bird" made its appearance in the unfathomable Land of Up.

No wonder they called her the "Dizzy Three." This DC-3 suffered wing damage from Jap gunfire in the spring of 1941. But CNAC crews were undaunted; they had a DC-2 wing available so they slapped it on to replace the damaged wing. The plane was flown back to the main base of operations. They called it the DC-2½. (Douglas Aircraft Co. Photo)

Chapter 15

"Dig That Dizzy Three!"

Captain Charlie Sharp, the pilot who flew Jimmy Doolittle out of China was talking about what happened to one of the China National Airways Corporation airliners. It was a DC-3 . . . or was it? "Well, it was and it wasn't," Charlie said with a wry smile. "You see, it was this way . . .

"In the spring of 1941 one of our DC-3s on a flight between Hong Kong and Chungking made a forced landing at a field near Kiuchuan. Crews were working on the ship when a flight of Jap Zeros swooped down and sprayed the whole area with machine gun fire. When the shooting was over, the plane's fuselage was riddled with bullet holes and one wing had been blasted off.

"We first heard about it when the plane's Captain, H. L. Woods, radioed back to the CNAC base. *'The plane's a wreck,* Woods reported, *'But if we can get a new wing, I think I can fly her out of here.'*

"The hell of it was, we didn't have a DC-3 spare wing and we didn't know where to get one. We did have, however, a DC-2 wing. It was ten feet shorter and it wasn't designed to support the loads of the DC-3. But we thought it might work, and we needed that airplane in the worst way."

According to Sharp, they bolted the DC-2 wing to another DC-3's underbelly and flew it across the 900 miles of mountainous terrain to Kiuchuan. There, ground crews installed the DC-2 wing on Wood's damaged airliner. It looked a little lopsided, but the ship took off and flew as though nothing had been changed.

"We called her the DC-2½," Sharp concludes his story.

What they did to the twin-engined DC-ships, themselves, was almost as fantastic as the job the planes did in their role as aerial pack-horses and skyfreighters. There were so many in-the-field modifications that even the Douglas tech representatives couldn't keep track of them all. The DC-3 or the C-47 became an ambulance plane especially fitted for litter patients; a "flying tank car" that hauled gasoline and/or milk and sometimes, even, fresh water, to isolated airstrips and stranded ground forces; an "airborne photo lab" used by reconnaissance groups which could fly over the enemy, take their photographs, and develop the pictures enroute back to base; a "flying wrecker" which consisted of a complete airborne machine shop. The miracle was that this machine designed specifically as a luxury airliner could be so quickly adaptable to perform so many different missions.

In the evacuation of the wounded, the "Gooneybird" wrote a new page in modern warfare. They called her the "Flying Hospital." (USAF Photo)

II

Deep in the heart of New Guinea, a spanking new C-47 cracked up a wing on a rough jungle landing strip. Harry Booth, veteran Douglas Company trouble-shooter was on the spot. "We got our heads together to see if we couldn't figure out a way to fly a wing over the Owen Stanley Mountains and get that C-47 back in the air again," Booth reported. "It had never been done before but after careful study we decided it could be done and proceeded to do it."

Booth's report continued:

"We took out twenty-six bolts from the lower forward gas tank stress plates. Then we took chunks of flat boiler plate, bent angles on them, and made holes to fit the attach bolts and bolted four of these plates to the belly of the plane on the gas tank stress plates. We lifted the inboard end of the wing and bolted the boiler plate strips to the attack angle of the wing. Links of cable between the lower angle of the wing and the nacelle held the wing firmly in place.

"Next we took a (2 x 12-inch) board, cut it to fit the contour of the wing on the bottom side and the fuselage on the upper side. This served as a buffer between the outboard end of the wing and the fuselage. Then, we hoisted the outboard end of the wing up to the fuselage and held it firmly in place by bolting a cable to one side of the fuselage, running it around the wing and then up to the other side of the fuselage where it was again secured. To cut down wind resistance and drag we faired the inboard end of the wing with strips of wood salvaged from boxes and crates. The wooden fairing was covered with fabric and doped. In a few days the C-47 with the wing slung to its belly was ready to fly.

According to Booth a six-man crew flew the "triplane" (it had three wings) on its initial test flight. Booth, himself, went along as a technical observer. The others were: Major L. Imparato, pilot; Captain Charles R.Baer, co-pilot; Tech. Sgt. D. C. Payton, flight engineer; Pvt. Q. E. Steen, radio operator and a Captain John Boyle. Before the decision to fly the wing over the mountains to the stranded C-47 they ran several test hops. It was learned they had to put more ballast in the tail because the ship showed unstableness on the controls. This done, they climbed aboard, for the hop through the 10,000 foot pass over the Owen Stanleys.

"The take-off was normal," Booth wrote, "using very little of the runway. There were only two obvious and notice-

With spare wing slung under its belly the "Gooney Bird" introduced a new kind of maintenance technique. For flying this C-47, Major L. Imparato won DFC. Citation reads: "On Feb. 13, 1943, a damaged C-47 at Buna Buna was in need of a complete left wing to make it flyable. The spare wing was suspended beneath the fuselage of a second C-47 and despite danger of the wing tearing away or setting up a vibration to wreck the airplane or change its flying characteristics, he flew the wing 285 miles to an advanced area, where the damaged plane was repaired and flown out." (Douglas Aircraft Co. Photo)

able effects of the unusual cargo — the ship stalled at a higher speed, and it settled faster during the landing. But the C-47 came in without a hitch. The wing was unhooked from its belly, and in a few days two C-47s flew off the strip.

"Since that time," Booth concluded his report back to the company, "we have made-up special kits and issued them to different service units. The kits consist of boiler plate fasteners, fairings, cable cut to exact length, bolts, fabric and dope. They permit flying C-47 wings, P-47 wings, B-25 wings and even B-17 wings from the major depots to the advanced air bases.

"The practice has become so common that nobody even turns his head when a "Gooney' takes-off with a wing slung beneath its belly. It is paying off, too. One small outfit reported their group, alone, had ferried twelve wings across the mountains and saved the lives of twelve airplanes."

III

In the Mediterranean Theater, Colonel "Monty" D. Wilson, commander of a Depot Group for the 15th Air Force was having maintenance problems galore. Typical was a grounded P-38 *Lightning* which had been shot down near an advanced fighter strip, but needed only minor repairs to get back into the air again under its own power. The problem was it would take a week or more to send a repair crew overland to get to the disabled aircraft. Wilson couldn't spare the men for that long a period. Still, they needed that airplane. Moreover, there were tens of similar situations all around him; planes that could fight again if they could just have a quick repair job.

"Monty" Wilson had an idea. He remembered a time when he was driving cross-country and had a break-down with his automobile. All he did was call the nearest Triple-A garage and a wrecker came out to tow the car in for needed repairs. Only, this was a special kind of "wrecker." It wasn't just a tow-truck. The crew had rigged up a small machine shop in a truck bed and they fixed Wilson's car right on the spot. Why not do the same thing with a C-47 — turn it into a "flying wrecker," a machine shop with wings? That way they could fly the repair crews to the downed planes, work on them right on the spot, get them back into the air again.

The idea grew into reality. There emerged a modified C-47 which they called "Depot Belle." Inside its fuselage was a 24-volt generator for driving machine tools, an instrument test stand, a hydraulic systems test stand, a drill press, air compressor, lathe, grinder, welding equipment and all the necessary tools.

"When the flying repair shop went into operation, "Colonel Wilson reported, "we were accomplishing Third Echelon maintenance on planes in 36 hours which previously would have taken a week to fifteen days."

Before long there were "Flying Depot" planes operating all over the world.

IV

Man's ingenuity stretched from Dayton to Dakar and back again on the wings of the DC-3 and C-47. There is the record of one ship they modified as a propaganda plane. It carried a complete printing press and they printed their own newspaper aloft.

Air Transport Command pilots such as Captain Eddie Jones of United Airlines, pictured above, flew the mail in planes that were literally "Flying Post Offices." Some interiors were outfitted like railroad mail cars. (United Air Lines Photo)

Sometimes, the plane flew in advance of the ground armies, dropped leaflets to citizens in the towns ahead in the path of the advancing forces. Another C-47 was fitted as a "flying laundry" – washing machines, dryers and ironers aboard. Once a week it made scheduled stops at advanced bases. They called it the "Dirty Underwear Special." Airborne canteens, complete kitchens, were as common to some of the forward bases as the chuck wagon on a round-up.

If newspapers could fly, so could radio stations. In India, Supreme Commander Lord Louis Mountbatten was having difficulty directing his forces spread out over such a wide area. The Burma Campaign moved so fast in 1944-45 that Mountbatten had to be constantly on the move to command his armies. Colonel Harold W. Grant came up with the answer – a C-47 with a complete Signal Corps radio station inside its hulk.

During an engagement at Rangoon (May 2, 1945) Lord Mountbatten was 1500 miles away at an emergency field. But he directed the movements of the troops, according to Colonel Grant, from the C-47 parked on the advanced airstrip. Later, when Mountbatten was called to London for a conference with Churchill and other leaders, he maintained contact with his Pacific Operations from the "Flying Command Post" parked on the airdrome outside of England's capital city.

Stateside, another C-47 played an important role in the improvement of air-to-ground and ground-to-ground communications. Flying over the Great Smoky Mountain Range in October, 1944, the plane laid a two-way telephone line 16 miles long in the record time of seven minutes. It was especially modified with a Center Guide Wire-Laying System. Giant spools of wire in the fuselage permitted trailing the wire and linking up ground posts with a telephone hookup in a matter of minutes.

On its trial run the plane swooped low over a command post, dropped one end of the wire to the ground communications personnel. Then, roaring across the mountanous terrain trailing its telephone line – unreeling at the rate of 200 feet per second – the plane strung its line of communication. Within three minutes after the start of the run, the men in the plane were talking with the men on the ground. Seven minutes later the telephone hook-up between the two command posts were established.

"You guys take it from here," said the pilot of the *Dizzy Three*.

V

There was no guessing what the DC-ships might do or what they might look like; crazy, mixed-up "Goonies," these C-47s, R4Ds and DC-3s. One day during the height of the war, for instance, residents around Wilmington, Ohio were startled to see an airliner without engines or propellers gliding and banking in the summer clouds, and then gracefully coming to rest on the nearby army airfield. The next day they raised their eyebrows still higher when they saw two airliners hitched together towing a large transport-type glider.

What they saw on both occasions was no illusion. They were looking at a conventional airliner, more specifically an Air Force C-47 made into a glider and the first "tandem tow" by which two airplanes were used to haul a giant glider.

Behind the story was a strange twist of fate. Since the outbreak of the war, the Army Air Forces had developed a series of gliders (CG4-A's) as troop carriers. These gliders, however, were designed for towing behind twin-engined transports, in most cases, the DC-3 or the C-47. The *Skytrain* was born.

As the war progressed, however, air transport was going through a transformation from the twin-engined DC-3 to the bigger four-engined planes like the Douglas *Skymaster* (C-54) a military version of the DC-4E. (See Chapter Twenty). It became evident that in time there would have to be a larger glider development for towing behind the bigger transports.

The Troop Carrier Command was rapidly switching over from twin-engined to four-engined operations. None of the existing gliders could meet the demands. The problem of finding such a glider fell to the Glider Branch of the Aircraft Laboratory at Wright Field, Dayton, Ohio.

Major William C. Lazarus of the Glider

Branch put it this way – "We started by figuring the reserve power available in the C-54 and trying to determine a desired cruising speed for the locomotive plane and the glider. Then, we began to conceive a purely theoretical design and configuration of a glider which would meet these requirements. . . . As the specifications for this glider evolved from the drafting boards and slide rules, it became more and more apparent that the size and gross weight of the glider we wanted would coincide with that of the airplane we had been using as a tow-ship – the Douglas C-47!"

Two former glider pilots, Bernard J. Driscoll of Hartford, Connecticut and Chester Decker of Glen Rock, New Jersey (both were captains in the AAF at Wright Field) came up with a revolutionary idea. "It's never been done," Decker, one of America's leading sailplane proponents, declared, "but let's take a C-47, jerk out its engines and see if it will prove to be the glider we have been trying to design."

They told Bill Lazarus about it and the trio took the idea up with Brig. General Frank O. Carroll, Chief of Wright Field's Engineering Division. "Well, they've done everything else with the Old Girl," Frank Carroll said reflecting a minute about the C-47. "What the hell are you waiting for? Go ahead and try it."

Officially, a C-47 became the XCG-17 Glider.

It wasn't easy. First, they ran a series of glide tests with the C-47 to see if it really had the potential of being a glider. With only fuel and crew aboard Decker and two other pilots, Captain Lloyd Santmyer of Latrobe, Pa. and Capt. Norman Rintoul of Pittsburgh – both former airline jockeys – took the C-47 up to 5,000 feet, cut both its engines and deadsticked to a landing, time and time again. Finally, they were convinced the C-47 without power could

With engines out and nacelles plugged, this C-47 became a glider, officially designated the XCG-17. (Douglas Aircraft Co. Photo)

glide in and hit the spot consistently, regardless of winds and the amount of payload.

Next, they had to determine if the C-47 was stable in towed flight. Up to this time, all gliders had been specifically designed as gliders with more aileron, elevator and rudder control than the conventional airplane. But, here was a C-47, designed to be flown only as a powered airplane – would it stand the test on the end of the nylon tow rope?

There was another question, too. Where could they attach the tow rope? According to Bill Lazarus they soon learned that the versatile C-47 even had built into it the answer to this "knotty" problem. The Douglas engineers who had never dreamed they were building a glider when they designed the DC-3, had provided a rectangular inspection door on the belly of the plane through which mechanics could readily examine the main wing structure where it passed beneath the fuselage. By simply unbolting this inspection panel and replacing it with one specially fitted with a tow release mechanism the hitch could be made. The tow hitch was quickly designed and installed in the experimental C-47 at Wilmington's Clinton County Air Force Base which the AAF had designated as its new glider branch test field.

With Santmyer, Rintoul and Decker doing the flying they hooked one C-47 behind another at the end of a 350-foot nylon tow rope. The lead plane applied power to take up the slack in the rope. Then the towed C-47 applied power, but not quite as much as the tow-plane so that the tow rope remained taut. Down the runway the two airplanes came, up went the towed C-47 first and then, the tow ship was airborne – the first towed flight of a C-47 plane was a success.

When the two ships gained safe altitudes the second C-47 – as the glider – cut its engines, and feathered its props. It was now in full towed flight. Decker, who was at its controls said she handled beautifully. Shortly he cut the plane loose from its tow plane and glided it safely to a landing.

Lazarus, who was watching the experiment saw in it something else other than a glider tow. He saw the possibility of using two C-47s in a tandem tow (like hooking two diesel locomotives onto a long freight) just what was needed for the bigger gliders that were already in the experimental stages. A few days later they tried it with two C-47's in tandem yanking the world's biggest glider – the all-wooden XCG-10A – off the ground and towing it through the air. At altitude, the lead "locomotive plane" cut loose and one C-47 was towing the giant glider.

One C-47 could tow a glider that was bigger than the "locomotive." It took two C-47's to yank the big XCG-10A glider off the ground, but once in flight, a lone "Gooneybird" took over. (USAF Photo)

This was the craziest ever; the glider, a whale-like monster with a profile like a meat cleaver, dwarfed the towing C-47. It was like the caboose towing the locomotive. Yet, it was. It did happen. The "tandem tow" made it possible. Once airborne, and with one of the tow planes cut loose, it was no trick at all for a single C-47 to tow the big glider.

"Here was a real *Skytrain*," Major Lazarus remarked to General Carroll. "We've got the answer to towing the bigger gliders."

"What about the XCG-17?" Frank Carroll wanted to know.

"We're ready to make a C-47 into a glider," Bill Lazarus reported. "But we need a plane to make certain modifications."

Carroll went down the list of aircraft on the line at Wright Field. He came upon a war-weary C-47 that had recently returned from combat. It was "Old Miscellaneous."

"Take this one," Frank Carroll said, "She won't let you down."

The Glider Branch accepted the plane gratefully and proceeded to tear out thousands of pounds of weight. The first thing they did was yank out the engines. Then, they added hemispherical streamlined cones to the empty nacelles to reduce the frontal area. Next, they eliminated the forward baggage compartments, and they put in a new floor so that cargo could be loaded farther forward to compensate for the loss of weight up front when the engines were removed.

Tests with the XCG-17 were so successful that Major Lazarus wrote in his report to General Carroll – "The XCG-17 is the only AAF cargo glider which requires no ballast when flown in minimum-weight condition.

"It is America's largest glider, carrying a payload exceeding seven tons.

"It has a long flat glide angle, a ratio of 14 to one. (That meant it could glide forward 14 feet while dropping only one foot.) By comparison, the small CG-4 Waco wood and fabric gliders had a glide ratio of ten or twelve to one. This means that the XCG-17, big as it is, will outglide even the smallest conventional AAF glider.

"The XCG-17 has a remarkably low stalling speed – 35 miles per hour while the stalling speed of the CG-4 is 55 miles per hour.

"Most important of all, the XCG-17 can be towed as fast as 270 to 290 miles per hour. The top speed of the conventional gliders is 200 miles per hour."

He might have added that the C-47 made into the glider was also the only all-metal glider in existence.

There were other implications. When word of the experiment reached combat units they were quick to see practical utilization of the idea. It was something that made Colonel "Monty" Wilson chuckle to himself when he read about it in *Air Force* Magazine.

Our GI mechanics were right on the ball. When a C-47 was downed and needed repairs, out went a sister ship to the scene of the disabled Gooney. The second aircraft, fitted with special "glider snatch" equipment yanked the damaged plane off the ground and towed it back to base for repairs. The day of the "flying wrecker" was here.

VI

The adaptation of the C-47 as a glider (XCG-17) was one of the major modifications made to these aircraft during the war years. By the time it was perfected and ready, however, the day of glider invasions was *passe*. But there were other modifications that turned the C-47s into strange configurations. One of these was the Y-123, an amphibian version of the flying packhorse.

They called it the "Duck" because it could fly high, low, fast or slow, and take off or land neatly on the water. This, pilots said, was due to the weight of the ship which approached 29,000 pounds. The float gear, alone, weighed almost a ton!

Equipped with huge pontoons and wheels, they turned the Gooneybird into a Duck. Officially she was designated the X-123. (USAF Photo)

The land-water versions of the C-47 were used in Alaska and to some extent in jungle areas where large rivers and lakes provided suitable landing areas.

VII

Perhaps, the greatest change of all came after the war was over and the airlines wanted their converted DC-3s back, and all the C-47s they could get to meet the increase in air travel which the war had brought about. It was a strange paradox. The DC-3 became the C-47 and the C-47 became the DC-3 again. "This airplane went around in design circles," remarked one veteran United Airlines captain, "which is probably why they called her the *Dizzy Three*."

The war over, out came the heavy cargo

For snow operations they fitted the C-47 with skis and wheels. (USAF Photo)

plane floors, the cargo bulkheads, the bucket seats, the parachute racks. Off came the olive drab paint. In went plush carpeting, sound-proofing, air conditioning units, lounge chairs, galleys, hat-racks and lavatories. It took less than twenty days to convert a war-weary aircraft into a virtually new, gleaming silvery commercial transport.

The "Old *Dray* Mare" of wartime fame was a Lady again.

By the end of 1946 – ten years after the DC-3 went into service – there were more than 500 of these planes in domestic "non-sked" and scheduled airline service. As usual they were carrying most of the traffic.

To one passenger, riding east in a rebuilt wartime C-47 there was a special satisfaction as he looked around the cabin, leaned back comfortably in the soft, reclining seat and listened to the hum of the engines. His name was Donald W. Douglas, "Father of the Modern Airliner."

It was the first time since the end of the war that Douglas had made a trip to Washington. "I remember that trip for two reasons," Douglas relates, "I'll never forget looking down as we flew near Davis-Monthon Air Force Base in Arizona, at the graveyard of the B-17s, B-24s, and B-29s. There were thousands upon thousands of these planes which had been retired from service and were awaiting the blow torch to cut them up and turn them into aluminum pots and pans.

"Then, suddenly, the thought occurred to me that this machine in which I was riding, a DC-3, also had been through the wars. But here she was, still up there, still flying, still performing a vital role in the air transport of people and things.

"You can't forget a thing like that, not when you've been as close to it as I have through the years. The other reason, in a way, was linked to the first.

"I was going to Washington to talk with the military people and others about a new proposal we had worked up to make the DC-3 an entirely new airplane."

Chapter 16

The Shadow Of Extinction

"The pace of aircraft development is swift and relentless," Don Douglas once told a group of engineers. "Before one model plane goes into scheduled operation, a newer, more powerful and probably even swifter member of the same family already is taking shape on the drawing boards, in the laboratories and shops. In the air, as on the ground, progress, like opportunity, does not linger very long."

"Probably the most compelling characteristic of our industry," he added, "is that it cannot stand still and rest on its laurels. Always, we, and the airlines, must move ahead."

Perhaps, as Douglas surveyed the air transport industry after World War II, he was reminded of these statements. The very thing he was talking about was happening all around him. Progress catching up with progress. The war effort, just as it had created a giant of the Douglas Aircraft Company also did the same for other airframe manufacturers. Everybody benefited from the design and production know-how which the war needs brought to the fore. There was no limit to the dollars that went into experimental models and prototypes. In the process, it was only natural that many of the companies should come up with new ideas for post-war airliner designs and prototypes – paid for in part by defense dollars – which would challenge Douglas' leadership in the field of commercial airliner design. As a result, immediately after the war, for the first time in more than a decade, there were some twin-engined passenger planes going into service on various airlines *besides* the DC-3.

Here and there at airports once served exclusively by the DC-2's or DC-3's, there appeared a new family of skyliners. Consolidated-Vultee of San Diego, builders of the famous B-24 *Liberators* introduced its ***Convair Model 240's.*** The Glenn L. Martin Company of Baltimore, whose B-26 *Marauders* were our fastest medium bombers in the early stages of the war, got into the picture with its ***Martin 202*** model. Republic Aviation Corporation where the famous P-47 *Thunderbolt* fighters were born even tried its hand with passenger transport – ***"The Rainbow,"*** built originally as a high-altitude photo-recon ship for the military. Curtiss-Wright, whose C-46 *Commandos* flew wing tip-to-wing tip with the DC-3's and C-47's "Over the Hump," quickly offered the airlines a plush-job version. And there was talk that the late Tony Fokker's Dutch company was working with the Fairchild Aircraft Corp. in the design, the Fokker-F-27, "Friendship," a turbo-prop airliner that *would do anything the DC-3 could do and better.*

So said the advance notices. The growing breed of air traveler, who sprouted wings with the DC-3, suddenly found himself faced with a glittering array of shiny new airliners to choose from for his aerial journey.

Moreover, the new designs introduced things that were appealing to the public. They were bigger with much roomier cabins for added passenger comfort. They could carry half again as many passengers as the ***Threes*** which raised the eyebrows of the operators, who saw a rosy future in the added payloads. The new designs, for the most part rested on tricycle undercarriages which made them more comfortable for passengers on the ground (one didn't have to ride on a slanting floor over rough runways during taxiing) and pilots, too, liked their ground-handling characteristic. These new planes were much faster than the DC-3's. In short, post-war air transport was going through an evolutionary phase which would soon make the old, war-weary DC-3 an obsolete airplane.

The DC-3 had other ideas. So did Don Douglas and all those who loved this "Grand Old Lady of the Skies." They refused to put her out to pasture.

The winged veteran, proudly wearing her campaign ribbons from every theater, returned to civilian life to take up her job where she left off. While the new planes were going through their "public acceptance period," the chance to prove themselves along the airline system, and air travelers waited for the promised advent of big four-engined transports that were coming along, the faithful old *Three* was assigned the task of filling in to meet the upsurge in civil air transportation needs. Ten-to-one she outnumbered and outflew all the others along the world's far-flung air routes. Not satisfied to be relegated to the role of playing "second fiddle," she started another revolution in the new concept of air transportation's future.

II

The first shot in the "revolution" was fired by our returning GI's, many of whom had decided to build their postwar future on the art (flying) which they had learned so well in their wartime roles. Pilots who had flown the *Goonies* (for some the only avocation or occupation they had ever known) decided they wanted to stay in the game. They had their own ideas on how to go about it.

Writing in his book *"High Horizons,"* a history of United Air Lines, Frank J. Taylor summed up the situation – "Shortly after the war ended, the Army and Navy, by Executive Order from the White House, turned thousands of planes over to a new agency, the War Assets Administration, which was authorized to dispose of them in any way it could. Bombers, fighters, trainers, and transports were stacked up at Army air strips, where anyone, but veterans preferred, could buy them for a tenth of their cost, or even less. Hundreds of veterans took advantage of the offer. Some bought planes so cheap they made a profit by merely selling the fuel in the tanks and the instruments off the panels.

"Others, veterans of the Air Force, set up inexpensive charter flying services. They flew cargoes from anywhere to anywhere, and passengers, too, at cut rates, sometimes barely half those allowed by the Civil Aeronautics Board for airlines offering transportation over identical routes."

They called themselves "The non-skeds," this new family of airlines, an appropriate enough name, since their wildcat airliners flew at irregular departure times, to avoid being classified as airlines subject to airline regulations. The DC-3's (more accurately the converted C-47's which they bought from surplus) and the C-46's were the backbone of their operations. For better or worse, their very existence shook up the whole air transport industry. The "cry of the gooneybird" was heard across the land.

It was good for aviation, and it was bad for aviation. "This new, unregulated competition added to the confusion on the airways," Frank Taylor wrote in his history. And he was right. The "non-skeds" flying as they did taxed the already over-taxed facilities at airports and along the government-controlled airways. Too, the fly-by-night operators with a minimum of maintenance and ground crews, flew continuously on the fringe of safety requirements. There resulted another period when "crash fever" hit the non-skeds, and seldom a week went by that headlines did not proclaim – "ANOTHER AIRLINER DISASTER." But in most cases, it was one of the non-skeds that was down. The whole industry suffered. It so blackened the record of scheduled air transport companies that the CAB had to step in with rigid regulations for the non-sked operations. Many were forced out of business. But some survived, and the airline industry would never be quite the same. The DC-3 had made sure she had a voice in shaping the future of the air transport world she really started.

More important, out of all the chaos and confusion, she had forced the airline people to change their rate structure and she brought air travel within the reach of everybody's finances. Before the non-skeds came into operations, the price of a ticket by scheduled airliner from New York to San Francisco was about $150. The GI-airlines and their converted *Goonies* charged $88. And they proved, despite their ragged operations, the public liked the idea. Ticket offices sometimes were jammed – until the crashes thinned the lines. *Fare*, not *fear*, they proved, was

Near the end of the war American Airlines started converting some of its DC-3's into all-cargoliners. The Flagship Airfreighter was born. The DC-3 was pioneering another new field of transportation—cargo by air. It was to become booming business in years ahead. In ten years alone American would fly a total of 54,000,000 ton miles (in 1953) with new fleet of DC-6A Airfreighters. (American Airlines Photo)

keeping many potential air traveler on the ground. The result was when the "whole mess settled down" the scheduled airlines, themselves introduced the first *coach services* which are still with us today.

As somebody aptly phrased it – "The DC-3 in the postwar era forced the big operators to put wings on everybody's pocketbook."

She had long before taken the *fear* out of flying.

Something else happened right after the war. Another crisis of another kind developed in the delivery of the Air Mail. Only the certificated air carriers (this did not include the Non-skeds) could fly the mail. At some terminals the mail was piling up to such an extent that it overtaxed the capacity of the airliners, mostly DC-3's, that were Uncle Sam's flying postmen. Smart airline operators like United, for example, were quick to come up with a solution. They started *Cargoliner* operations using their DC-3's, returned from the war, without seats and flew these planes exclusively as cargo and mail transports. Other airlines followed suit. The mail moved on schedule. Applying the lessons learned during the war from the capabilities and performance of the C-47's (Hap Arnold's "Aerial Mules") the airlines quickly saw the value of all-freight operations. The DC-3's as commercial aerial freight trains became the backbone of all-cargo airlines. A role, incidentally, that was not new to the DC-ships since United, as early as 1940 had pioneered "flying freight cars" with some of its DC-2's and DC-3's.

The cargo business grew rapidly. The DC-3, "Jack of all trades" soon helped make money for the new all-cargo airlines and the regular skeds operating air freighters. "There was little she couldn't carry and almost no place she couldn't go," wrote Marvin Miles, veteran *LA Times* aviation writer. "Fresh fish, fresh produce, furniture, flowers, animals, birds, clams, clothes – a wide variety of cargo rode in her cabin, much of it refrigerated."

Wherever the action was, there was the DC-3, ready to perform whatever task they called upon her to perform. There was plenty of action. More and more people, most of them stimulated by first flight experiences during the war, wanted seats on the airliners. The new cargoliner services got top priority attention from shippers everywhere, a decided impact on the nation's commerce. Communities that heretofore had turned their back on air service, demanded they be considered in the airline structure. The big trunklines were not enough. There was demand for supplementary service to the smaller cities and towns. To meet this demand the Government created another family of airlines, The Local Service Carriers, granted subsidy from Uncle Sam to provide air mail service and a faster mode of communications to the smaller communities – a government responsibility under the Civil Aeronautics Act of 1938.

The Local Service Airlines came into existence in 1948. There were 18 smaller airlines granted temporary operational certificates and routes under the CAB regulations as regular scheduled airline operators. The DC-3 was the vehicle that put them into business. By the time these carriers were ready to begin operations, many of the big trunklines were getting their first new four-engined Douglas DC-6's, Lockheed *Constellations* and Boeing *Stratocruisers* – born during the war – which were starting to replace the DC-3's along the long-haul routes. The Local Service Airlines took the DC-3's from the big trunklines as fast as negotiations could be worked out.

When they got their *Threes* the Local Service Airlines "gussied" them up as never before. Once more the DC-3 became the Cinderella airplane. She was "Queen Mother" of the whole new family of airlines.

Then it happened. The Local Service Airlines began to taste a little success. They formed their own association, and they started shopping around for a replacement for the old DC-3's. Spurred on by irate citizens who "wanted something better than a fifteen year old winged workhorse" to service their communities, the fledgling feeder lines started a vicious attack on the DC-3. There was a lot of name-calling. They said she was "worn out and unsafe." They called her a "tramp," "The Shirt-tail Special," "an obsolete warhorse," and a lot of other names unprintable here. With paid ads in newspapers, they argued that a new plane operating at a lower cost per mile, would reduce their dependence upon government subsidy. In time, they could become

The Association of Local and Territorial Airlines (ALTA) started its own campaign to put the DC-3 out of the picture. This was typical propaganda, part of a pamphlet sent to Congress. (ALTA Photo)

self-supporting. Perhaps, this was true. The big problem was to find that new plane.

"After all, the design of the DC-3 was 14 years old by now," reported Harpers Magazine, *"If our aeronautical know-how hadn't advanced in fourteen years to a point where we could build a more efficient and economical airplane than the DC-3, we'd better throw in the sponge! So, the talk ran at any rate . . . The airlines, manufacturers, and sympathetic government aviation officials sat down and agreed on the broad general specifications for a postwar plane to replace the DC-3. Then, the manufacturers went to work to design such a plane."*

"But gradually, the cold, unpleasant truth emerged," the Harpers article continued. *"It couldn't be done! Although American, British, Canadian, French and Dutch manufacturers tried their hand at the DC-3 replacement design, the answer was invariably the same. The DC-3 built for about $7.00 per pound of aircraft weight, represented too much in the way of competition. A new airplane would cost $21.00 or more a pound to build. One after another, the manufacturers gave up."*

This is first Super DC-3 on maiden flight. Outwardly, except for new tail configuration, she looked very much like standard DC-3. But she was actually about sixty per cent all new airplane. (Douglas Aircraft Co. Photo)

All but one. Douglas had some ideas on the subject, too. The company had been keeping a close eye on things even though its plant facilities were devoted almost entirely now to the production of four-engined transports, the DC-4 passenger versions of the military C-54 *Skymasters*, and the new pressurized DC-6 airliners. They had made their own survey of the DC-3 The Douglas conclusion was that *the only replacement for the DC-3 was a better DC-3* – a somewhat larger and faster version. The only question was: Could they stretch "the rubber airplane" just one more time?

III

"Our studies revealed that a replacement showing any vast amount of improvement over the DC-3 would be far more costly than would be the process of modernizing the DC-3 itself," said a Douglas spokesman. "Our idea was that we could take the basic DC-3, give it improved performance, economy and utility which would meet the demands of the short-haul airline operators, and at the same time pass the test of new Civil Air Regulations that seemed to be aimed at forcing the DC-3 ships out of the sky. Perhaps, there was some sentiment involved. We just didn't want to see the airplane that had put us in this business simply fade away."

For the umpteenth time Douglas got his "gang" together, the same crowd for the most part who had designed and developed the DC-1 and all her descendants. Arthur Raymond was there. And Fred Stineman. His chief designers, even though they were deeply engrossed in a design study of a DC-8 jetliner, Douglas' entry into the Jet Age which was just over the horizon. "Doc" Oswald and his aero-dynamicists also got in their two cents worth. The structures branch experts sat in on the conference – Donald W. Douglas presiding.

"It was like we were all called together to pose for a picture out of the pages of history," Arthur Raymond remarked. "But the past was the present and, ironically, we were about to tackle the same problem that had faced us in the beginning – come up with sound ideas to meet airlines' specifications and demands. The big difference was we were older and wiser in this business. But we went at it in the same way."

Whenever they could the group, taking time out from the other top priority projects, got together and thrashed out the things they would have to do to improve the basic DC-3.

There were many things that had to be

done. They knew, for instance, in order to be competitive with the *Martins* and the *Convairs* the fuselage would have to be stretched to provide for increased seating capacity. When they did this it would mean changing the wing and a need for the most powerful engines available. Changing the configuration and size of the plane, they also knew, would change its aerodynamic characteristics. They would have to "clean her up," get rid of a lot of unnecessary external perturbances and clutter; probably redesign the whole empennage to insure stability and control.

"Before we knew it," recalls "Doc" Oswald, "we were getting into the fringe area of designing a whole new airplane. Finally, we had to call a halt to all the ideas that were floating around the room. Somebody even came up with the suggestion that we all meet inside a DC-3 and work from the inside out. Maybe, it wasn't so crazy. After all, the big problem was to effect the changes within the basic framework of the DC-3 configuration."

It wasn't easy, held back by this restriction, but after many sessions the "replacement" emerged on paper and the decision to go ahead came down from Don Douglas. They were going to build a *Super DC-3!*

"At this point things deviated from the normal procedure in developing a new airplane," reminisced the late Ed Burton, a company V.P. who probably more than anybody else influenced Douglas to build the *Super Three*. "Remember, the whole idea was to take a standard DC-3 and rework it into an improved version. There wasn't any need to start from scratch. You see, we already had the skeleton framework right out on the ramp. We had purchased a couple of old DC-3's from the airlines. So, when we had worked the details out *on paper*, we turned loose a bunch of fabrication specialists and they put on their own version of "My Fair Lady." The stage was the mammoth hangar where the XB-19 was built . . . We rolled the old DC-3's in – and several months later – out came the new Super DC-3. But, believe me, it was some face-lifting job."

According to one source, Douglas paid about $8,000 apiece for the two DC-3's which were bought from the airlines. But when the *Super Three* was ready for the market she had a price tag on her of from $140,000 to $200,000 depending upon the interior configuration. But, it was pointed out, she was almost an entirely new airplane.

What they did to make it virtually a new airplane is best described by M. K. Oleson, whom Douglas named as chief engineer on the Super DC-3 Project.

"The first thing we did was to effect some aerodynamic changes," Oleson says. "That is, clean up the airplane. As a starter, we designed completely new nacelle fairings fully enclosing the landing gear. At the same time, we made the tail wheel partially retractable with a fairing to cover the larger openings. Then, we ripped off all the old external air scoops and air exhaust outlets, replacing them with flush-type units. The same thing was done with the high drag radio antenna and antenna masts, and we cleaned up the cockpit enclosure by flush mounting the front windows and eliminating sharp corners. The whole idea here was, of course, to slicken up the airplane's surface, built-in assurance to help increase her speed. We were going to have to come up with a faster plane, or the airlines would laugh us out of the picture.

"All of these things were done, of course, to the fuselage, wings and empennage after these basic structures, themselves, had been substantially changed . . . The fuselage, for instance, was lengthened by extending the nose section 39 inches forward, and the rear compartment partition 40 inches aft thus giving an effective cabin increase of 79 inches. In the process, the cabin arrangement thus provided for all of the cargo space in the aft section, with a waist-high loading ramp eliminating need for ground-handling equipment . . . Likewise, the entrance door was redesigned to incorporate built-in steps doing away with the need for ground personnel to move-up a gangplank for passengers to enter the cabin.

"The wings were next, and we came up with a completely new outer wing panel . . . The biggest change was to provide sweepback in the outer wing panels to move the effective center of pressure of the wing farther aft. It was necessitated by the change in the cabin arrangements for weight-and-balance reasons. We also beefed up the wing panels structurally and cleaned up their surfaces aerodynamically with flush riveting and flush skin joints."

These were major changes, but still to the layman the plane maintained its familiar profile. To the inexperienced eye, she was still the same old DC-3, maybe, a little larger perhaps, but no plane spotter could mistake her. But if you chopped her off at the fuselage just aft of the cabin door, that's where the big change met the eye. The new empennage which they designed for the Super DC-3 made her look like anything but a "Gooneybird." Looking aft at the new tail, she looked more like the Douglas B-26 bomber than anything else. There was a reason for this change.

Let "Doc" Oswald explain it: "Wind-tunnel tests told us to get the required directional stability we desired, we had to design a completely new vertical fin and rudder. This meant a completely new airfoil section for the vertical fin and the rudder. The rudder and fin changed their shape radically . . . For longitudinal stability we also increased the horizontal stabilizer, an increase of approximately 42 per cent over the area of the old surfaces."

"Satisfied with the airframe improvements, we turned to the consideration of the new powerplants," Oleson continues in his version of what happened. "It was decided to use either the nine cylinder Wright 1820-C9HE single-row engine, or the Pratt & Whitney fourteen cylinder twin-row engine, R-2000 D5 or D7. The horsepower for take-off was thus increased from 1200 to 1475 per engine using the Wrights, and to 1450 using the Pratt & Whitney engines . . . We also made use of the new short-type exhaust units on the engines to gain additional thrust from the discharging exhaust gases.

"There were other changes . . . We souped up the landing gear hydraulic system cutting the time for wheels retraction down to 5 seconds, thereby reducing the drag immediately after liftoff. The result was a faster acceleration and better climb . . . New engine mounts and redesign of cowling flaps greatly reduced vibration . . . A modified electrical system increased the plane's own power output. A new gasoline combustion heating unit installed in the fuselage below the floor just ahead of the wing improved cabin atmosphere, long a problem with standard DC-3's . . ."

"The fact is," Oleson concludes, "by the time we were through with all our improvements, the Super DC-3 emerged *sixty per cent all new airplane.*"

IV

The first *Super DC-3* was rolled out of the big hangar early in the spring of 1949. There wasn't much of a fanfare, according to those who saw the ship make its public debut. But she was a thing of beauty and pride. To a few, like Raymond, Oswald, and Douglas, himself, who could crank back their memories to the day the first DC-1 was rolled out of the hangar, she represented "a big chunk of our lives." For here was the past, present and future all in a single package.

Behind her in the same factory building where the DC-1 was born almost two decades before, they were laying the keel for the first DC-7. Taking off, roaring right over her, was a standard DC-3, an inter-company airline operation, loaded with engineers who were flying to the Long Beach facility for a conference about the DC-8 jetliner, already in the planning stage. Was it any wonder Grandma was so proud?

She didn't even show her wrinkles. There weren't any. Her skin was smoother than the day she was born. And by comparison with her daughters – the standard DC-3's – she was a fashion plate above their envy. A streamlined figure. Taller, three feet in height above the regulation DC-3. A new bustline with her streamlined engine nacelles. Slimmer in appearance, because of the elongated fuselage – three feet longer, a capacity for 10 more seats. Vocal chords – Excellent. And the roar of her increased horsepower proved it. The only thing was, she had put on some weight. The Super Three (empty) weighed 19,751 pounds, as compared with the original DC-3, 21-passenger version, at 15,260 pounds. But nobody really cared. The weight was distributed in the right places.

And when they called upon her to perform, she came through like a trooper. On her maiden flight with Douglas Chief Test Pilot Johny Martin at the controls, she earned the comment – "Better than our highest expectations." After that, they put her through a rigid physical. Breathing *normal* at altitudes up to 31,000 feet. Reflexes – *excellent.* Good response to the controls, Equilibrium – *good.* Stable as a high-wire artist. Muscles – *strong* as a lady wrestler, She could lift 30,000 pounds or more! And she could run – 270-mph top speed. The 500-yard dash in less than a minute! Some grandmother!

Understandably, everybody was pleased. The rubber airplane, stretched again, was full of pep and bounce. There remained, however two big questions (1) Would she meet all the requirements of the new Civil Air Regulations? (2) If she did, could they sell the *Super Three* to airline customers and others?

They got the answer to the first question in a hurry. CAB and CAA inspectors moved in and conducted their own tests. She passed with flying colors. Ed Slattery of the CAB commented, "They had somberly considered several times her age and her performance. In fact, on at least four occasions there was talk of not renewing her certificate to fly (referring to the Old DC-3's). But each time her record showed the old workhorse was safe, still airworthy. You can't argue with performance . . . And when we weighed the results of the tests with the *Super Three,* it was pretty well decided we'd stamp the case *Closed* and grant her a certificate to read 'GOOD, UNTIL SHE WEARS OUT.' "

But the question about airline acceptance still was unanswered. So far as her future life was concerned, perhaps, this was the most critical test of her long and colorful career. Douglas engineers were

The Super DC-3 interior. This particular plane No. 30000 (Douglas number) was especially plushed-up as a demonstrator. The Supers, sold to airlines and others, had various interior configurations.
(Douglas Aircraft Co. Photo)

never worried about whether or not they could hurdle the technical and mechanical barriers in the renovating process. They were confident they could do the job with the know-how at their fingertips. But nobody could "slide rule" what was going on in the minds of the airline people and others who were "on the other side of the counter, looking at the merchandise."

A lot depended on the outcome. How the new model on display moved over the counter. "If the market is there," Douglas told his people, "we'll go ahead with the production line. But if the customers don't like her, we'll have to forget it."

V

When the first *Super Three* had passed all her tests, she was primped and polished and primped and polished again, inside and out. Mechanics tuned-her up to purr like a kitten. She was to be the "flying showcase." They were going to take her around the country to show the airline people they didn't have to look any farther for that "replacement" everybody was talking about. This was it. Before it was over, she would fly more than 10,000 miles. She would make a hundred or more demonstration flights under the scrutinizing eyes of airline executives, engineering people, maintenance personnel, sales staffs. The "hard sell" was on. It wasn't like the old days when the first DC-3 rolled out, and customers were "standing in line to get their 'John Henrys' in the order book."

The *sales blitz,* literally, got off to a "flying start." Douglas had his "first team" on board. The plane was loaded with talent; his top engineers, structures expert, accoustics man, systems specialist, powerplant technician, men who could answer any questions. Ed Burton went along. So did Donald Douglas, Jr. and in Houston, Don Douglas, himself, joined the party. The Scotsman was damned proud of the *Super Three.* So much so, in fact, that he already had made up his mind this plane was going to be his own personal aircraft. No. 30000 wasn't for sale.

First reactions to the *Super Three* looked favorable. Leland Hayward, a director for Southwest Airlines took a ride in her and remarked, "She looks like a winner." In Houston, General Bob Smith of Pioneer Airlines made a few short hops and then, proposed a test. He laid out a two-and-a-half hour flight plan over Pioneer's route. "Here's a schedule, let's see what you can do with it," he challenged Don Douglas. Pioneer's own chief of flight operations took over the controls. Don Douglas went along for the ride.

In cockpit of Super DC-3, Donald W. Douglas (left) and Donald W. Douglas, Jr. They were part of "first team" on blitz sales tour to sell the new airplane. (Douglas Aircraft Co. Photo)

"There were a lot of stops," Douglas recalls. "We were up and down, up and down, and never much higher than 1100 feet. It was a damn rough sea. I never saw so many Texas towns. But when it was over, we had come within two minutes of the schedule. Bob Smith was satisfied. He told me he'd like to talk it over. But he didn't sign up."

In Washington, the story was different. Capital Airlines President J. H. "Slim" Carmichael, himself a veteran DC-3 pilot, took one look at the plane and "couldn't wait to get at the controls." When he came

The Navy bought more Super DC-3's than any other customer. They called them the R4D8's, used for various special missions. (Douglas Aircraft Co. Photo)

down he commented – "Just what we've been looking for." Jack Franklin, Capital's chief of operations who, incidentally, had been with Jack Frye when TWA bought the DC-2's, felt the same way about it. Capital placed orders for three of the planes, right on the spot.

While he was in Washington, Douglas also talked to his friends in the Pentagon. The Air Force didn't show much interest. But the Navy started contract negotiations for 100 *Super Threes* to be modified as R4D-8's. The future looked brighter.

They went back to Santa Monica. Douglas wasn't dissatisfied with the result, but neither was he overpleased. The *Super Three* hadn't set the world on fire. It was true, everybody thought she was a "fine airplane," and they had only the highest praise for her performance. But, he had only one firm commitment (Capital's) from the airline crowd. Three airplanes! All the rest were oral "expressions of interest" and at best, it looked like the airlines would go for only about 60 or 70 planes even if the verbal commitments got down on paper. The Navy order, of course, made things a little better. But Douglas decided to wait and see what happened before going ahead with any mass production plans.

"There was a lot of unexpected sales resistance," Ed Burton explained. "Airline skeptics pointed out that the plane didn't have any cabin pressurization. Its seating capacity was still short of that in the Convairs and Martins. They didn't like her conventional undercarriage, the slanting cabin floor when she was on the ground. Most of all, I guess, they shied away from the price tag. One airline executive, I remember, got pretty nasty – *What the hell,* he said, *we're buying a used airplane and paying the price of a brand new one!* We weren't exactly exhuberant about the reactions."

Douglas waited. And the picture did change somewhat in July, 1950 when Capital Airlines put its Super DC-3's into service. AVIATION WEEK, the publication that is regarded as aviation's Bible, reported in its October 9, 1950 issue – *"The Super DC-3 came into the airline world less than three months ago. Already its owner, Capital Airlines, wishes it had more . . . The Super-3 flies faster, costs*

USAF also bought several of the Super Threes (from other sources than Douglas) and used them for Air Rescue Service. This one was fitted with JATO assist take-off. Note dual landing wheels.
(Douglas Aircraft Co. Photo)

less to operate and handles easier than Capital President J. H. Carmichael expected when he placed the initial and only airline order to date."

Other excerpts from the article built up the *Super Three* sky high, and it might be added, sounded "mighty encouraging" to the Douglas crowd.

"According to Capital airlines," said AVIATION WEEK, *"the Super-3 is the best plane now available in these categories: Where traffic potential is the range from 15 to 31 passengers. Where intermediate stops are less than 100 miles apart. Where runways are too short to schedule planes like the Convair or Martin 2-0-2 without weight restriction (For example, Newport News, Va.) Where a plane is needed having postwar design, quality and economy."*

The article also quoted "Slim" Carmichael as saying – *"Any short-haul operation having stops less than 100 miles apart might well consider the Super-3 in preference to any other commercial plane presently available or in sight."*

Jack Franklin had this to say to AVIATION WEEK – *"The Super-3 meets all the CAA transport requirements. The plane handles easier than any other that Capital has ever operated."*

VI

All of this glowing praise was sweet music to Don Douglas' ears back in Santa Monica. But there was a sour note in the orchestra. Carmichael was also quoted as saying – *"The Super-3 is not the perfect replacement for the DC-3 – it's more of a stop-gap in that line."* Where were the orders for more *Super Threes*? The oral commitments never became written contracts. Even Capital Airlines which said they wanted more, didn't increase their order for the Super-3. There were no more airline commitments.

It was a hurtful decision that Don Douglas had to make. But the hurtful facts were all there. The airlines weren't interested in courting a "grandmother," even though she was a living doll and had money in the bank.

She was in the shadow of extinction with new planes coming into being—the DC-4's, the Martins, Convairs and Constellations. Major trunklines sold their Threes as rapidly as possible. This Eastern Air Lines DC-3 made a sentimental journey. She was hauled up Pennsylvania Avenue to the National Smithsonian Institution where she took her place of honor along with the first Wright Brothers airplane and Lindbergh's "Spirit of St. Louis." *(Eastern Air Lines Photo)*

The die was cast. The Douglas Aircraft Company, after twenty years of turning out its Model DC-3, more than 12,000 planes in all, including the wartime versions, would stop building the plane that had changed the world. Don Douglas "couldn't see the way clear" to keep the line moving. It was simply bad business.

"With that announcement," editorialized one newspaper, *"the shadow of extinction settled over a faithful servant to the airline community and the traveling public."*

Aviation writers, who loved the Old Girl, started writing her epitaph. It was just a matter of time, they said.

The DC-3 was dying a slow death.

Chapter 17

That Damned Gooney Bird Again

The thousands of C-47's – *Skytroopers* and *Skytrains* – that hauled our armies to Europe on D-Day had done their job well, for the beachead was secured and Allied might, like a gigantic tidal wave swept across German occupied Europe with the effect of the flood in Noah's time – cleansing the earth and the chaos upon it. There emerged, within the year, a free Europe and a Hitler-Germany defeated, with the task ahead of rebuilding *der Vaterland*, and all the other worn-torn countries. What to do with Germany posed the greatest problem for the victors. Berlin, in particular. What to do with it?

What was the right thing, what was the wrong thing to do, history alone will tell us. But what happened was that Germany was split into East and West Zones; the East Zone under Russian occupation, the West Zone under American, British and French occupation forces. Berlin, itself, was occupied by all four powers. Russia and her allies, in the high-spirit of friendship and victory, by gentleman's agreement, pledged there would be no interference with the transportation arteries – highways, railroads, canals – so vital to the reconstruction program and the life of the city. For a three year period, except for political and ideological differences, the plan worked smoothly – trains moved, and cars and trucks along the highways, barges on the canals. There was even a written agreement setting up three air corridors, each twenty miles wide, fanning out from Berlin. For the first time, in too long a time, Berliners could look skyward without fear in their eyes as transports, not bombers, reestablished the city's air link with the capitals of Europe and the rest of the world. Before long, even commercial airliners were flying regular schedules from the United States to Hamburg and Hanover in the British Zone, Frankfurt and Wiesbaden in the American Zone. There was bright hope in the sky and the future. The wing had, indeed, changed the world.

Then, it happened. Berlin became a trouble spot.

According to General William H. Tunner, writing in his book *"Over The Hump"* (Duel, Sloan & Pearce) – "It was the reform of currency in West Germany which triggered the Berlin trouble. On June 19 (1948), the day after the reform became effective, Marshal Sokolovsky, Soviet Military Governor of Berlin, issued an angry statement in which he referred to Berlin as *part of the Soviet occupation zone*. The Germans residing in the American, British, and French zones of the city making up West Berlin were terrified. They remembered all too well when the Russian troops poured into the city to rape, loot, and murder. It was obvious that the Soviets intended to drive the Western powers from Berlin and engulf the whole city.

"By June 24 the blockade was complete," Tunner continues. "Reason given for the termination of rail service was *technical difficulties*. Bridges were declared unsafe, and one hundred-yard stretch of railroad was torn up. No foodstuffs, or any other supplies could be brought into the three western zones of the city by surface transportation . . .

"There was no recourse but to take to the air."

The rest is history. General Lucius D. Clay, at that time the United States Military Governor in Berlin, called Major General Curtis LeMay, the USAFE Air Commander. According to Tunner in his book the gist of the conversation went like this:

"Curt," he (Clay) asked abruptly, "can you transport coal by air?"

For a moment there was silence on the line. "I beg your pardon, General," LeMay said, "but would you mind repeating that question?"

When the Russians slammed shut the gates to Berlin for ground transport, the C-47's opened the supply line. They were first to land inside the isolated city to start "Operation Vittles." As this photo shows, the field at Tempelhof is alive with the Goonies. The line kept moving in a steady stream. Hitler had designed an ideal terminal for the modern technique of airlift. (Official USAF Photo)

Clay did.

This time LeMay answered promptly. "Sir, the Air Force can deliver anything."

The die was cast. Clay had not been too worried about supplying American forces in Berlin by air. He already knew that many items were being shipped by air, and he was well aware of the miracle of military logistics that had been performed by air transport during the late war. But there were serious questions pertaining directly to the Berlin situation. Could airlift provide an entire city with sufficient supplies, a city larger than Chicago, Illinois? He knew planes could carry foodstuffs and the basic commodities and machinery. But he also knew that Berlin was dependent upon the one item – COAL – for light and heat and power to keep the city alive. He wasn't sure that airplanes would make good coal cars.

Curt LeMay's answer was reassuring. General Clay did not hesitate. He told LeMay to start mobilizing all the aircraft at his disposal. When LeMay took inventory, he found in all of Europe the Air Force had just exactly 102 of the C-47's or about 306-ton airlift capacity. The British also had some C-47's or *Dakotas*, and, of course, they would be in on the job, too. Along with a couple of C-54's (Douglas Skymasters), this was the air fleet he had to implement an airlift to supply the entire city.

Most of LeMay's C-47's were a part of the 60th Troop Carrier Group, veterans of World War II campaigns in Algeria, Sicily and Italy. Some of them even had the white stripes still painted on them, signifying they had taken part in the Normandy inva-

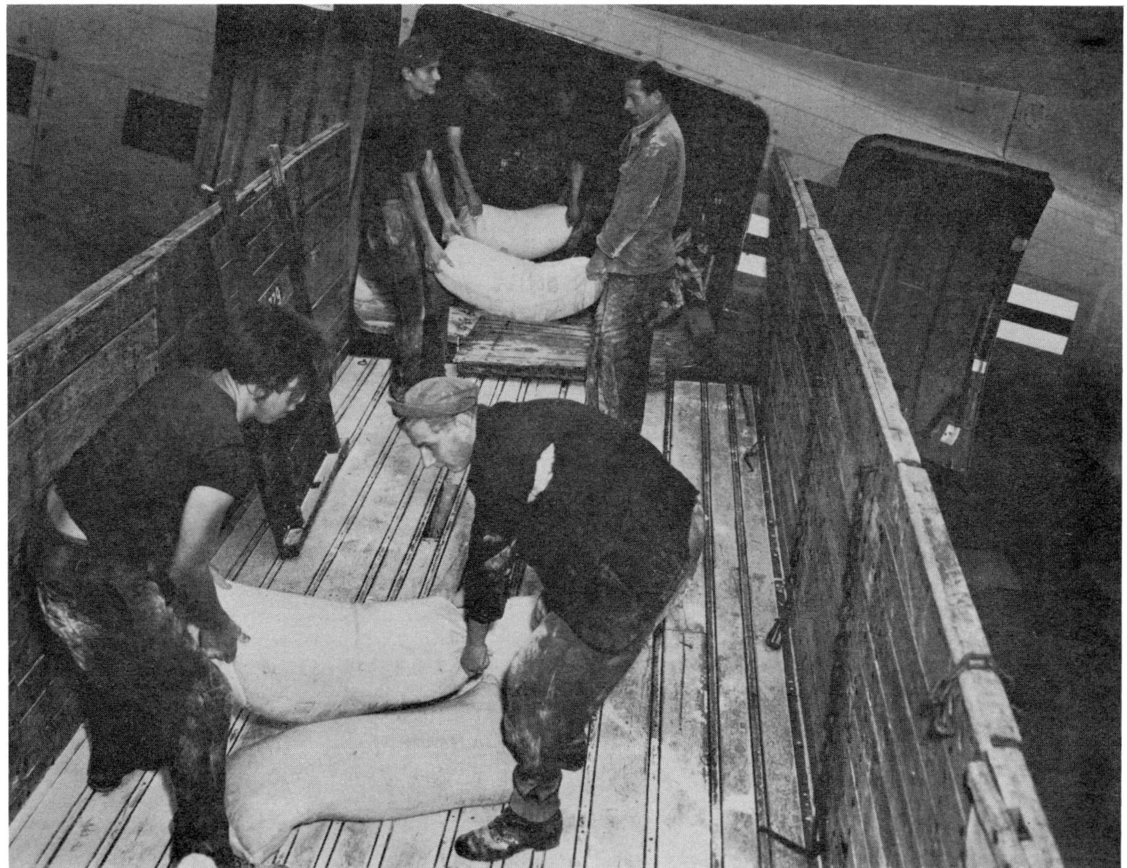

The C-47's flew in anything and everything. They "put wings on the staff of life," someone said. Here's proof: German workers at Tempelhof Airdrome are shown unloading flour from a U.S. Air Force C-47. (Official USAF Photo)

sion. It was one of the 60th's old reliable Gooneybirds that made the first flight into the city loaded with foodstuffs and medical supplies. When it landed at Wiesbaden, General Joseph Smith, post commander there, saw the foodstuffs being unloaded and coined a name for the operation.

"What the hell," Smith is reported to have remarked. "We're hauling grub. Let's call it *Operation Vittles.*"

In the first forty-eight hours of *Operation Vittles,* the C-47's shuttling back and forth along the American and British air corridors, flew in eighty tons of flour, milk, and medicine. By July 7th, they had reached the *one thousand ton* mark! And this included the first shipment of coal. It came in the stripped-down fuselage of a C-47 with the coal packed in GI duffle bags.

Later, as it was apparent the air supply of the city would have to be extended – at the whim of the Russians – the C-47's were joined by bigger planes, the four-engined Douglas *Skymasters* and others. But the Gooneybirds never were out of the picture from the very beginning of *Operation Vittles* until it was all over September 1, 1949. Unbelievable statistics showed that in all a total of 276,926 flights, the entire airlift capacity, had hauled 2,323,067 tons into Berlin. In the last month of the operation one DC-3 never missed a single day in the air; three hundred twenty-seven hours and thirty minutes recorded in its logbook. The Old Workhorse, working overtime.

There were many incidents. An outstanding one, because it illustrates the design integrity of the C-47 aircraft and certainly the capability of the high-lift wing, concerns a C-47 that took-off with an unprecedented load.

The story goes that it was a mix-up in materiel nomenclature, an alphabetical *goof* that resulted in a flight which almost ended in disaster. The *goof* came because somebody didn't know the difference between "PAP" and "PSP" which stand for, respectively – *Pierced Aluminum Planking* and *Pierced Steel Planking*, for the layman's education.

Anyway, the plane took off with a load of "PAP", so it said on the manifest. It was anything but a normal take-off. She rolled and rolled and she rolled along the 6000-foot runway. But something was wrong. Pouring on all the power she could muster, the Gooney wouldn't get off the ground.

Then, finally the tail lifted. The wings took hold. The plane staggered into the air. There wasn't any runway left!

Fitting itself into the flight pattern, sandwiched between other C-47's and the bigger planes, another link in the endless chain, the plane churned her way Berlinward. According to the pilot she just "lumbered along". It seemed she was just tired out.

But she made it and the pilot started the final approach. Only, when he put the gear down, the airspeed dropped too drastically, dangerously so. He had to use almost *full power* to keep her from stalling. In fact, he negotiated the landing virtually with engines wide-open. The ship slammed down hard, almost snapping the landing gear. The tail wheel hit with an even harder thump, and she almost broke her back.

"This bird is done. She just doesn't want to fly anymore," the pilot remarked.

One thing was sure.

Something was wrong.

They quickly found out. It wasn't *Pierced Aluminum Planking* back there in the hold; it was *Pierced Steel Planking*. The Gooneybird had performed a Herculean task. Designed to carry a max load of 6500 pounds, this one had carried a load of *steel* weighing 13,500 pounds!

They checked her over, and she was back in the sky again in 24 hours.

There were crashes. In the early days of the airlift one of the first C-47's coming in with a full load of food crashed in the heart of the city. Pilot and co-pilot perished.

General Tunner writes the epitaph:

"The entire populace grieved. Mayors of the six boroughs in West Berlin together visted Colonel Frank L. Howley, the military commandant, to express their sorrow. A plaque was erected at the site of the crash paying homage to the two American fliers. – YOU GAVE YOUR LIVES FOR US."

The German people will never forget the C-47 and her role in the Berlin Airlift, certainly not these youngsters who today make up the new Germany. It was all part of "Operation Kinderlift," and naturally, the "Gooney Bird" started it. Groups of children from the Western Sector of Berlin were airlifted to the Western Zone of Germany where they were placed with various families to enjoy pleasures of a vacation. Here, one group is shown on its return to Tempelhof Airdrome. The smiles tell the story as the Gooney stands there proudly. (Official USAF Photo)

The people of Berlin will never forget.
The Gooneybird was an angel in disguise.

II

Capt. Louis Droste of Detroit, Michigan at the controls of his C-47 aircraft was circling the communist-surrounded battle area awaiting his turn to land at Hagaru, a tiny airstrip hacked out of frozen hills near the North Korean reservoir. Suddenly, his co-pilot, Lt. John MacDonald of Missoula, Montana spotted two groups of men streaming across the treacherous ice of the nearby reservoir. The first group of about two hundred were plodding along, so exhausted they seemed oblivious to the pursuing horde behind them. Droste and MacDonald were almost certain these men were U.S. Marines. The second group, they were almost equally sure, were Chinese Reds trying to attack the American force from the rear.

The two C-47 pilots thought they had a sure way to find out. Droste revved up the twin propellers, shoved the nose of his battered old Gooneybird toward the first group of men below, roared down to investigate. The plane flared out at virtually zero altitude roaring over the heads of the marching column. The column stopped in orderly fashion. The leader waved his arms at the Gooneybird.

"They're our guys," remarked Droste.

He headed the Gooneybird toward the second group of marching men. As the plane flashed low over the heads of the men, they broke rank and in wild disorder fled in every direction. The two pilots were sure now – this was the enemy! MacDonald thumbed the radio control buttons to a fighter frequency and started calling for Navy Corsair fighters working in the area to *come to a strafing!*

That might take time. Droste had another idea. He racked his unarmed transport around into a steep turn and drove in for another pass at the fleeing Reds. Propellers churning wickedly in the cold sun-

An Air Force evacuation plane (C-47) takes off from an advanced airstrip in Korea, as an Army "twin forty" mobile gun stands guard at the north end of the runway. The plane was within range of enemy gunfire almost before wheels were pulled up. Many were hit but all landed and took off safely. (Official USAF Photo)

light, less than a man's height off the ground, he scattered the Chinese column like a rotor snow-plow going through a snow mountain. For a while at least, until the Corsairs arrived, the Reds wouldn't be concerned with too hot of a pursuit after our guys.

Stirring up the Reds into panic and disorder, Stout Droste and MacDonald flew their C-47 back over the Marine column, circling and circling to see if they could be of any help. It was obvious they could.

The Marine leader, while Droste and MacDonald had "deck-topped" the Reds, was busy stamping out the words WHICH WAY in the snow. The marines were lost!

Lieutenant MacDonald related later: "When we realized this, we wrote directions on a piece of paper, and then hunted all over the damn cockpit for something to tie it to or put it in. Finally I grabbed my old GI canteen, drank the water from it and stuffed in the note.

"We flew over again and dropped the canteen to the Marines below. Then, just to make sure, we made a long pass overhead in the right direction, pointing the way. The message got through, all right. We saw the Marines turn around and start for our own positions on the other side of the frozen reservoir.

"Just then, the Corsairs came in like a stinging horde of wasps, and we identified the Marines and the Reds for them. You should have heard those fighter pilots go wild. One of them yelled over the radio – *Hey, I've got me some Chinks. I'm in business!* The whole flight slammed into the fleeing Red column, strafing them all the way across the reservoir.

"We had to leave the scene, then, because we got our instructions to go in and pick up some casualties – our prime mission being the evacuation of wounded."

They called it a *police action,* but Korea was anything but just that. It was full-scale war. The Gooneybirds just couldn't stay out of it. This was their kind of fracas.

The above story of the "Gooney and the GI Canteen" that saved the lives of 200 Marines was told to the author by Ray Towne, Director of Public Relations, Douglas Aircraft Group, Long Beach. He should know. He was there.

Towne was also in the Berlin Airlift, as a pilot and as General Bill Tunner's Public Information Officer. Tunner at the time had taken over command of *Operations Vittles* when LeMay was called stateside. Probably more than any other man, General Tunner is credited with the successful planning of the Berlin Lift and final result. And it was he who fought against tremendous odds, even going over the heads of higher-ranking officers, for the giant cargo planes like the C-74, the Douglas C-124 *Globemasters,* and others to come. The man who could *airlift anything, anytime to anywhere.*

It was quite natural, that when the Korean thing broke in the summer of 1950, with Red Chinese troops crossing the dividing line in Korea to invade South Korea, Tunner was the man picked to head the Korean Airlift. Ray Towne went with him.

Today Towne recalls – "The Korean lift never got the publicity that *Operation Vittles* did, but it was one of the great achievements of our time, spanning the vast expanse of the Pacific Ocean, the longest air supply line ever attempted."

"It was up to the big babies, the *Globemasters, Curtiss C-46 Commando's,* the C-119 *Flying Boxcars,*" he adds, "to fly the long over-ocean routes.

"But in the battle zone itself, the good old reliable C-47 Gooneybirds – some of them in their fifteenth year with tens of thousands of hours of flying behind them – proved a most vital, essential, sometimes indispensable member of the team."

It was a time, for example, when the entire Eighth Army had crashed into Pyongyang and the North Koreans were on the run. Our 187th Airborne Regiment, Paratroops, was itching to get into the bout. This was their hour of destiny, the high command decided. "A successful drop of the Regiment at the crossroads of the towns of Sukchon and Sunchon some thirty miles north of Pyongyang," General Tunner wrote later, "would seal off the major escape routes, trap the fleeing enemy, and perhaps effect the rescue of Communist-held prisoners of war."

The transports that would carry this airborne force were the C-119's and C-47's. There were seventy-one C-119's and forty C-47's lined up and ready on the field at

In Korean action sometimes the C-47's were called upon to operate from almost impossible landing areas. They were, however, the only type aircraft that could land in some regions, which once more proved them indispensable. Here at an advanced airstrip, a "Gooney Bird" lands on gravel runway. Note the Operations Office at right of picture. It's another Gooney that refused to die, but would rather serve on and on and on. *(Photo Courtesy Ray Towne)*

Kimpo between Inchon and Seoul that October 20, 1951. The planes and the men were ready, but the weather wasn't. Heavy overcast came right down to the ground. The Air Armada waited. There was a five hour delay before it could take off, and even then, the planes roared aloft into thick clouds and disappeared. But Tunner in a "trailblazer" plane had flown ahead and over the target area, found it was clear.

"The 111 planes, flying in precise formation made a beautiful sight," he writes. "We flew along with them to the drop area . . . At 1400 hours over Sukchon, the planes suddenly blossomed, and white petals fell to earth. Just a few moments later the same scene was reported over Sunchon. We put the troopers down exactly where they wanted to be, in drop zones only a mile long by half a mile wide. Within one hour we delivered 1,860 men and over 301 tons of equipment, including jeeps and artillery."

That day the C-47 earned another battle star.

Another time, later on, things weren't going so well for us. Vast numbers of Red Chinese troops had slipped across the Yalu River determined to destroy the United Nations Forces in Korea. In white uniforms invisible against the new snow, they swarmed down on the UN troops, a flanking maneuver that collapsed a ROK division, annihilated many of our Seventh Infantry, and virtually isolated one of our Marine regiments which finally managed to fight their way out only to get bottled up again near the village of Hagaru. The situation was desperate.

The Marines stranded in this Chosin Reservoir area needed urgent supplies to carry on their fight for life. The more important thing was to try and get the Marines out, especially the evacuation of the wounded.

The drop situation and the relief of the 1st Marine Division is most urgent, General Tunner was told. The Marines had hacked out a 3200-foot landing strip from the frozen earth. It was their only avenue of escape. The planes had to come in, get down on the short field, get off again. There were some 900 to 1000 casualties awaiting air evacuation.

Tunner alerted every available C-47 in Japan. He knew it was a C-47 operation, the only plane that could do the job because of the limited size of the landing area. The C-47's flew in, landed on the strip which pilots said was only 2500-feet, not 3200-

One of the Evac C-47's taking on wounded at Hagaru. The runway was reportedly less than 2500 feet and made of gravel. But planes got in and out until all wounded were removed. (Official USAF Photo)

feet, flew in supplies, unloaded, and flew out the wounded. Back and forth, day and night the planes shuttled; right in the face of the enemy all around the perimeter. Some of the ships came back bullet-riddled from ground fire. But they kept right on flying.

There were stories, according to Tunner, of pilots permitting thirty-five even forty wounded men on board. One pilot claimed to have flown out forty-two. The operation continued for six days until there were no wounded left at Hagaru. And not a single casualty during the whole operation!

In all there were two planes lost. One crashed at the end of the runway during take-off, but no one was injured. The other developed engine trouble. It was intentionally destroyed to keep it from falling into the hands of the enemy.

The miracle was that a total of 4,689 casualties had been removed from the area. In addition, they flew out hundreds of Chinese Communist prisoners.

In high-praise, General Tunner said — *Without the C-47, it would have been impossible to evacuate the five thousand casualties from the Chosin Reservoir.*"

Wherever in the world, in all the history of mankind, were there such strong, merciful wings dedicated and ready to serve such a humanitarian task?

III

After Korea, things settled down for a while even for the Gooneybirds although they were far from inactive in the skies around the world. They were, for example, still the mainstay of the local service carriers — five years old now — providing much-in-demand air service for the smaller communities across the nation. And more and more of the C-47's and DC-3's which were being retired from the bigger airlines found themselves in the important role of aerial freighters. Everywhere, they were doing about everything. According to writer E. J. Kahn, Jr., again, in *The New Yorker* — "trundling emigrants from Italy and Cyprus to Australia, beef from inland Australian abattoirs to coastal ports, and sheep from Australia to grazing lands in New Guinea. . being used to spread fertilizer in New Zealand . . to harass brown-tail moths in the United States . .

DC-3's on skis patrolling the DEW line . . DC-3's on floats wafting fishermen to remote trout-packed lakes . . ". And delivering newspapers for the Sydney Morning Herald in Australia!

But still just about the only real excitement was when Arthur Godfrey – one of the few private owners of a DC-3 – buzzed a control tower much to the irritation of the FAA which admonished the redhead to "slow down a little."

Arthur did to some extent. But the Gooneybird was getting restless again. There were new worlds to conquer.

On duty with a construction gang building the DEW line, our early warning radar system in the far north regions, she played a star role in several Arctic rescue missions of downed crews that were setting up a weather station near the North Pole. And before it was over, on May 3, 1952 it was a C-47 that landed on top of the world to establish a base at the North Pole itself!

An historic moment is reached when two members of the U.S. Air Force party land at the North Pole on 3 May 1952, and place Old Glory on top of the world. (USAF Photo)

A statue-like symbol of her invasion of the Far North, this C-47 still stands on a mound of ice 30 feet above the remains of Ice Station Bravo. The aircraft was cannibalized and only the shell remains on this wind-eroded iceberg. Ironically C-47's played major role in helping to establish Ice Station Bravo (also known as T-3) located 95 miles north of Point Barrow, Alaska. It was used as a weather station and scientific research outpost by the USAF from 1952 until the fall of 1961. Deactivation became necessary in late September 1961 when a 2500-foot runway began to break up and drift away. (Official USAF Photo)

She was roaming in the Antaractic skies as well. Participating in the Navy's "Operation Highjump" (1946-47) Commander "Trigger" Hawkes led a flight of Douglas R4D's – the Navy version of the DC-3 – off the flight deck of the carrier *Philippine Sea* during the first carrier operations in deep Antarctic waters.

She showed up again (1956-57) in the Antarctic taking part in "Operation Deepfreeze" which saw another historic event with the R4D as the star attraction. This time it was "Trigger" Hawkes again along with Lt. Commander "Gus" Shinn at the controls of their plane *"Que Será Será"* (a Navy DC-3) and after an 840-mile flight from Ross Island, they landed at the South Pole.

Aboard the plane as a passenger was Admiral George J. Dufek, the ranking officer for "Deepfreeze". When the DC-3 landed at the South Pole it left there three scientists who became the first humans to inhabit the region at 90-degrees South. Paradoxically, they camped within yards of the spot where both Amundsen and Scott had once briefly stayed.

The full import of the event is thus described by Rear Admiral Dufek – "Since the arrival of *Que Sera Sera*, the South Pole area has been continuously occupied by the United States Navy in support of the permanent civilian scientific teams which come there to study various aspects of the Antarctic."

Proudly, the DC-3 could now proclaim that she was the only aircraft ever to have landed at both Poles.

The ends of the earth were hers!

Navy R4D aircraft "Que Será Será" on the deck at the South Pole. Pilots were Commander "Trigger" Hawkes and Lt. Commander "Gus" Shinn. On board was Admiral George J. Dufek, the ranking officer for Navy's Deepfreeze Operation. (Official U.S. Navy Photo)

The plane that landed at the South Pole "Que Será Será" buried in the Antarctic winter. They are starting to dig her out to fly again. (Official U.S. Navy Photo)

IV

That same winter of the landing at the South Pole, was one of the worst for blizzards and cold that had swept the midwest in more than two decades. Whole communities were isolated by the blinding snowstorms. Cattle were starving on the ranges. There was only one way to help – air drop supplies to the marooned areas.

Naturally the DC-3 was in on the show. Flying at low altitudes over the rangeland she dropped bales of hay to the starving beef herds. It is said she helped save tens of thousands of cattle from a frozen death.

The irony of it all! One need only recall (Chapter Twelve) when a similar situation occurred and "Hap" Arnold dropped supplies from the air to save the Indians on reservations. How Arnold had told Don Douglas that his bombers simply couldn't do the job. What was needed was a real cargo plane. How Don Douglas had listened. He must have. For the DC-2 was the first Army cargo plane and "Hap" Arnold, then Assistant Chief of the Air Corps gave the green light for the first C-32's. How his "aerial mule" became a reality and the C-47 was born.

Such is the way that history is made. And the cycle, never ceasing, keeps repeating itself.

V

Almost thirty years after the first American Airlines/Douglas DST flew on its maiden flight – December 17, 1935 – there was held in the Pentagon, November 26, 1965, an important press conference about the DC-3. Only they didn't call it the DC-3. They called it the AC-47 and it wasn't a transport plane, anymore, it was very much a combat airplane. That's what the press conference was all about. The Gooneybird was turned warhawk with probably more firepower – rounds of

United States Air Force C-47, piloted by Captain Milford Peck, drops hay to cattle on a ranch 12 miles northwest of Chadron, Nebraska. (USAF Photo)

bullets per minute – than any other aircraft.

"The AC-47 type aircraft is being used in support of friendly forces in all four military areas in the republic of Viet Nam" spokesman for the Department of Defense told the gathering of newsmen. "They are assigned to the 4th Air Commando Squadron as a Fire Support weapon under the command of Lt. Col. Max T. Barker of Jaroso, Colorado.

"This organization was initially formed last summer at Forbes Air Force Base, Kansas. A prototype of the aircraft has undergone a test program in the Republic of Viet Nam for the past year where it has become known to ground forces as "Puff the Magic Dragon." The nickname is derived from the roar of the guns which have a combined firepower of 18,000 rounds per minute, and the flame from the tracer bullets which often forms a steady stream of fire from the aircraft to the ground.

"The AC-47 aircraft is equipped with three side-firing Mini-Guns each capable of firing 6,000 rounds per minute. The aircraft carry sufficient fuel to loiter for extened periods of time in the target area and are equipped with flares in order to allow

U.S. Air Force personnel check a 7.62mm mini-gun aboard one of the AC-47 aircraft assigned to Viet Nam. Airman First Class James H. Schmisser loads the gun as Airman First Class Ronald Snyder, left, and Airman Third Class Allen W. Sims, right, look on. (USAF Photo)

In VietNam the "Gooney Bird" surprisingly turned up in a new role, an actual combatant. This is the AC-47, so designated because she is an attack weapon. Note the three open ports on left side, each a gun station for the rapid-fire mini-guns. (Official USAF Photo)

them to provide fire support on a 24-hour basis.

"The squadron of the new AC-47's is assigned to the 2nd Air Division located at Tan Son Nhut Air Base, Saigon," the DOD spokesman concluded.

That night on television, millions of viewers listening and watching the newscast saw "Puff the Magic Dragon" in action. They saw a C-47 aircraft that looked very little different from the thousands of C-47's which took part in the Normandy Invasion. The fact is, some of the *Dragons*, actually had been a part of that action in World War II – they were twenty years old and older. The big difference was noticeable when one looked closer at the rows of windows. The sides of the Gooneybird's fuselage was lined with gun ports. Her interior was bare of everything but thousands of rounds of ammo and armourers to feed the cartridge belts. Literally it was a flying machine gun nest.

Scenes from the official USAF news film showed close-ups of the pilot, who in the AC-47 is also the gunner. All the guns fire automatically, triggered much the same as a fighter pilot fires his fifty-caliber wing guns by pressing a button on the control stick or column. A specially designed gunsight mounted in the cockpit, by the use of mirrors, enables the pilot to fly his aircraft straight ahead but still aim at targets in the line of fire of the side-firing guns.

In this particular action, viewers saw an AC-47 take-off and search out target areas where Viet Cong were believed in hiding in thick jungle and foilage. Actually no Cong soldiers could be seen as the TV viewer rode along in the aircraft on its mission. But they were there.

Over the target area – located and radioed from the ground – *Puff The Magic Dragon* suddenly fired her broadside of guns. It was raining bullets from the sky.

Veteran of two wars, a dozen airlifts, conqueror of both Poles, the DC-3 at long last had become an actual combatant. She was no longer just a transport, but a winged gun platform.

Additional roles for the aircraft in Viet Nam include supplementing strike planes and long endurance escort of convoys.

That damned Gooneybird had found herself another war, determined, so it seems, to keep her world from too drastic a change by anyone else's hands.

Meanwhile, stateside, the DC-3 has found herself another character part to play. All gussied-up in frills and finery once again she's the queen of the ball.

The production line for the DC-3 was long ago shut down; but in this hangar in Miami, Florida, another production line modifying AC-47's for the VietNam mission is very much alive. Before they are through with her, this "Gooney Bird" will pack a lot of firepower—18,000 rounds per minute—three side-firing mini-guns. More and more squadrons of AC-47's are being sent to the war zone. (Courtesy Air International, Miami, Florida)

Chapter 18

The Flying Sophisticates

When the DC-2 production line was at its peak, in the summer of 1934, a visitor to the Douglas plant on an escorted tour stopped in front of one of the planes in final assembly. His face registered surprise at the markings on the ship's fuselage. All the other ships bore the insignia of airlines with which he was quite familiar, himself, being in the airline business. But this one was different from any airline identification that he ever had seen before.

"Who's plane is that?" he asked the guide.

His escort wasn't quite sure. So, the guide asked the shop foreman. The answer he got was – "I'm not sure, but I think it's being built for one of them rich oil barons."

He wasn't far wrong. Later, the visitor learned that plane Number NC-100, a DC-2, was on order for the Swiftlight Corporation of California, a subsidiary of the big Cities Service Petroleum Company. Although outwardly the plane looked like any other DC-2 except for the Swiftflight insignia, inside the ship was literally an executive suite with wings. The interior furnishings included a desk, large swivel chairs, a secretariat, filing cabinets and a small galley. It was probably one of the first planes of this size ever to be furnished so completely as a "flying office."

Company records show that it was the first DC-2 sold to a private corporation. Shortly afterwards, the Standard Oil Company ordered an even more plushed-up executive version. The DC-2's were pioneering a whole new field in air transportation.

Their impact on our way of life, particularly in the industrialization of many rural areas and in changing the economic climate of the business world, indeed, how we do business with each other, may be chalked up as another "revolution" started by the DC-skyships.

Back in 1934, however, Douglas, himself, is said to have remarked to Harry Wetzel when they were discussing the Swiftlight Corporation order – "Well, it's a market we certainly hadn't counted on to this extent."

Perhaps, he said that with tongue-in-cheek, because the idea of the plushed-up

First of the DC-2's to be sold as a corporate aircraft was this plane NC 1000, purchased by the Swiftlight Corporation of California, a subsidiary of Cities Service Petroleum Company. Note the CITCO insignia on nose. (Douglas Aircraft Co. Photo)

In the early thirties Douglas modified one of these "Dolphin" twin-engined amphibians for a French industrialist. It was probably one of first specially-equipped executive aircraft. Certainly the idea of "stylized" aircraft for individuals and executives was beginning to germinate. (Douglas Aircraft Co. Photo)

interior, specially-fitted aircraft wasn't exactly new with the Douglas Company. It is likely he reflected a moment on something that had happened a few years previous, before even the DC-1 went into its design stages.

Crosby Maynard recalls the incident in his book "Flight Plan For Tomorrow" a Douglas publication.

"In 1929 Douglas started production of flying boats," Maynard writes. "Perhaps, the most famous Douglas flying boat of the era was the *Dolphin*, foresightedly pointed at the commercial markets. The high winged amphibian monoplane was powered with two Wright *Whirlwind* 300 horse-power engines and priced at $45,000.

"The early 30's, however, were not propitious years for the sale of such special luxury items as amphibian transports to

Chevrons are clearly distinguishable on this Standard Oil Company DC-2 which was delivered in 1934. (Douglas Aircraft Co. Photo)

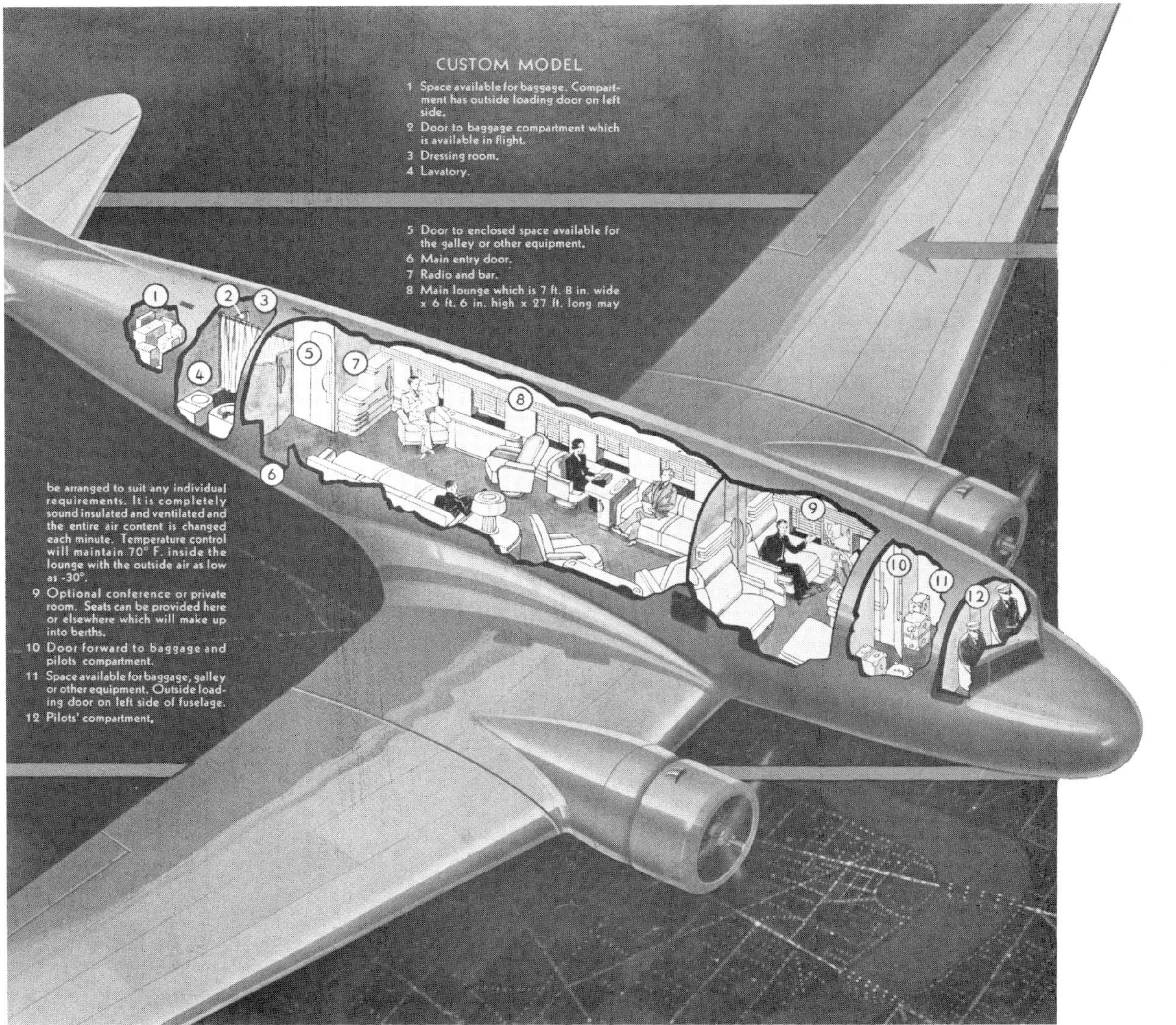

Cut-A-Way Drawing of DC-3 Custom Model. (Douglas Aircraft Co. Photo)

private users. ...But there was a single *Dolphin* sale which is still remembered at Douglas...

"One day, a sleek, chauffeur-driven car stopped in front of the main entrance of the Santa Monica plant and out stepped a trim young man who sought audience with Don Douglas.

"After certain delays, it was granted. The young man asked somewhat apologetically if he could buy a *Dolphin*. Mr. Douglas said that indeed he could but that it was a fairly costly vehicle. In reply, the visitor produced a check for $57,000 and made known that among his ideas was a specially-built *Dolphin* including such conveniences as a bar.

"If Donald Douglas was understandably dubious, it was not for long. The check was perfectly good. The purchaser was a French industrialist with a direct approach and a whim for the comforts of aviation!"

The Frenchman's "posh-posh" *Dolphin*, significantly marked another milestone in Douglas history. Certainly, it was a successful probe into a vast new market.

The day of the "Flying Sophisticates" was here.

"It would be a few years before the executive airplane came into its own," Maynard concludes his anecdote. The Swiftflight Corporation's DC-2 – less than five years away – shortened in time, at least, the import of these prophetic words.

Awareness of the potential market, and the ideas he had on the subject was in a very short time to influence Douglas' thinking when they were designing the DC-3. In the Douglas Company brochure announcing the DC-3, there is a cut-away illustration and considerable copy devoted to selling the CUSTOM MODEL (see Chapter eight) and there can be little question Douglas was going after the business of building planes for the business community; planes tailor-made for the busy executive.

Describing the CUSTOM MODEL, DC-3, the brochure says: "The main lounge which is 7 ft. 8 in. wide x 6 ft. 7 in. high x 27 ft. long may be arranged to suit any individual requirements. It is completely sound insulated and ventilated and the entire air content is changed each minute. Temperature control will remain 70-degrees F. inside the lounge with the outside air as low as minus 30-degrees . . . Optional conference or private room . . . Seats can be provided here or elsewhere which will make up into berths."

It is also significant that almost fifteen years later, when the company presented its *Super DC-3*, there was a CUSTOM MODEL available. NO. 30000 was plushed-up with an executive interior, and several of the *Super Threes* were sold to big corporations as executive transports. Had there been more orders, it might have influenced Douglas to keep on building the famous line.

As it was, the idea of the custom-built aircraft, geared to the whims of the executive clan helped to prolong the life of the standard DC-3 ships. In the process, it put some companies into the business of modifying these planes. Sales to corporations and individuals proved an Old Gal prettied up could hold down an important job in the business world.

II

The big boom in business flying started almost immediately after World War II and, unquestionably, was ignited by the proven capabilities of air transport during the war years. The old saw – "Necessity is the mother of invention" – undoubtedly had a lot to do with the explosion. In the immediate postwar years the upswing in air travel made it virtually impossible to get a seat on the busy trunkline carriers. The entire airline fleet numbered less than 400 planes, and the air transport system itself was readjusting to the aftermath of the war. The big new planes like the DC-4 (commercial version of the Douglas C-54 Skymaster) and the Lockheed *Constellations* and Boeing *Stratocruisers* were just beginning to appear along the commercial airways. Overworked *Threes*, some of them war wearies back in commercial service again, simply didn't have the capacity to meet the growing demand of traffic.

Salesmen and high-paid executives, rushing here and there and everywhere to rebuild the nation's peacetime business and industrial image, found themselves wasting many hours around airports trying to get a seat, or gearing their trips to limited airline schedules. Yet, the business community was first to admit that the flexibility of flight, the advantage of speed and timing could save time, and make money. Air transport became a major factor in planning sales campaigns; the art of the "Blitzkreig" so dearly paid for in human lives at the beginning of the war, became the heart of the "Sales Blitz" with the flying salesman able to cover much more territory in a day's time. The same was true for the over-worked company executive. The practical convenience of owning their own planes made it possible for key company personnel to move around more and keep in closer touch with branch offices and factories.

"The difference between flying the commercial airlines and flying in the company plane," one business executive summed it up, "is the difference between taking the train and driving your own car. When you take the train you have to go when the train goes. With your own car you can go when you damn please. Besides, you never miss a plane when you own your own!"

It was soon evident that the "plane to own" was the DC-3 so far as the big corporations were concerned. And there were plenty of DC-3's – more accurately wartime C-47's – on the war surplus list. Some of them, in flyable condition, could be purchased for as low as twelve hundred dollars! The job of having them refurbished into plush "flying offices" and the cost, brought a glint into many an auditor's eye as he saw the mounting dollars being spent for commercial airline tickets and counted the "wasted time" between planes and the limited availability of seats and restricted airline schedules, especially to small communities and rural areas. Suddenly, the war surplus DC-3 was in great demand.

Big corporations like General Motors, Ford Motor Car Company, National Cash Register Company, Alcoa, Standard Oil, Campbell Soup, Coca Cola, U. S. Steel and many others were quick to grab up the bargains and start their own corporate fleets. Good pilots, many of whom because of the war had been trained for no other trade, were eager to stay in the flying game and take over as company chauffeurs. The new breed of plane and pilot soon began to appear in ever-increasing numbers at airports across the nation.

Once more, the DC-3 – now more than 12 years old – became the prime mover in an entirely new utilization of air transport. The impact of this new role would effect many people in many places, creating thousands of new jobs, in some cases, giving birth to entire new communities in areas which never before had been considered as factory sites or as locations for branch offices of major corporations. In this way the *Three* helped to change the face of America.

This is what happened in many instances: A big company expanding to its beams because of the postwar business had to seek new location for branch offices of new factory sites. Plans called for building a new factory to meet the demand. Normally, this meant that the factory would have to be located in a community already on the air map, so that corporate executives could be only hours away from their new plant in order to "stay on top of things." In the selection of sites this virtually ruled out some smaller communities and rural areas. But with the advent and utilization of the so-called corporate airplane, which put the executive only hours away at any time of day, new consideration was given for plant location which in many cases opened up new areas for industrialization. The result was many communities today enjoy economic benefits of big plant payrolls and branch office buildings, regional sales staffs and other big business outlets which previously would never have been considered as suitable locations for these facilities. The executive plane, overnight, became an important tool generating new business, dictating the policies of big corporations, and carving great new physical plants out of the wide-open spaces.

In the process it generated a new business of its own. Because of the demand for the modification of the DC-3's and their transformation into "flying offices" aircraft firms specializing in the refurbishing of old and used aircraft suddenly found themselves doing a land-office business. It was salvage work of a kind, but it became big business for such companies as Remmert-Werner in St. Louis and the Garrett Corporation's AiResearch Aviation Service

Division, Los Angeles, California. Paradoxically, their big hangars where the modification work was done soon began to look like the assembly lines at the Douglas factory where the DC-3's were born.

Who said the DC-3 was dead?

The race was on, and the companies vied with each other to locate DC-3's anywhere, in any condition, to fill orders from corporations that wanted them as soon as possible. What happened sometimes was hilarious, as was the revivification process itself.

They found a DC-3 in South Africa that was being used as a roadhouse, its wings ablaze with neon signs. They bought it on the spot, shipped it back to California and soon it emerged as one of the "flying sophisticates." Another was a chicken house in Alabama, but they turned it into an executive suite for the heads of one of the biggest corporations in the country. Sometimes, they picked up one wing in Florida, another wing in California, the fuselage in Texas – put them all together and a Sky Queen was the result.

Writing in the *New Yorker* (September 10, 1960) E. J. Kahn, Jr. describes the harrowing pursuit of a DC-3 by an agent of Remmert-Werner sent to Ankara when they heard that Turkish State Airlines wanted to sell seven old Threes. "Inquiry revealed that they (the planes) had been stripped of engines, radios, instruments, panels, interiors, floors, windows, and fuel and hydraulic systems," says Kahn. "But so serious was the supply of DC-3's at the time that this seemed no serious drawback."

When the Remmert-Werner man arrived in Turkey, Kahn reports, "he learned that he would have to compete in the bidding against agents from England, Egypt, Israel, Brazil, Italy, Germany and Canada. After many complicated negotiations, he got the nod from the seller, and then discovered that the sale would have to be sanctioned by several echelons of Turkish officialdom, including the Cabinet and the Prime Minister. Before the appropriate papers could be signed, a pistol-brandishing debate was staged on the floor of the Turkish legislature, and the government fell.

"Dazed, the Remmert-Werner man renegotiated successfully with the new government, but it wouldn't issue an import license to fly the planes out, so they had to be shipped by rail and sea. Enroute, four wings were destroyed when a freight car overturned on a mountain curve. Three and a half years after the start of the dickering, the seven plane skeletons arrived in St. Louis, with the Remmert-Werner people looking on, as pleased as punchy."

So it went. And as fast as companies like Remmert-Werner and AiResearch could locate a DC-3 that was for sale, in almost any condition, they bought it and started the beautification process. The irony is that when the modified planes rolled out onto the ramp, in spite of their years in time and service, they brought prices on the market *more than double* the price that American Airlines paid for each of its first twenty DST's ordered back in 1935!

Some of the "Sophisticates" sold for as high as two hundred and sixty thousand dollars! These were, of course, the ultra-ultra, plush-plush jobs. But at the height of the boom the average used DC-3 fitted as a "flying office" seldom sold for less than $150,000.

III

What happened to the Old Girl during this transformation process, engineering-wise and structurally, gave her the muscles of greater power, the reflexes of better control, the vitamins of more fuel. Typical is what AiResearch Aviation Service did at its vast, varied and comprehensive engineering and service facilities for overhaul, maintenance, rebuilding and modification of all types of aircraft at the Los Angeles International Airport.

For the executive ships, AiResearch installed larger engines that boosted take-off horsepower from 1200-hp to 1350-hp, substituting Pratt & Whitney R-1830-92's for R-1830-94's in powerplant terminology. This change jumped the Three's cruising speed by 20 mph because of the power increase. At the same time it gave the airplane a safety factor bonus through better single engine performance, adding 1700 pounds to the permissible gross weight for a total of 26,900 pounds.

Taking advantage of this increased gross, AiResearch Aviation Service engineers found a way to install extra fuel tanks in the transport's outer wing panels. With 200 ex-

This was typical scene in Garrett Corporation's AiResearch Aviation Service hangar at Los Angeles International Airport when DC-3 refurbishing program was in full swing. Planes were virtually rebuilt inside and out, but they were still DC-3's. (AiResearch Manufacturing Co. Photo)

tra gallons in each wing the plane's range at average cruise and in average weather was extended 800 miles. Furthermore, there was no waiting for the job to be done. The division kept modified wings in storage and quickly exchanged them for old wings which in turn were equipped with the new tanks to await the next customer.

The larger engines were also "teamed" with geared rudder and aileron trim tabs incorporating mechanical boost systems. Cutting down required control forces by one-half provided better single engine control (in the case of the rudder) and increased flight safety under all conditions.

Perhaps, the greatest single advance in modernizing the DC-3 was to be found in the new (and exclusive with AiResearch) maximizer" kit, a company innovation. With NO increase in engine horsepower, the kit provided an increase in speed of 20 mph while adding a measurable margin of safety, payload, economy and revenue. The "maximizer" kit included a completely integrated and newly designed system of engine cowling, engine baffles, oil cooler ducting, wheel well doors and exhaust system.

Understandably the kit was a kind of a "shot in the arm" for the DC-3. Small wonder, it came from a design team headed up by famed pilot Benny Howard, longtime racing pilot, aircraft designer, and engineering consultant to many of the country's leading airframe manufacturers – including the Douglas Aircraft Company.

Secret of the "kit" was that it reduced drag through adaption of modern principles not practiced – and little known about – when the original DC-3 was produced. The chief change and the biggest benefit was derived from new knowledge gained from experience with streamlining, particularly in the area of engine housings (cowlings) and new air-cooling techniques which came about during the war years. By improving pressure distribution of incoming air across the face of the engine, AiResearch engineers, decreased the drag or frontal air resistance of the radial engines, while at the same time increasing the cooling effect of this moving air. They did it by installing a new cowling design with smoother contouring. Another result was less buffetting and vibration.

Through a patented new engine baffle design utilizing an entirely new concept, they reduced the drag effect in the engine area, providing better engine reliability and performance, especially in hot weather conditions. Improved oil cooling was obtained by changing the contour of the oil cooler diffuser entrance.

At the same time the "kit" called for a streamlined, lightweight enclosure for the wheels relieving another drag problem.

To bring their modified Three up to par with more modern radar-equipped aircraft, AiResearch designed a nose modification kit and radome for weather radar installations of RCA, Bendix or Collins equipment without change in basic air speed limitations as some such domes require. The installation of this new feature was unique in that it permitted easy accessibility to the nose and instrument panel. The radar scope itself was mounted either in the panel or in a special mounting where it could be pulled up between the two pilots when in use. Indeed, the renovation of the Three taught us many things.

Another AiResearch modernization brought the new Madsen light system to the DC-3 to substantially lessen the chance of mid-air collision by brilliantly indicating the ship's position, altitude and direction of movement.

They did something else. Some AiResearch modified DC-3's introduced four large panoramic windows which would become a popular feature of most of the executive-type planes. Whereas the conventional DC-3 had 14 windows (12x16 inches in size) the AiResearch version introduced the Viewmaster version with eight (17x17 inch) windows and four giant (17x57 inch) panoramic windows of extra-thick "Plexiglas" – much to the delight of photographers. And tired business executives, who liked to do a little sightseeing!

Inside, they made a peacock out of the "Gooneybird." Special fabrics, colors of any

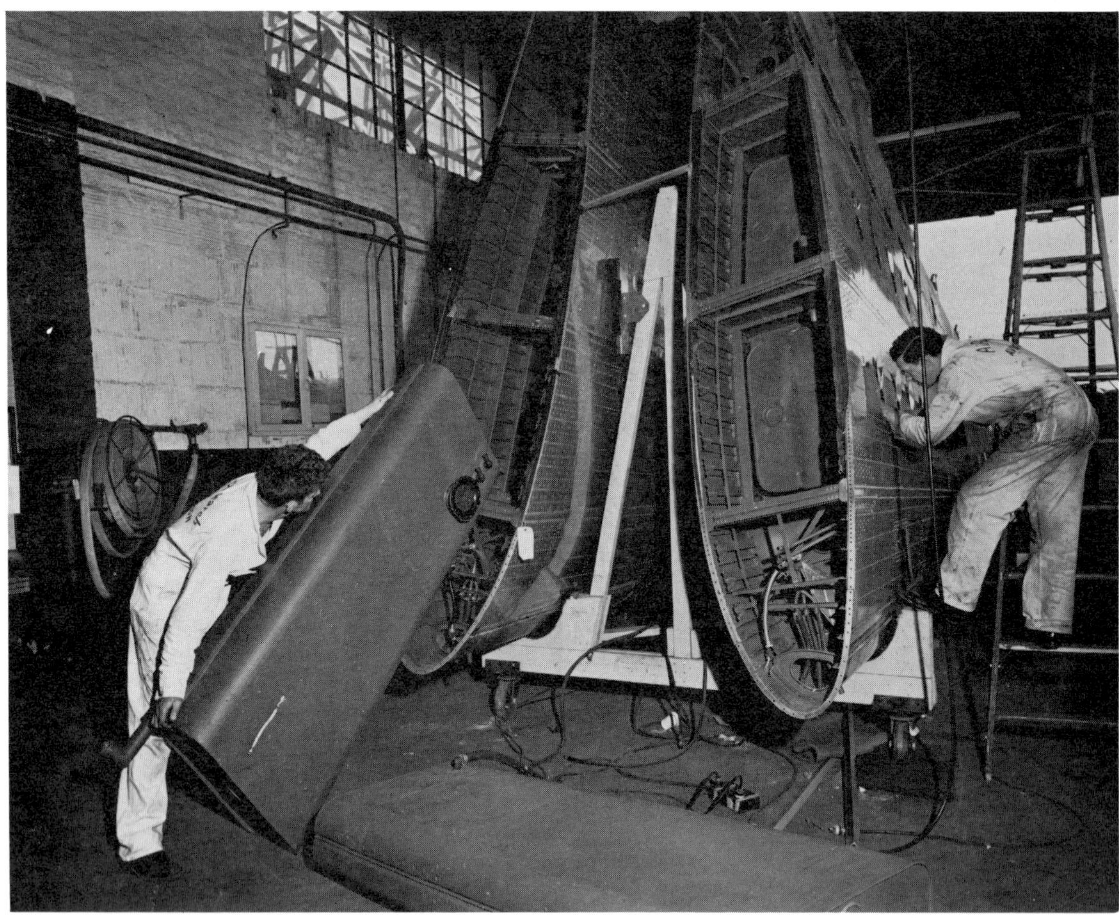

One of things AiResearch modification did for Three was to put additional tanks in the wings to increase range. (AiResearch Manufacturing Co. Photo)

hue, wood paneling from any land, wing-backed, contoured, reclining chairs; luxurious divans, private sleeping quarters if you wished, special fittings throughout in any design you were pleased to have – the whole decor and furnishings lightweight, fireproof and blended to individual taste with infinite care and skill.

This is what happened to the DC-3. The plane they said was dying a slow death suddenly became one of the most beautiful planes in the skies. Once more, in the dress of big corporation colors she became a "showcase" in the air. A Lady of Distinction – not extinction.

Writes E. J. Kahn, Jr. again: "Some of these (DC-3's) are elegantly fitted out. Houston Lumber has one with mink-covered doorknobs. The furniture in Alcoa's is all of gleaming aluminum. A rancher in Texas, one of dozens of individuals with DC-3's at his beck, has upholstered the interior of his in unborn calfskin . . . It is not uncommon for such private aircraft to be fitted out with hi-fi and tape recorders and air-to-ground telephones . . . and of course, bars, which in the aircraft trade press are called refreshment consoles . . . Pillsbury Mills has equipped its DC-3 as a laboratory to test the quick-rising properties of biscuit mix at varying heights and a number of other firms use the planes as traveling showrooms, in which new products are demonstrated aloft to customers consoling themselves with refreshments . . . A few Middle East sheiks fancy-studded the paneling with precious jewels – their value impossible to compute."

Their presence in the skies, unquestionably, brought a big smile and satisfaction to Don Douglas, and those close to him like to tell the story of the day he stood on the observation deck, a specially prepared platform loaded with dignitaries, (Memorial Day, 1958) at Long Beach to see the debut of his new DC-Eight jetliner. After the first flight was over, the DC-8 – a queenly representative of the Jet Age which the DC-3 in its own right, and the DC-1 before it, had helped bring into existence thrusting Douglas into the air transport field 25 years before – made its fly-bys Douglas was talking with the pilot of the plane, "Heimie" Heimerdinger. The strange thing is they weren't talking about

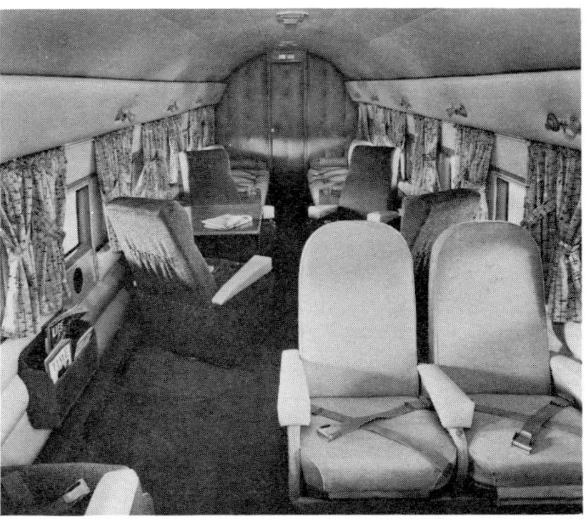

Interior of DC-3 modified by AiResearch. Overnight, the flying sophisticates became new sky queens. (AiResearch Manufacturing Co.)

the DC-8!

"Heimie," who is Chief Pilot for Douglas Aircraft Division at Long Beach, told his boss – "You should see the DC-3 that's sitting over there on the ramp at the AiResearch hangar. She's the prettiest thing you could ever feast your eyes on. Come on over and see for yourself."

What Douglas saw was a DC-3 that had been modified for Conrad Hilton. It was one of the "plushiest of the plush" airplanes, inside and out.

According to Heimerdinger – "The boss had a glint in his eye that I swear he'd sure like to own that airplane!"

Last year, in 1965, the Douglas Company bought the same plane and started using it to shuttle key personnel and executives between its California plants.

IV

Today, according to the NATIONAL BUSINESS AIRCRAFT ASSOCIATION – an outgrowth of the business and executive aircraft trend started with the first DC-2 – there are some 40,000 planes ranging from single-engine ships to planes like an executive Douglas DC-9, roaming the world's skies. The FAA lists in the hundreds the number of these corporate planes that are DC-3's. Some of them have been flying in this role for more than ten years.

One of the first big corporation's to buy a DC-3 executive aircraft, Montgomery Ward & Co., is still operating two DC-3's

This DC-3 was one of the "Flying Sophisticates" sold originally to the Hilton Corporation. As late as 1965, however, she was back at the place where she was born, Douglas Aircraft Company, Santa Monica, to join the small fleet of Douglas corporate aircraft. It is reportedly being sold. Picture is significant because in background (right) is Douglas DC-9, also being made available as a Custom Model and the plane which Mr. Douglas himself says comes closest to a DC-3 replacement. (Douglas Aircraft Co. Photo)

and an executive of the company, quoted in NEWSWEEK (February 1964) reported on their value. "Montgomery Ward & Co. has found that flying its executives in a pair of DC-3's," he said, "costs one-third more than putting them on commercial flights but saves 58 per cent of the executives' travel time."

Likewise, Sears Roebuck & Company has a DC-3 that flies a shuttle run between its big store outlets up and down the length of California. They call it, "The Needle" because store managers never know when the top executives are going to drop in and *needle* them about operational procedures. The "Needle" is very pleasantly furnished and executives say that they would rather fly in her than they would in the bigger planes, even jets.

Ford Motor Car Company, although it has a fleet of much bigger planes, including some jets, still operates three DC-3 aircraft for short-haul flights. Recently, riding with a Ford Company executive on a coast-to-coast trip in a DC-8 jetliner, the author was pleased to hear him say – "This is air travel deluxe, but I still like the Old Three. In one that we have, equipped with dictaphone and typewriter, I get more work done than I can on any commercial airliner. Besides, I like looking out the big windows, and flying at the lower altitudes so I can see something."

Perhaps, however, the greatest tribute of all comes from Richard L. Spaulding, President of Boreas Corporation, New York City, one of the leading buyers and sellers of airline and executive transport aircraft.

"The DC-3 and/or C-47 equipped for an executive operation," says Dick Spaulding, "with a plush sixteen place interior and with the latest radios, autopilot and radar, has brought as much as $125,000 cash – and that is as late as February 1966!

"The executive market for this type of aircraft is slowing down a bit in the United States. However, there is a definite trend for this type of flying more and more each day in Europe and South America. Therefore, many of these airplanes in executive configuration will find their way to these markets.

"It is our firm belief," Dick concludes, "that we will be buying and selling Douglas DC-3's and C-47's for many years to come. *There just isn't a replacement aircraft that will do the same job for the same money on the world market today!*"

Chapter 19

On Wings Of Time

The flight was smooth and quiet. A bright morning sun's rays bounced off the silvery wings. Below stretched some of the flat fields of some of the richest farming and fruit-growing countryside in the world. This was North Central Airlines' Flight #926 southbound from Manistee on squash-shaped Lake Michigan's eastern shore to Reed City, more inland, to Grand Rapids, thence to Chicago. The plane was a DC-3.

Inside, the cabin was refreshingly cool. Comfortable seats, a bright and friendly decor. Passengers were doing things they do in the living room. Some were reading. Others were enjoying a cigarette. A few of us were munching a light breakfast snack and sipping hot coffee served by a pretty stewardess. The plane droned on, the throbbing beat of her propellers, almost a nostalgic sound, reminding the seasoned air traveler there still were prop-jobs around in this day of the swooshing jets.

Then, suddenly, it struck me. I was riding in a machine that was more than 25 years old!

Later, on the ground at Grand Rapids to pick up some more Chicago-bound passengers, I asked the pilot how old she really was. We looked at the small metal placard on the wall just behind the cockpit. Her certificate of airworthiness. Her license to fly. There were two metal placards. One was North Central's certification date – January 26, 1951. That would make her fifteen years old. This was January 1966!

We looked at the other placard. It was hard to decipher the date, but we finally made it out. This particular DC-3, North Central Plane No. 10, Serial Number N17320, had won her wings in August, 1939! By the time this is in print, she will be 27 years old – and still going strong!

Checking closer into the plane's history, I learned that Number *Ten* was the first DC-3 ever to be equipped with the automatic pilot. Thus, because the DC-3's were the first commercial airliner to introduce the "Third Pilot" aboard, she, in her own right, had a claim to history. Certainly, it was an important pioneering step in both safety and the utilization of many new flying aids and navigational devices.

Around the shops at North Central's home base in Minneapolis, Minnesota (Minneapolis/St. Paul International Airport) mechanics tell a story about Old Number 10 that somehow seems to belong here. They tell it straight-faced because they swear it really happened.

She had been flying for sometime on the western plains segment of North Central's system, shuttling back and forth above the Indian Reservations of the Dakotas. Then, one day she came home for a major overhaul. Unloosening an inspection plate on one of the nacelles, much to his surprise, a mechanic found an old flint Indian arrowhead!

"Godamighty," he exclaimed, "I knew this was an old bird, but I didn't think she was that old!"

Surprisingly, Old Number 10 despite her vintage years isn't the oldest airline DC-3. Douglas historians, who have kept a record wherever they could, say this honor belongs to Ozark Airlines' plane Number N133D. She was formerly an American Airlines' DST delivered to American in July, 1936. Sold to Ozark in September 1950, twelve years later she had logged more than 51,000 hours in the air and, four years later in 1966, she is still flying in daily scheduled operation!

Records also show that the oldest non-airline DC-3 belongs to North West Schools, Inc. in Oregon. It, too, was one of the first DST's, plane No. N67000, delivered to American in July, 1936. The first DST ever built, incidentally, crashed and burned shortly after take-off from Chicago's Midway Airport during the war years. It was operated by a non-sked charter service.

This DC-3 belongs to the Federal Aviation Agency (picture was made before change was made from CAA, note tail letter) and it is used for checking various airport radio and electronic aids facilities. Reportedly it is one of oldest planes in existence, certainly the oldest known military version. Some say it was a C-41 which at one time was General Arnold's personal ship. (Official Federal Aviation Agency Photo)

Interior of FAA's DC-3 used for inspection of airport aids. It is a virtual "flying laboratory." (Official FAA Photo)

Oldest ex-military (C-41) still flying, so far as actual records are concerned, today belongs to the Federal Aviation Agency. The plane was delivered to the Army Air Corps in October, 1938 with an especially fitted interior as a personnel transport. Only one C-41 aircraft was ever contracted for. And it is believed to have been used at one time by General Arnold as his personal aircraft.

The FAA today has it outfitted with special electronic gear and it is used extensively for checking various airport navigational aids.

There are, perhaps, many other DC-3's which can claim longevity records. But for purposes here, these are illustrative of the fact that thirty years after the DST made its appearance machines of its vintage are still busy and active, daily performing many varied missions.

II

The Federal Aviation Agency, which keeps tab on such statistics, reported in 1965 that there were 217 of the DC-3's flying in commercial airline service in the United States. Among the users were: OZARK ("The Businessman's Airline"), LAKE CENTRAL ("America's Only Employee-Owned Airline") SOUTHERN, TRANS-TEXAS, FRONTIER, CENTRAL

Ozark Air Lines which is retiring most of its DC-3's is now flying this Fokker/Fairchild "Friendship" F-27, a jet-prop airliner, as a replacement for the faithful Three. Paradoxically it was a Fokker F-10, in which Knute Rockne was killed, that played a major role in the decision to design and build the original DC-1 aircraft. (Ozark Airlines Photo)

("Serving The Ozarks Playground Area") and NORTH CENTRAL ("America's Leading Local Airline"), and as late as mid-spring of 1966 they are still flying *Threes.* Trans-Texas even calls its DC-3's – *Super Starliners*!

The Russians also are still flying their version of the DC-3. Talking with a K.L.M. pilot, the author learned that Russian-built DC-3's – the Soviet calls them the L1-2's after builder Lissunov – are not an uncommon sight landing and taking off at Amsterdam's Schiphol Airport which is a West terminus for some airlines flying be-

This DC-3 owned by Ozark Air Lines is reported to be the oldest DC-3 still in regularly scheduled service. (Ozark Airlines Photo)

hind the Iron Curtain. It is interesting to point out that the Russian DC-3 is not a "Chinese Copy."

Back during World War II, the Russians were given 700 DC-3's – probably C-47's – under the Lend-Lease Agreement. Along with the 700 airplanes Douglas supplied parts and tooling. Reportedly, the Russians built about 2000 more DC-3's for themselves. In the civilian version, after the war, these planes became virtually the backbone of Russian air transport.

So far, however, even though it is making money for its Russian users, Douglas has never received any royalty payments. The Russians claim it is their airplane – the LI-2 was *made in Russia*!

By any name, the DC-3 just keeps on flying.

Threes are very busy abroad. In 1960, according to the British magazine FLIGHT, a recognized authoritative aviation journal, there were more than 1600 of the DC-3's in scheduled airline operations around the world. The same year, the International Air Transport Association, a trade group representing the international airlines, reported fifty-seven different airline companies around the globe, were still flying *Threes*.

As recent as 1965, a survey made by North Central Airlines' public relations manager, Richard A. Woodbury revealed that DC-3's were proudly flying the flags of some fifty nations. Indian Airlines Corporation, for example, owns more than fifty DC-3's. These planes are still "flying the Hump." Other foreign carriers still using *Threes* include Air Vietnam, Indonesia's Garuda Airlines, Iranian Airways, Jugoslovansk Aerotransport, Real Aerovias in Brazil. The list could go on and on – Woodbury's unofficial report contains more than fifteen pages!

North Central, incidentally, provides some other interesting statistics. The largest domestic local service airline, it also has the largest fleet of DC-3's still in service in the summer of 1966 – eighteen DC-3's. Aggregate flight time of these

Some of foreign airlines have modified their DC-3's with turbo-prop engines. "The Gooneybird has joined the jet age," someone has said. "She could not be left out of the show." B.E.A. (British European Airways) also had turbo-prop DC-3's. (Douglas Aircraft Co. Photo)

planes totals more than an estimated 1,280,000 flying hours. And using an average speed of 150-mph, slide-rule calculations say that means they have flown more than 230,500,000 miles.

For it is safe to say that there are more than three times as many DC-3's still doing yeoman's tasks every day than there are jetliners flying the world air routes. Nor does this include the hundreds of DC-3's and/or C-47's that are still in military service, here at home, and in many foreign countries.

Why does the *Three* hang on — the plane that simply won't wear out and never seems to lose her popularity?

There are many answers that go far beyond her basic design integrity and the durability of her metal-skin and frame.

Here are three explanations, however, that seem to tell the story best. The reasoning comes from the author's interviews, over the years, with airline operators, DC-3 passengers and pilots, all of whom swear by the Old Girl as — *the plane that will live forever!*

(1). There are some localities where no other aircraft yet in existence can do the job of the DC-3. Pound for pound over specific routes, performing specific tasks, there has never been — and probably never will be an aircraft which can operate so economically. In specific cases, this applies where fields are so small that no plane of any comparable size can land or take-off. There are some airports in foreign lands that are still little more than "cow pastures" — the *Three* can get in and get out without too much difficulty. Even here at home this is true.

The airport at Manistee, for instance, has short runways which in the winter-time often get pretty slick with ice. The adverse condition, sometimes, means a switch in equipment at Chicago for northbound North Central flights. A DC-3 can get in when bigger planes are instructed to fly over.

Moreover, the DC-3 can land and get away again without too much fuss and delay on the ground. Some airlines don't even cut one engine — the engine on the oppo-

Largest domestic fleet of DC-3's, as of spring of 1966, is operated by North Central Airlines. This scene taken at North Central's home base, Minneapolis/St. Paul International Airport, shows trio of DC-3's readying to take on passengers. Tail in foreground (right) belongs to North Central Convair which is replacing Threes on most of line's routes. (North Central Airlines Photo)

site side of the loading door is allowed to idle — when they land at small airports to take on passengers or mail. Landing, loading time, and take-off have been accomplished in under five minutes! It is probably why the *Three* is regarded as the best short-haul airliner.

Typical is the MacRobertson-Miller Airlines operation in Australia. One of its route segments calls for forty stops — some of them less than 10 miles apart — over a long 1750-mile line of flight. To even consider any other airliner but the DC-3 would be impractical.

Today's modified versions of the passenger-carrying DC-3's are also good money-makers for the short-haul operators because of built-in improvements. Increased horsepower and other design changes have given the *Three* added payloads which in turn means a more profitable operation. Some *Threes* today have four rows of seats, seven on each side, two abreast to give them a passenger capacity of 28 persons. (The original *Three*, remember, was designed only as a 21-passenger airliner.) In the new configuration, there is added revenue.

An acid test was when two local service carriers a few years back decided to retire their DC-3's and buy bigger and faster planes. They did. But after using the new planes for several months, the lines sold them and went back to the DC-3. Their route structure simply called for too many stops. The bigger planes were on the ground more than they were in the air! The return of the *Threes* got things back to normal.

(2). The DC-3 is still around because so many thousands of air travelers, pilots, mechanics and just about everybody who has come in contact with her for more than a quarter of a century simply *love that airplane*. An American Airlines ticket agent reported recently that she received a call from one potential customer who said indignantly, when told American hadn't been flying *Threes* for years — "Well, if I can't take a DC-3, I won't fly." Such calls are not uncommon with other airlines. People know the *Three* by name and reputation.

The passenger sitting next to me on my flight in North Central's Old Number 10, I was pleased to hear remark — "The jets are very wonderful, but *this is flying!*" He went on to explain that whenever possible he would take a DC-3 even though there were faster schedules. By way of explanation "It means, usually, we fly at lower altitudes and I like to see the countryside. Any other way is too damn fast. Moreover, I like the sensation of flying which you get in a DC-3 and don't usually get in the bigger planes. Somehow, you feel like you're a part of this airplane. The others are cold and indifferent; they don't have any personality. Me? I guess you'd say I'm a DC-3 buff!"

There are untold thousands just like him.

There have been odes written about the DC-3. One sample entitled "The Ballad of A Bush Pilot" concludes with these lines:

"Before I die
"I Want To Fly
"A Douglas DC-3."

One letter which Donald Douglas received from a Canadian banker, is a prized possession. It describes the DC-3 as *"a beautiful mechanical beast" . . . in flight, smooth and firm and straight and level . . . a person, not a piece of machinery . . . If ever an inanimate object earned, deserved, and received the love of a man, your DC-3 was that object."*

Suffice it to say anything against her.

(3). "She probably will be around for a long, long time for other reasons than sentiment," says Art Hinke, Chief pilot for North Central Airlines. "The *Three* is a very forgiving airplane . . . She almost flies herself . . . But to fly a DC-3 and fly it well makes a good pilot into a better pilot . . . For this reason she is ideal for pilot training with particular emphasis on emergency procedures . . . I can see a long life ahead for her in this category!"

This role of "trainer" would really not be new for the DC-3. On the list of Senior Captains, the Airline Pilots Association says there are few who did not win their Commercial Pilot's Certificate in a DC-3. The difference is, all things relative, while they were getting proficient at the art of flying they were helping to build the greatest transportation system the world has ever known — on the wings of the DC-3!

This is "flyingest" aircraft, North Central's famed 728. Note the panoramic windows. (North Central Airlines Photo)

III

The saying goes among pilots that "You can crack one up, but you can never wear one out!" and the proof lies in one of North Central's DC-3's, Plane No. 21728. It has never been involved in even a minor mishap, but at latest count (as of June, 1966) she has logged more than 84,000 hours of time in the air. More than nine years aloft! More time in the air than any other airplane in history. And during that time she has flown more than *twelve million* miles, the equivalent of 24 trips to the moon and back. It is estimated she has worn out 550 main gear tires, 25,000 spark plugs and 68 pairs of engines. She has burned more than *eight million* gallons of gasoline, enough to run the family car 10,000 miles a year for 11,000 years. On the ground, she has taxiied well over 100,000 miles. Her pilots joke that "everything has changed but the serial number and the shadow" but the truth is 728's airframe is 90 per cent original. She just won't admit she's getting old, that's all. One look at her and nobody could tell she's aging at all. The fact is, N21728 is one of the most beautiful planes in today's skies.

Before she was plushed-up, 728 was just plain "Old 18," flying the regular run for North Central. (North Central Airlines Photo)

The Saga of 728 began on August 11, 1939. On that date she was rolled out of the Douglas Plant at Santa Monica a bright and shiny thing with wings. Brand new, the 2,144th DC-3 to come off the assembly line. The customer was Eastern Air Lines which logged more than 50,000 flying hours on the aircraft before selling it to North Central in July, 1952.

Wearing her new colors, 728 known then, simply, as Plane No. 18, flew up and down North Central's route system, at one time or another, stopping at every airport – more than ninety cities from Sault Ste. Marie, Michigan to Sioux City, Iowa; westward into Montana and eastward into Ohio. On off-line charters she flew to such places as Washington D. C.; Windsor, Ontario, Canada; Jefferson City, Missouri; and Jamestown, New York.

Then, on Monday, April 26, 1965 she was retired from regularly scheduled airline operations. It was a busy day for 728. Typical, perhaps, of any day in the life of any DC-3 that is still flying.

The day began at 6:25 A.M. when, as Flight 2, she left Milwaukee airport southbound for Chicago's O'Hare Field. Captain Jim E. Robb and Flight Officer Jay Thomas were at her controls with Stewardess Charlotte MacKenzie back in the cabin attending to her 22 passengers. She landed at Chicago at 7:00 A.M. right on schedule.

At 7:30 A.M., they were off again. This time as Flight 467 with 18 passengers on board, back to Milwaukee. There, she picked up a full load of 24 passengers; sixteen bound for Madison and eight for LaCrosse. Operations were normal at Madison and LaCrosse, but she had to over-fly Winona because of high water conditions. At 10:59 A.M., however, she landed at Minneapolis/St. Paul with six passengers. This was home.

By mid-afternoon, she had been reserviced and cleaned, made ready for more work. A new crew took over. They were: Captain Herman C. Splettstoeser, Flight Officer James R. Topping and Stewardess Jean Krebechk. She became Flight 757. At

In its shops at Minneapolis, North Central gave its "Old No. 18" a complete face-lifting. Here she is partially torn apart, getting a thorough skin test. In the process they did not change her basic airframe or dimensions. Major modifications were interior furnishings, surface paint job. (North Central Airlines Photo)

3:30 P.M. she took off with 12 passengers for Brookings. There she picked up another load of 12 passengers bound for Huron. She arrived at Pierre with two passengers at 5:12 P.M. So far in her daily operation she had touched down in cities of five states — Wisconsin, Illinois, Minnesota, , Michigan, and South Dakota.

At 6:50 P.M. with the same crew, as Flight 758 she headed home for the end of a long, long journey. She carried six passengers to Huron, another six to Brookings and landed at 10:19 P.M. at Minneapolis with seven on board. She had maintained on-time schedule all day.

As of the moment when her wheels stopped rolling, Captain Splettstoeser recorded in her log book that N21728 had flown 83,032 hours, 52 minutes since she first spread her wings in 1939.

Although she would no longer be in scheduled service, she was really just beginning a new life. They had decided to make Old Number 18 a "showcase," and she went to the North Central shops for a beauty treatment — emerging as one of the "flying sophisticates."

She made a second debut in July 1965, almost 26 years to the day from the time she first was rolled out of the Douglas Santa Monica plant. This time, although her airframe was essentially the same, and her outward appearance — except for a sleek new paint job — the interior was something to rave about.

There was blue wool carpeting from Puerto Rico on the floor, a light beige ceiling of vinyl-backed fabric wall covering, lightweight walnut paneling with contrasting band of bamboo mat. The big viewmaster windows replaced conventional DC-3 windows, one on each side, with six other large-size windows on each side. And inside, her seating arrangement was entirely new.

Instead of 26 seats which Old Number 18 formerly carried (the Standard North Central configuration for its *Threes*) 728

Inside, 728 is one of the most luxurious DC-3's ever to spread its wings. Note the television. She also has hi-fi and stereo. (North Central Airlines Photo)

now had accommodations for only eleven persons. A large down-filled blue divan seating three; four more in double reclining seats of blue; two in two single reclining seats of gold; two in two single reclining swiveling seats, one blue and one gold. Other furnishings included three tables, table lamps, television, AM radio, stereo tape recorder for hi-fi music. Lighting was indirect, similar to the system used in the Boeing 727 jets.

In the front of the cabin there was a large galley complete for serving meals and beverages. To the rear a lavatory was installed — a modern lounge, with hot and cold running water and a special flushing toilet!

This is 728 today. Although it is used to shuttle company executives back and forth to important VIP functions, it is also used as a "flying laboratory." She is, for example, being used to test various paints which accounts for her always glistening appearance. Likewise the cockpit is fitted with the latest in-flight and navigational aids for testing before they are adapted for use in North Central's other aircraft. The airline's first DME (Distance Measuring Equipment) was tested in 728. The same holds true for various color schemes and cabin accessories.

The plane's measurements, wing span, fuselage length and so forth, are exactly the same as the standard DC-3. So is her horsepower rating. But 728 weighs a thousand pounds more than the standard *Three;* she has a two hundred gallon more gas capacity. She can fly almost 1,000 miles non-stop. And in her new role as "Queen" of the North Central fleet — even though she does not fly a regular run — she has run up a lot of hours visiting almost every city along the route, plus flying here and there around the country.

Donald W. Douglas (left) presents historic plaque to Hal Carr, North Central president. (North Central Airlines Photo)

In March, 1965 she made an historic flight from Minneapolis to Santa Monica, California. Twenty-six years, seven months, after she was born there, she had returned to her birthplace and landed at Clover Field, adjacent to the Douglas plant from where she had made her maiden flight. There was a big homecoming celebration for her.

She had a busy week. Flying down to the big Douglas plant at Long Beach – which wasn't yet built when she was born – where they are building the new DC-9's that will join North Central's fleet in 1967, she took time out to have her picture taken with the new jets. Then, she flew to Palm Springs where Donald W. Douglas was vacationing, and it was a proud Mister Douglas, who showed it with a glint in his eye, as he saw her standing there in the warm desert sun. The "Father of the DC-ships" had a big surprise for her.

At a special ceremony he presented Hal Carr, President of North Central with a bronze plaque which recognized Aircraft N21728 as having spent more hours in the air than any other plane, and as a symbol of all the DC-3's and their contribution to aviation. No other aircraft, so far as is known, could ever match her high-time record.

During the presentation ceremony, Carr asked Douglas a question: "Did you have any idea thirty years ago that there would still be some of these DC-3's flying around the country?"

"No, I must say we didn't," Douglas admitted. Then, he added with a wry smile, "But we think now, that the DC-9 is really the only replacement for the DC-3. It has been a long time coming."

That same day, 728 played host to Arthur Raymond and Frank Collbohm, both of whom had played major roles in the design, development and testing of the DC-1 more than 33 years before. Both were most impressed with this Jet Age version of the "Rubber Airplane."

Also on board for a courtesy flight was Dr. James H. "Jimmy" Doolittle, who remarked that this airplane was "a helluva lot different" from the DC-3 which had brought him safely out of China after the Tokyo raid.

And it was Doolittle who said – "The DC-3 without question is the most versatile, fixed-wing aircraft ever built. I know of no other machine that has saved so many human lives."

Perhaps, that is the greatest tribute of all to this Grand Old Lady, and accounts for the reason so many people feel the way they do about the DC-3.

"The *Three* is certainly the best and best-loved airplane we've ever produced," says Don Douglas. "But the circumstances that made it great just happened. They were not of our making. I doubt whether any airplane will have the same impact, or the same opportunity again."

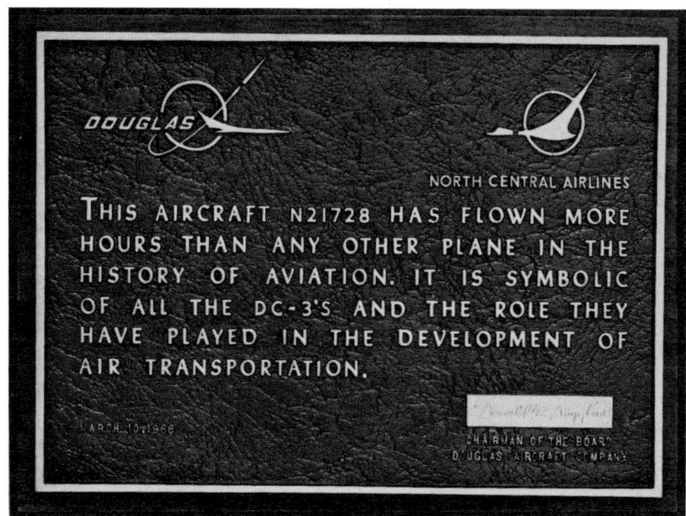

This bronze plaque now hangs on a bulkhead in plane N21728.
(North Central Airlines Photo)

FAMILY PORTRAIT

In this rare photograph taken at Douglas Long Beach, a DC-3 poses with the new generation of airliners which she helped bring into being. Indeed, here and there, in the nose, the tail, the wings, there is evidence of look-a-likeness which shows family resemblance. Left to right, rear row, Pacific Southwest Airways DC-4, USAF DC-6, United Air Lines DC-7. Front row: Stewart Air Service DC-3, and first Douglas DC-8. At the time picture was made, the DC-3 was more than 20 years old and still flying. DC-8 was just sprouting its wings. (Douglas Aircraft Co. Photo)

Chapter 20

The New Generation

Back in 1935 when he delivered his Wright Memorial Lecture to the Royal Aeronautical Society in London, Donald Douglas revealed some of his thoughts about future developments in transport planes. Studying his technical paper entitled – THE DEVELOPMENT AND RELIABILITY OF THE MODERN MULTI-ENGINE AIRLINER – one finds that the famous aircraft designer already had in mind the building of planes much larger than the DC-3.

"We can reasonably expect to continue to improve the reliability of our engines, instruments, radio, plumbing and other vital gadgets," said Douglas. "But at the moment we can only visualize a general betterment in the airplane itself by such changes as a four-engined transport capable of flying on any two engines . . .

"Further, it seems that the most important advance in safety that we should be concerned with is in better protection against icing up, against electrical storms, and in better development of blind landing facilities . . . The icing problem is partially, but inadequately, solved at the moment. Its better solution may be mechanical and may also be along the line of greater altitude capabilities of the airliner.

"Comfort development, certainly, is an open field and includes the problem not only of comfort, but sustention of life at high altitudes at which we may soon wish to fly . . . Pressure cabins and/or free oxygen in the cabins, are both being experimented with today. Our airlines are working diligently with our designers on these points and we look with confidence to some solution soon."

From these statements, it is evident the design and development of the four-engined, pressurized-cabin airliner was a challenge to the man whose DC-1, DC-2 and DC-3 skyships had revolutionized air transportation.

Douglas was to accept that challenge sooner than even he expected.

II

During the negotiations between United Air Lines', "Pat" Patterson and Don Douglas the following year (1936) the two men began a lifelong friendship. On many things particularly the future of air transport, they saw eye-to-eye, and before long they were talking about a "dream plane" that Patterson had in mind – a four-engined Super Skyliner. It just happened that Patterson had the specifications in his brief case. And he confided to Douglas that he had been shopping around the various aircraft companies to get somebody to build the giant, but there wasn't much interest. They talked a lot about it.

When Douglas heard from Patterson that Commander Jerome C. Hunsaker of M.I.T. (Douglas' former teacher and one-time boss) had helped work up the design study, the Scotsman became very interested in Patterson's project. He called in A. E. Raymond, now Chief Engineer at Douglas, and they began to put some ideas down on paper. Their own ideas about a superplane.

The next time Douglas, Raymond and Patterson met there was only one question. Raymond put it this way to Patterson – "Engineering such a plane will take a lot of time and a lot of money. Are you just looking or buying?"

Patterson wasn't bluffing.

"We'll put up $300,000 for the engineering cost if you'll foot the bill for the rest," he told Douglas.

Douglas remembered the experience he had had with the DC-1. The $125,000 TWA put up was just a starter. He had lost money until they were well in the production stages with the DC-2's. Then, it was the foreign business and additional airline

The Douglas DC-4E, first of the truly big commercial airliner prototypes. She was far ahead of her time in 1939, before outbreak of World War II that spurted development of bigger planes. Note the triple-tail. (Douglas Aircraft Co. Photo)

orders that had finally got the company off the hook. It was true, the gamble had paid off handsomely – but how many times does such a lucky number turn up on the wheel of chance.

Conceivably, tackling such a giant project as Patterson was proposing could wipe out all gains, and put the company's prestige position on the block. Unless? Could Patterson guarantee enough orders for the design so that the risk would be minimized?

Patterson had an answer for that one, too.

He had called a meeting of the top engineering experts and executives of TWA, American, Eastern, and Pan American airlines – and, of course, United's own engineering people. They had already agreed to split the $300,000 engineering cost which Patterson had promised. Furthermore, he assured Douglas, these carriers had all agreed that there was a need for such a plane, the sooner the better.

"We talked it over and decided that it was a waste of money to go at this thing with everybody going off half-cocked in every direction," Patterson explained. "It was evident there was a need for a bigger transport. If we tried to finance it individually, we'd all go broke, one by one."

Patterson had got the "Big Five" to sign a pact that none of the group would spend any money with any other company in the design and development of a plane in this weight category until they had first evaluated the Douglas design.

The DC-4E was born, prototype of the DC-4, the C-54 and the Navy R5D.

Probably for the first time in their short history, the airlines, always at each others' throats to sell tickets, were banding together on a "technological front" to provide a better, safer air transportation package for the air traveling public.

Credit for the unprecedented action of togetherness must go to Patterson of United. How he did it, Patterson once told a group, was simple. "I said *United* we fly; divided we lose money!" he said.

Airline people admit this, but competitors seldom use the word *United*. Everybody claims the credit. Fortunately for the public, the DC-4 merely gave the airlines a new weapon to use in their war of competition. They have never stopped building progress.

To the credit of the air transport industry, however, history tells us the four-engined airliner, as we know it today, was the result of a collective effort on the part of major airlines. As Raymond puts it – "Vast as was the experience of the Douglas Company in building transport planes, the DC-4E was to be the result of the fused experience and ability of some of the nation's greatest airline engineers along with the Douglas men."

The fusion process did not come easy. Neither did the giant grow without many difficulties and problems that sometimes seemed insurmountable.

III

The super transport – roughly three times the size of the DC-3 – came to life behind huge canvas curtains that screened off a section of the Santa Monica plant. Workmen called the place – "The Holy of the Holies." There was a bit of irony in all the secrecy. The big competing airlines knew all about what was going on. They were paying part of the bill.

The magnitude of the task is, perhaps, best described by these facts gleaned from a Douglas press release put out about the new Leviathan of the skies: "More than 500,000 hours in engineering and design, another 100,000 hours of ground and laboratory tests, eighteen months to build. Some 20,000 different pieces of metal framed to different shapes, 1,300,000 rivets. Total cost – $992,808 for labor and engineering, $641,804 in materials and overhead."

During the building of the DC-4E, once more the plant took on a new appearance. Douglas himself, walking through the shops one day and looking up at the maze of scaffolding around the jigs and forms for the huge wing made the remark – "That looks like a part of a ship's superstructure, not an airplane wing spar. It's hard to believe." Perhaps, he remembered childhood days long ago in Brooklyn when his father took him to visit the shipyards and see the ocean-going ships under construction. Indeed, the plant looked more like a shipyard than an airplane factory.

Another time Douglas confided to Raymond – "I knew we could design planes as big as this and bigger; but I frankly didn't know how we would ever build them."

The big $-sign went into the design and building of tools and dies and fabrication techniques that made possible the construction of the airplane itself.

The size of the DC-4E posed a new problem with every progressive step. Take the matter of the engine controls system. Each of the two outboard engines was seventy feet from the cockpit. Yet somebody had to work out a means that would permit engine power adjustments to get the same positive, sensitive response that is possible when the powerplants are only a few feet away.

There was the same old problem again. It will be remembered engine controls, specifically engine carburetor controls, was a big bugaboo in the early stages of the DC-1. Now, powerplant trouble was haunting Ivar Shogran's crowd once again.

"We had to start from scratch," Shogran explains. "It meant designing a whole new control system. But finally, we whipped it with a combination of push-pull rods, and cables that ran through the internal structure of the thick wing. It was rather ingenious, but it worked.

"We worked out a new fuel feed system, too," Shogran recalls. "Each engine had a 100-gallon tank of special *take-off* fuel and another 300-gallon tank of *cruise fuel*. You could switch from one tank to another with the flip of the wrist. It meant the plane had extra power for take-off, the critical moment of any flight. Yet, once the ship was airborne and set for cruise speeds she was ready to start an economy run."

Working out the engine control system and the new fuel-feed technique brought about a major innovation in "big ship" design, – the Flight Engineer's station.

"We felt from the very beginning," Douglas explains, "that an airplane of this size was just too much for one man to handle. It seemed we were asking that a pilot or co-pilot have four hands.

"To eliminate the need for conditioning *freaks*, we built duplicate engine controls and hydraulic system controls and installed a second control board just behind the pilots' station. It meant putting a third flight crew member up front, but it took a great load off the pilot and co-pilot during the critical flight moments when their attention is required to the fullest on the flight attitudes of the airplane. In short, the man at the helm didn't have to worry about the horsepower factor when he needed to keep both hands on the wheel."

It was an added safety feature that would pay big dividends.

There was another control problem closely related. The control surfaces themselves – ailerons, rudder, elevators – were bigger than the wings on the trainers Douglas was building. Only a Superman could be expected to move these huge "barn doors" in the face of the manmade hurricanes whipped up by the powerful engines and propellers – air rushing back over the large control surfaces.

Control "boosters" were applied. The standard control cables were replaced with small diameter hydraulic lines. Electric motors driving pumps, used the principle of the hydraulic automobile brake to operate the ailerons, rudder and elevators. The DC-4E introduced "finger tip control" to the cockpit.

"Doc" Oswald and the aerodynamicists had their hands full when they studied the wind tunnel results during the early design stages of the giant.

"We weren't getting very good lateral stability using the normal rudder configuration," Oswald says. "It got to a point where we had blown up the DC-3 rudder to almost five times its normal size and still we had instability.

"Then, I don't know who it was, but somebody suggested we try a new idea – three smaller rudders and vertical stabilizers instead of one.

"The result gave the ship remarkable stability especially during two-engine operation. This was a *must* requirement; that the plane be able to fly on any two engines. It was similar to Lindbergh's one-engined take-off requirement for the DC-1. We laughed about it. Things don't look so tough when you've faced them before!"

There were other problems that did not pertain to engines, wings, speed, seating capacity, safety.

Patterson was out at the plant one day talking to Raymond. They had just gone through the wooden mock-up of the DC-4E. Raymond sensed there was something bothering Patterson, who seemed to be rather sullen as he walked over to the executive dining room for lunch. Raymond learned about it when they were eating the swordfish steak – fresh caught the day before by Douglas.

"Mighty tasty," remarked Patterson. "But I was just thinking, you know, we have to do something about that galley in the big ship . . ."

Then, he went on to explain that he had hired a young Cornell-trained food and dining service expert named Don F. Magarrell to make a study of in-flight feeding problems along United's system. They had come to some pretty definite conclusions.

Patterson put it bluntly:

"With the galley in the tail like it is in the mock-up," he said, "the pretty stewardesses are going to run their pretty legs off trying to serve forty passengers on a short flight – say, from Cleveland to Chicago.

"We think the galley should be located amidship . . . Why can't we put it near the cabin door . . . That would make it easier to load on the food and beverage containers . . . It would also save time between the kitchen and the diners."

Engineers don't like food experts telling them how to design airplanes. But admittedly Raymond, Douglas, and the others pricked up their ears. Patterson had a point. He pressed it further.

"I'm going to send Magarrell out here and let him talk to your engineering people. Maybe you can get some ideas."

Later the engineers had to admit it was a good move. They learned a lot from the food man. As Patterson once said – "The men who knew all about aerodynamic flows listened to the fellow who knew all about the flow of food from the kitchen and when they got together we had put wings on the dining room table."

IV

They called her – "The Grand Hotel with wings." She could accommodate 42 guests by day and 30 by night. Cabin decor and passenger appeal offered chairs, color

Galley on DC-4E was big enough to make possible cooking meals aloft. (Douglas Aircraft Co. Photo)

blends, lighting, sound-proofing and other modern conveniences. And, of course, her size made all of this luxuriousness magnify itself many times in the eyes of those who stepped through the door into a new world of comfort in the clouds.

Giant she was, indeed, with a wing span of 138 feet, three inches; fuselage length of 97 feet, seven inches; wing thickness, 4 feet, six inches; 14-foot diameter propellers; gross weight of 65,000 pounds! And Luxurious!

There was a comfortable Ladies' Lounge, a Men's Dressing Room, a private compartment up front called the "Bridal Suite." The big lounge type chairs – two abreast seating, twenty seats on each side of a wide aisle – were arranged like the seats in a Pullman car so that they could be easily and quickly make up into sleeping berths. Other features included air conditioning, steam heat, hot and cold running water, electrically operated kitchen, complete with home appliances (curling irons for the ladies, electric shavers for the men) and a telephone system connecting with any exchange in the world while the plane was in port.

Aerodynamically and mechanically the plane also represented the acme in design, safety and performance. Virtually every new improvement and innovation then available to the aircraft builder had been incorporated into the DC-4E. And there were some which it introduced for the first time. It was far ahead of anything in the air transport line anywhere.

For one thing, the DC-4E was the first aircraft of its size to incorporate the tricycle landing gear. Instead of the familiar tail wheel and main landing gear (two wheels) arrangement, the DC-4E rested on two main wheels and a nose wheel. The tricycle undercarriage had many advantages. It meant that the big ship's fuselage was level even when the plane was parked on the ground. No longer did the passenger need walk up an inclined aisle in order to take a front seat.

More important, the tri-gear greatly improved the big plane's take-off and landing characteristics. The airplane, being in a normal level flight attitude presented the control and lift surfaces to the airstream right from the beginning of its taxi run – cutting out the need to "lift the tail high," angling the lift surfaces into the airstream. Likewise, in landing, the new gear enabled pilots to literally "fly" the ship in for a landing, rather than let it settle at the last minute. "Positive control right to touchdown," airmen call it.

On the ground, taxiing capabilities of the giant far exceeded the maneuverability

They called her a "Flying Hotel." The DC-4E could sleep thirty people. (Douglas Aircraft Co. Photo)

of small planes because of the kiddie car type undercarriage. You could literally turn the big ship on the proverbial dime.

Retracting the nose wheel and the dual-wheels of the main gear posed new design and mechanical problems. But the ship had two auxiliary engines working independently of its four powerful Pratt & Whitney *Hornet* engines.

Developing a total of 600-horsepower, the two "extra" motors drove generators to provide electricity and actuated pumps for the hydraulic controls that operated the booster system, auto pilot, landing gear, wing flaps and de-icers. They also drove the compressors for cabin air conditioning and heating.

"We manufactured enough electricity to light a large office building," Shogran explains. "It was the first time a generating plant of this size ever sprouted wings."

"In the DC-4E the Pratt & Whitney gang finally got their chance to prove the prowess of their engines," Shogran adds, recalling the 'war of the horses' back in the days of the DC-1. "The P & W crowd back in Hartford had made tremendous strikes in engine improvement without which we probably wouldn't have had the power available to get the thirty-two-and-a-half ton airplane off the ground.

"Higher compression ratios, supercharging, tougher alloys permitting faster crankshaft speeds, redesigned fins for cooling, gave us the first 2000-plus horsepower aircraft engine."

The DC-4E's quad of engines, 14-cylinder, twin-row air-cooled, radials, produced a total of more than 5600 horsepower — equal to that of two diesel locomotives.

One thing was certain. There was enough power at his fingers when Carl Cover climbed into the pilot's seat on June 7, 1938 and took the giant up for its maiden flight.

"She flies herself," Cover told Douglas. "I just went along for the ride."

Commented Don Douglas after the ship had landed — "The story of the DC-4E is the story of the organization that made it possible. To us it is more than just the outstanding airplane of its time. It is a symbol — a goal achieved and a task fulfilled. Here in our plants, where other wings of commerce and defense have taken shape to spread over the world's skyways, engineering and craftsmenship find their highest expression.

"Scientist and mechanic alike have a heritage and tradition with which there can be no compromise. Together they work, together they plan ahead and look ahead. The DC-4E is a tribute to the men who designed and built it. The ship is our token of a job well done and the promise of progress to come."

V

The DC-4E proved to be everything they had hoped for and more. Early in the test program the company released performance figures — Useful load, 20,000 pounds. High speed, 240 miles per hour. (Faster than any bomber of that period) Cruising altitude 22,900 feet; absolute ceiling, 24,000 feet — almost five miles above the earth. Maximum range, 2,200 miles.

The ship flew in June of 1938, but it was not until May the following year that Douglas turned the plane over to United and the other participating airlines for their flight evaluation tests. First one, then the others — United, American, TWA, Eastern, Pan American, in that order — assigned their flight test crews to put the big plane through its paces.

Up and down the airways, east, west, north and south, landing at big metropolitan cities and intermediate populated areas — wherever airports were able to accept it — the plane made its public debut. Wherever it went people looked at the giant with awe, almost disbelief, that such a huge machine could lift itself into the sky and hurl through the air at four-miles-a-minute speeds. Surely, this was the modern magic carpet.

Pilots liked it, praised it. "Flying the DC-4E," said United test pilot Benny Howard, famed racing flyer and plane designer (the "Mister Mulligan" racing designs), "is about as exciting as a game of solitaire."

Airline operations' people thought it was the answer to their prayers. At Cheyenne, Wyoming, elevation 6200 feet, Howard, during United's flight tests, roared down the runway in take-off, reached up and cut out two engines. The plane soared aloft as though nothing had happened.

Watching this unprecedented demonstration of power reserve, Jack Herlihy, vice-president of operations for United, beamed – "That's the plane for us!"

The airlines were ready for the big step into the true Air Age. The DC-4E had the range. She could fly non-stop from San Francisco to Chicago, high above the treacherous Rocky Mountains. Tons of radio, communications and navigational equipment aboard led her by the hand across the limitless sky. She had the capacity to haul great loads – a crew of five; two pilots, flight engineer, steward and stewardess; forty passengers by day; 32 berths. There was plenty of room to spare for mail, express, baggage. Most important, she could do all this for about the same operational cost of the faithful DC-3's. Where the cost went up, the performance and capabilities made it negligible.

Results of the airline test program brought about many recommendations for improvements in passenger comfort and in design suggestions.

The principle change recommended was that the production models have a pressurized cabin.

Pictured in flight is a Boeing 307 Stratoliner, first of the pressurized cabin skyliners. It was, however, smaller than the DC-4E and the Douglas production models on the planning boards, which were also to be pressurized. (Pan American World Airways Photo)

Douglas agreed with the changes. Frankly, they had anticipated this requirement and the pressurization system had already been worked out on paper.

The truth is, they were "forced" in this direction by competition. Two of the airlines which had signed the pact with Patterson had bought a Boeing design, the four-engined 307 *Stratoliners* which had a pressurized cabin. The *Stratoliners* were in service actually *before* the DC-4E was turned over to the airlines for evalua-

First to demonstrate the "new age of air travel" to the public was United Air Lines whose president, W. A. Patterson, was chiefly responsible for the development of the DC-4E. (United Air Lines Photo)

Outbreak of World War II curtailed production of the planned DC-4 production models already ordered by some of the airlines. The airliners had to give way to military transport version, the Douglas C-54 SKYMASTER. Before the war was over the C-54's were taking over many long-range airlift tasks which had been pioneered by the DC-3's (USAF Photo)

tion tests. The Boeings were smaller ships and good ones. They set the pace for over-the-weather flying.

Their tests completed with the prototype, both United and American placed orders for the improved DC-4 type airliner. The order went down to the shops to start building the production models.

History had other ideas.

It was the year 1940 before they got the green light to go ahead with the production program. Britain was fighting for her life. France had fallen. The Luftwaffe was bombing Coventry, Birmingham, London and other English cities. England, alone, stood between the U. S. and Hitlerism and Nazi conquest.

Britain needed bombers – not transport planes. Lend-Lease was in effect. The order came down from the top military chiefs – *no more transports, build combat aircraft.*

"Hap" Arnold, U.S. air chief, on a visit to the Douglas plant saw the work progressing on the DC-4. A few days later Douglas got a teletype directing him to stop work on the big transport plane. It riled the Scotsman's blood. He was already producing fast, twin-engined Havoc bombers for Britain at a rate faster than they could deliver the ships across the sea. He wanted to tell Arnold to go to hell. This was his money and the airlines' money, his plant, and if he wanted a new Board of Directors it wouldn't come from the top military top brass. Besides, Douglas believed there would come the day when the military would need a ship the size of the DC-4.

Once more Douglas took the initiative and the gamble. "We're going to keep on building the DC-4," he told Raymond and his production people. "We'll step up the bombers and the other military (Navy) production lines. But we're going to build the big transport."

Something else happened that more than justified his foresight. The Germans with a great aerial armada invaded the island of Crete. U. S. military observers returned with reports of the giant gliders and huge four-engined Junker transport planes that made the invasion lightning swift and successful.

The teletype from Washington clacked out another urgent message – "Top priority on the big transport."

Douglas must have smiled to himself that day. He had kept the DC-4 production line going because he already had orders from United Air Lines and American Airlines for the commercial version. There had been a lot of changes made in the original triple-tailed DC-4E. The production airplane was emerging as a single-tail configuration and there were many other internal modifications. Everybody was pleased and virtually certain that this plane would be the answer to a global network of airlines. Only a major war could delay the new-era civil air transports.

A major war did. On a visit to the Douglas plant Robert A. Lovett, Assistant Secretary of War, saw the commercial DC-4's which United and American had ordered, going down the assembly line. He reported back to the Chief of Staff in Washington that this was the airplane the military needed for warfare logistics. The higher-ups, the White House even, agreed, and both United and American were asked to cancel their orders so that the Douglas plant could concentrate on a military version. The airlines complied.

Overnight, the plush commercial DC-4 became the rugged, Douglas *Skymaster*, the Airforce C-54 and the Navy R5D. She was soon to join her predecessors the DC-2's, DC-3's and the other military transports like the C-47 in the skies all over the world – a bigger "workhorse of the air."

In her war role the C-54 did a tremendous task. She hauled VIP's – Roosevelt, Marshall, Churchill, Eisenhower, and the other wartime leaders – all over the world. Probably more than any other machine she was responsible for the long-range, over-water flying, proving that landplanes could do the job the "Flying Clippers" had previously performed. The fact is, the "Clippers" vanished from the airways. In Transocean travel Douglas once more had won the race with Boeing. It was the same story of the DC-1 and the 247 all over again.

And when the war was over, the DC-4 became the prime commercial carrier on the new commercial air routes that linked together the capitals of the world. Because of her size and range, she started another revolution in air transportation.

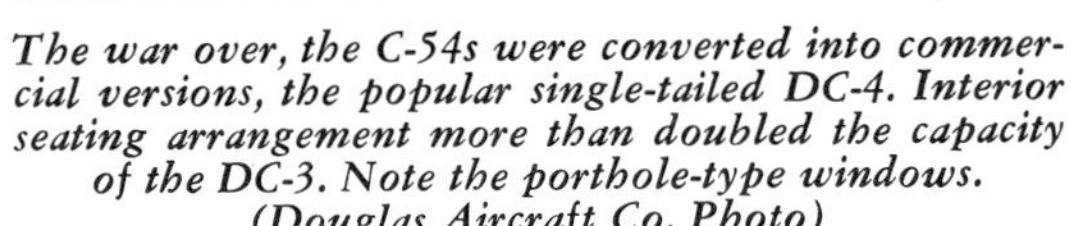

The war over, the C-54s were converted into commercial versions, the popular single-tailed DC-4. Interior seating arrangement more than doubled the capacity of the DC-3. Note the porthole-type windows.
(Douglas Aircraft Co. Photo)

The art of "stretching a design," learned with the DC-1, DC-2 and DC-3, was applied once more and Douglas found another rubber airplane in the DC-4. The result was the DC-6, one of the first long-range, high density (seating), pressurized-cabin airliners.
(Douglas Aircraft Co. Photo)

The Douglas DC-7 ("Seven Seas") so named because she was the first truly intercontinental airliner. First plane to have range for full-load non-stop coast-to-coast travel. (Douglas Aircraft Co. Photo)

There would follow a whole family of four-engined Douglas airliners: The DC-6, bigger and faster, one of the first pressurized cabin airliners. The DC-7, first airliner to permit non-stop, coast-to-coast schedules. The DC-8, first Douglas jet transport, and the DC-9, the medium range jet, which paradoxically, was designed to operate from airports that once could only be served by the DC-3's!

The original DC-4E, however, was the beginning of the age of the skygiants. And

Douglas entry into the jet age was marked by the advent of the DC-8, four-engined jetliner. (Douglas Aircraft Co. Photo)

The Douglas DC-9, medium range jetliner, is one of the hottest planes in today's skies. It has been said that nothing like it had happened to Douglas since the advent of the DC-3. Orders poured in for the NINE, paralleling the days of the DC-3 avalanche. Reason: the DC-9 has built-in performance that will allow it, within minimums, to operate from almost any field that once was the exclusive domain of the DC-3. (Douglas Aircraft Co. Photo)

when it made its public debut there was irony in this official Douglas announcement: "The all-metal design and construction of the DC-4 follows closely that of the DC-3."

The press release said further – "The DC-4 in no way replaces the famous twenty-one passenger DC-3 . . . Rather, it is an independent development anticipating future needs for long distances . . . It represents Douglas' contribution to the science of aeronautics – a new and significant milestone in aviation's progress."

Moreover, a quarter of a century later, at the Long Beach plant where the new DC-9 – latest of the family of DC-ships – was rolled out of the hangar, Donald Douglas couldn't help referring to the long line of predecessors.

Unquestionably, he was thinking of that letter he had received from Jack Frye so long ago, a piece of paper he refers to as the "birth certificate of the modern airliner."

"I see her here and there, in the shape and design and features which have gone in the DC-3's, DC-6's and DC-7's, even in the jetliners," he remarked. "Certain things the DC-1 pioneered will be with us as long as planes still keep their present configuration."

He might have added, that if it hadn't been for the DC-1, the traveling public probably would not have been ready to accept the 600-mile-an-hour Jet Age. It was the "flying showcase" that put modern air travel on display and the public bought the merchandise.

World's largest commercial jet airliner—the Douglas DC-8 Super 61 takes off from Long Beach Municipal Airport Monday, March 14, 1966, on its maiden flight. The huge transport is 187.4 feet in length, 37 feet longer than the standard DC-8's and can carry 251 passengers—ten times the number that the first DC-3 could carry. (Douglas Aircraft Co. Photo)

Epilogue: It is 1965, almost thirty years since the first DST spread its wings from Clover Field, Santa Monica, and we are riding in North Central's "728," the modified luxuriously furnished DC-3. There are VIP's on board – the City Officials of Saginaw. They are here for a ride in the DC-3 because on this day North Central is phasing out its DC-3 service to the city. This is sort of a testimonial occasion to the Old Gal – the DC-3 – that brought air service to this Thumb Country of eastern Michigan. The airline will inaugurate only *Convair* service nest week. In 1967 North Central's DC-9 jets will be landing here.

On board there is nostalgic talk about the DC-3. Two of the "city fathers" were C-47 pilots in World War II. Everybody gets in his two cents worth. The plane itself seems to be listening and singing a happy song. The Hi-Fi even drowns out the roar of its engines. And the newscaster seen on the TV screen in the cabin is telling about her exploits.

Pretty Carol Shanahan, North Central stewardess, is talking about one trip she remembers in a DC-3.

"I was standing in the doorway," she relates, "waiting for this passenger to come up the steps. When he got up to the door he patted the ship's aluminum skin. Then, with a big grin, I heard him say – *Good Old Gooney. I'd take this baby to the moon. She'd get you there – slow but sure.*"

Later, Mrs. Shanahan said her passenger identified himself. He was a NASA scientist enroute to the Houston Space Center. One of the project engineers on *Gemini Seven* and *Apollo*.

The DC-3 was the only way he could make connections in Chicago with a jet flight for Houston.

It seemed the old DC-3 persisted in having a final role and a part in man's landing on the moon.

She will probably be around when he does.

On June 28, 1966, almost 33 years after the unveiling of the TWA/Douglas DC-1, Douglas presented to the world its DC-8 Super 62 at special ceremonies in Long Beach, California. The Super 62, newest member of the family of Douglas Commercial (DC) skyships, is capable of carrying a capacity load of 189 passengers and luggage nearly 6,000 statute miles without re-fueling. Plane has an extended wingspan of 145.4 feet, six feet greater than preceding Douglas four-engine jetliners. The wing configuration, however, except for a sharper sweepback, certainly reveals its proud heredity from "The PLANE that changed the WORLD!"
(Douglas Aircraft Co. Photo)

Index

Index

Index

E

F

G

Index

Index

Index

Index